T O

F R O M

D A T E

A Moment to Breathe: A 365-Day (in)courage Devotional Journal

Copyright © 2018 by DaySpring

First Edition, January 2018

Published by:

DaySpring

P.O. Box 1010
Siloam Springs, AR 72761
dayspring.com

Printed in China.

Unless otherwise noted, all Scripture quotations are taken from the Christian Standard Bible®, Copyright © 2017 by Holman Bible Publishers. Used by permission. Christian Standard Bible® and CSB® are federally registered trademarks of Holman Bible Publishers.

Designed by Jessica Wei
Typesetting by Greg Jackson of thinkpen.design

Prime: 71922

ISBN: 978-1-68408-213-1

Introduction

We are so glad you're here. Come on in. We may come from different places, but when we come together, we find one thing to be true: Our heartaches may be different, but our hearts are the same. And that's what you'll find in these pages — stories from women in every season of life, women who have been there, women who understand.

We're so honored to include the beautiful voices of eighty writers — many voices, one heart. You can find out more about each women and the devotional book at *www.incourage.me/a-moment-to-breathe*.

As you turn each page, imagine a friend opening her door, welcoming you into her story, and inviting you to share your heart. Each day includes a story of everyday faith, passage of Scripture, and journaling space for reflection.

Let us know how God uses this devotional journal to bring hope and encouragement to your everyday.

We're All Worth a Second Look

Mark and I wander over to our favorite fruit stand laden with discounted merchandise labeled "seconds." A wiry woman says, "These are here because they have some kind of trouble."

I look at her and say with a half grin, "Don't we all?"

We know she means there might be a bruise from a hard landing on unrelenting ground. Or there could be a tiny hole where a bug helped itself to dinner.

But that doesn't deter us, so we choose our imperfect peaches and cart them home with anticipation. I set one on a small plate and split it right down the side with a silver knife. I put the piece in my mouth for an explosion of sweet and tart and summer.

I look at the remaining portion and whisper, "Who would have thought you had that in you?" Then I think about how this rings true to life—we all have parts of our hearts or stories that we think don't measure up. We call them unworthy and "less than" and put them to the side. But I have found that those are the places where glory and beauty are likely to show up and shout "Surprise!"

I thought "seconds" meant "not best." Maybe it really means "worth a second look."

I am sure of this, that He who started a good work in you will carry it on to completion until the day of Christ Jesus.
PHILIPPIANS 1:6

JANUARY 2
Praying for Rain

Late at night while the household sleeps, I straggle into the kitchen to a sink full of waiting dishes. As I rinse a pan, I find myself praying desperate dreams for the future. I pray for what I want but then feel convicted that I rarely pray for what I have.

I then recalled this verse in Zechariah, and suddenly my thoughts go back to a dry game farm with farmers who haven't seen rain in months. The sun-weathered men sit in their rough clothes at a long table outside for a meal. But with first bites come cold, hard drops of rain. And as the rain falls, the men carry on with their meal. Then the Lord said to me, "They won't leave the rain, because they don't want it to leave them." In the season of rain, they want more rain.

Now with soap suds up to my elbows, *I realize that what I wanted so desperately in the past is what I have now*: a healed marriage, healthy children, the beginnings of meaningful work. And I don't want to lose sight of these in the chase after my next prayer request. I want to revel in what God has provided here and now. Between soap suds and dirty dishes, I decide to pray for what I have.

Ask the Lord for rain in the season of spring rain. The Lord makes the rain clouds, and he will give them showers of rain and crops in the field for everyone.
ZECHARIAH 10:1

JANUARY 3
Dear John

The plane started to climb into the air when the man next to me knocked his elbow against mine. I turned to him and smiled. His hand flapped toward his chest, and he very slowly said, "My name is John." "Hi, John. It's nice to meet you."

He then asked, each syllable a marathon, "What is your name?" I felt guilty when the word slipped easily from my lips. "Aliza."

He looked at me and said, "I apologize. I haven't always been like this. I was in an accident." I felt a deep sinking in my gut. He thought he needed to apologize because I might think him different.

I saw the looks he was given on the plane and my heart hurt, because the truth is, John is no different from me. We were both searching and hoping and laughing and struggling, and so who is to say that he is different and I am normal?

I discovered that John reads a lot of books and loves Netflix, and he used to be an avid biker. Before we got off the plane he elbowed me again, and I'll never forget his final words. In the sincerest voice I've ever heard, he said, "Aliza, I hope that you are able to do everything I can't."

Therefore accept one another, even as Christ also accepted you, to the glory of God.
ROMANS 15:7

The Hidden Stain

Draped in white lace, I stood ready. The bridesmaids clutched their bouquets and the mothers adjusted their corsages, when suddenly an eerie silence descended. The faces of my girlfriends showed expressions of shock and horror. "What happened? What is it?!"

I followed their eyes to the train behind my bridal gown. A few creases had formed, and there, kneeling beside it, my 13-year-old cousin lifted a hot iron to reveal a dark orange triangle smoldering on the white satin. Apparently, she tried to iron out the creases, but the iron was too hot for the fabric.

In the sanctuary, the music began. I looked up and told my mortified cousin not to worry and then plotted with my maid of honor how we could hide the stain. Instead of spreading out the train behind me, I asked her to fold the fabric over to cover the stain. And down the aisle we went. No one in the sanctuary knew the bride had an ugly stain on her dress.

In Scripture, the church is the bride of Christ. By God's grace, the stain of our sin no longer marks us. We are cleansed and set free. The bride of Christ isn't perfect—none of us are—but Christ's forgiveness is complete. He's removed every spot and wrinkle.

Christ loved the church and gave Himself for her to make her holy, cleansing her with the washing of water by the word. He did this to present the church to Himself in splendor, without spot or wrinkle or anything like that, but holy and blameless.
EPHESIANS 5:25–27

What Will the Neighbors Think?

"Would you please just be quiet?" I hissed as my daughter raised her voice once again. My eyes darted back and forth, searching for any evidence that our neighbors were outside and within earshot. Since we'd moved here, I worried about what our neighbors must think of us. Life with a tween and a toddler is awfully loud a lot of the time, and it can be embarrassing.

One day, as I buckled my youngest into our car, I heard voices. I saw an open garage door and realized that another mom was just as exasperated (and expressive) as I often am. She hollered at her kids to get in the car, and it hit me: I'd been wasting time trying to control my family's appearance when I could have been walking across the street to introduce myself (and my noisy kids). I'd neglected the chance to connect in my effort to impress.

It's impossible to love our neighbors when we're worrying about what those neighbors might think of us. Choosing love requires humility and honesty instead of perfection and protecting reputations. It might even mean letting our kids run wild in the front yard while we decide to meet that mom across the street.

For am I now trying to win the favor of people, or God? Or am I striving to please people? If I were still trying to please people, I would not be a slave of Christ.
GALATIANS 1:10

Trust the Path

One day I went walking around a lake and decided to follow a path I had never walked before, so I looked at a map before heading out.

I walked for ten to fifteen minutes, thinking, praying, and processing. There were two decisions in life I was faced with, and neither had a clear right or wrong answer. I was worried, though, that I was going to miss the one God had planned for me. "Just show me, Lord," I said, "and I'll do what You want. I just don't know where either of these paths are going."

Then I looked down and realized I didn't know where I was, which was the case in many areas of my life. I felt a little lost, a little unsure, a little concerned that I was missing the mark. In a blink, God said: "Trust the path." As I looked down at the path, I remembered seeing the route on the map, so I knew it would eventually take me back to the road.

Trust the path . . . I knew God didn't mean just the one at the lake. So I'm now choosing to trust the next steps of my life path—to trust that it is going somewhere and wherever that is, God is there.

Make Your ways known to me, Lord; teach me Your paths.
PSALM 25:4

When You Need Permission to Let It Be

One night I sat on the couch staring at the blinking cursor on my laptop. Just staring. Thank goodness my husband broke into my reverie: "Let it rest," he said.

"Huh?" I said to him, trying to pull myself away from the hypnotic beat.

"Let it rest," he said again. "Close the laptop, and let it be. It will still be there tomorrow," he said. "Nothing will have changed, and nothing is going to change, just because you sit there staring at that screen."

So I closed it. Let it rest. Let it be. And an entire world opened up in front of me. There was music and food and laughter and the sound of snow melting from the roof overhanging our front porch. Outside was fresh air and sunshine. We hopped on our bikes and rode a few miles to the lake nearby. We sat on a bench that faced the setting sun, and we talked about where we've been and what we hope will be.

On the way home, we pedaled hard and laughed out loud as the sun spilled pink and orange across the horizon.

Sometimes the best thing to do is step away from the tasks and look up. Go outside and "lift your eyes to the mountains."

I lift my eyes toward the mountains. Where will my help come from?
PSALM 121:1

On Being the Truest Version of Me

Even her sweat was cute. Her cheeks flushed a blushing pink like a peony petal. Her hair curls in damp wisps around her face as she lifted a water bottle to her glossed lips, and my gaze flicked away from her to the full-length mirrors lining the walls of the gym.

My face was cherry-splotched and my ponytail hung limp and greasy. My oversized T-shirt was soaked through, and I could see where it clung to the bulges beneath my industrial-sized sports bra. I wouldn't be showering at the gym . . .

I see "gym girl" everywhere when I let envy dictate my dreams, my goals, my reality. I see her in all the ways I come up short. Not to change into a me that's good enough, but to believe that just showing up is part of the journey . . . not just to a fit self, but to a fit soul.

I am back to exercising. And when I look in the mirror bypassing the scale, I feel spent, yet whole, flushed, and alive. I'm not looking for a better version of myself, but a truer version of who I have always been: loved, cherished, beautiful, strong.

The Lord will fulfill His purpose for me. Lord, Your love is eternal; do not abandon the work of Your hands.

PSALM 138:8

JANUARY 9
If You Know Him

Here I am, on my couch crying, again. I will never get myself together. I am such a failure. I am so tired of making plans, lists, and self-help do-overs that land me right back where I started. I cannot fix myself.

It's been five years since my last "failure" breakdown. I was done—I was so over trying to be better, do better, get better. I just kept missing my mark, my perfectionist, pull-myself-up-by-the-bootstraps, get-it-together mark. So I sat on my couch and cried out to the Lord. I threw my hands up and said, "I'm done."

It was as though the Lord was waiting for those very words, because when I finally gave in to my deep weakness, I was able to begin relying on His strength. I am clay, and clay cannot mold itself. He alone is the One who molds and perfects me.

And the most wonderful life-giving news of all? As He's still intimately molding me toward maturity, He doesn't look at me as a failure. He looks at me and sees perfection and completeness because of Jesus Christ. Yeah, there's still work to do with my humanity here on earth, but this is not my final home.

Done deal. Perfect. Complete. Right now.

What sweet freedom. What grace. What an exhale!

_____

_____

_____

_____

_____

_____

_____

For by one offering He has perfected forever those who are sanctified.
HEBREWS 10:14

Because Life Is Hard

Brown paper bags lined the walkway to my front door. Food, toiletries, diapers, and gift cards overflowed. Our family was approaching a year without a paycheck, trying to keep our business afloat and avoid foreclosure on our home. But we were nearing the end of our rope. I begged God for clarity but heard nothing. I cried out, wondering how much longer this season would last, but answers weren't coming. In the midst of this, my mother-in-law was diagnosed with a brain tumor and given months to live.

But through some bags of groceries, God reminded me that He is greater than the circumstances we face. My circumstances do not determine my peace. The world can neither give us peace nor take it away. Life is hard. And it will probably get harder. Jesus said as much when He promised we'd have trials in this life (John 16:33). He wasn't trying to scare us; He was trying to prepare us.

God knows our pain and He understands our problems. So we have to trust Him, even when we can't trace Him. It's during those times we must choose to fully lean into our Lord Jesus. It's a choice. We can't do life alone, but we can be there for each other. And maybe bring a bag of groceries too.

You are from God, little children, and you have conquered them, because the One who is in you is greater than the one who is in the world.
1 JOHN 4:4

JANUARY 11
Peace Over Productivity

There is a hummingbird that regularly visits my flower—pot. When she hovers over a flower and dips her slender beak deep into a blossom for a nectar drink, her wings beat infinitely faster than my eyes can account. She is constantly in motion, zipping to and fro.

But now she sits on a telephone wire, a tiny dark silhouette against the pale blue sky of early morning, and rests.

In this moment, she is not striving. No flying or trying. Just being.

Every creature is given the gift of pause. Every living thing is led to rest, if under the Creator's view.

I am up early to steal a handful of quiet moments. There are e-mails to check, a work task to tend to, and a Bible study to complete. I feel pressed on all sides and need productivity to triumph.

I look up again from my desk and my wire friend is gone. But I gaze upon her empty spot and know that she is cared for as part of God's creation. She is carried by Him in her heart-wildly-beating, wings-frantically-fluttering day.

And I claim the truth again: it is worth putting aside my desire to be productive in order to rest in knowing that God is with me.

_You will keep the mind that is dependent on You in
perfect peace, for it is trusting in You._
ISAIAH 26:3

It's a Bad Day, Not a Bad Life

I gave in to unreason and colored my hair a new shade right before bed. And then at 11:00 p.m. I washed my hair 37 times before falling into bed with damaged pride and fitful sleep. The next morning was church, but I was in a bad-hair mood so I went back to sleep. Yes, I skipped church because of hair. Please, don't judge.

After I got up, what started out as a simple "Don't do that" to one of my kids ended up in a full-blown tantrum. The day went from lazy Sunday to the end times. and I longed for a do-over.

"Can we just pray together?" I asked my husband. And what I really meant was *Can my family just pray with me, for me?* So we all willingly piled up on our bed and held hands. I could see that our kids wanted a do-over as much as we did.

Our youngest prayed first, and then my husband led us in a simple prayer. I couldn't hold my tears back because it was exactly what I needed. My teen daughter rubbed my hand when she saw my tears and whispered, "It's okay, Mom." I nodded. Because now it was.

Man is like a breath; his days are like a passing shadow.
PSALM 144:4

JANUARY 13

The Difference Between Asking and Doing

Timing for a girls' weekend couldn't have been more perfect. I'd been home from Germany for four weeks, and the conversation swirled. I gave a condensed, practiced response about Germany, but one of my girlfriends wanted to know more about me. Her eyes penetrated mine, and she asked, "How are you doing with all the changes you've gone through the past year? How's your heart doing?"

I hadn't seen it coming. I didn't realize my guard was completely down. Unable to speak, tears began to reveal secret hurts—void, disappointment, rejection, loss.

Her question was a match lighting a soggy fuse, and I couldn't stop the waterworks. "Come right here," she said, patting an empty spot on the bed next to her. "We're gonna pray for you." I shook my head again and whispered "I can't," and she gently insisted, "Yes, you can, right here." (Pat. Pat. Pat.)

All the others gathered round and close. They touched me with their hands and their compassion and their words. They pressed blessing and understanding and healing deep into the marrow. I hadn't given them details, but in the beautiful, mysterious ways of God, He led them through the veins of my ache and ministered love through the hearts of these sisters.

And let us be concerned about one another in order to promote love . . .
HEBREWS 10:24

That Which We May Not Know

One hot Houston night, a young father stood up from his padded pew to beg for prayers for his newborn daughter. The middle soft spot of her cranium was closed, and the doctors said she needed immediate neurosurgery plus two blood transfusions. The man was a preacher and carried his burden into a crowded gathering of believers on a Wednesday night service. It was a night of prayer, and he needed to believe his God would answer his.

He didn't know the older man sitting in the crowd who heard his request and sensed a stirring in his spirit to help a young father in need. And so it happened, that life in a secondhand sense was given to me. I was that baby. Because in the sovereignty that can only be God, the older man paid for my surgery. He was a man I would never get to meet.

This piece of my true-life story is a reminder that we may never know the heart behind the words, the struggle behind the request, the private story that lives behind the eyes of the person. But let's pause to honor those who respond without knowing. Let's give glory to the God who sees everything and works to bring the two together.

For we are His creation, created in Christ Jesus for good works,
which God prepared ahead of time so that we should walk in them.
EPHESIANS 2:10

Stepping Out of the Way

One evening after an intense "discussion," my husband told me that no matter what he did or how hard he tried, it was never enough for me. He was right. I had a bad habit of finding fault with him as a husband and as a dad. Then he implied I was impossible to please . . .

I grabbed my coat and stormed out the front door. As I replayed our conversation in my head, I started filing complaints to Jesus against J.J. in what you might call a prayer.

When I finished, I then started crying out to God for help. When I stopped talking and started listening, I realized I wanted J.J. to make up for all the ways my dad had fallen short.

Growing up in a broken home led to a significant loss and deep disappointment, and I had never grieved the happily-ever-after I wanted but didn't have. I had become controlling and critical. Instead of expecting my husband to make up for my losses, I needed to cry out to God with my hurts.

As I continued to process how my childhood affected my marriage, I learned to ask God for help through each step of my healing journey. It took time, prayer, and courage, but God was so very present and faithful to help me.

I called to the Lord in my distress, and I cried to my God for help.
From His temple He heard my voice, and my cry to Him reached His ears.
PSALM 18:6

The Good News

I needed my friend that day. Life was running off the rails with my 60-hour workweeks and my avoidance of anything spiritual. Overwhelmed with exhaustion, I called my friend. I clearly needed Jesus in my life, but I didn't know it yet.

She knew. So she did what friends do: she showed up. I don't remember exactly what she said about Jesus, but when she handed me some tissues, my heart instinctively knew that I needed what she had: Jesus Christ.

Years later, I ran across a story in II Kings 7, where lepers had discovered a deserted camp with lots of food, silver, gold, and clothing. At first, they kept the good news to themselves. But then they remembered that others were starving, so they went back and told the others. That's what my friend did for me. She knew where the feast was, so she gently led me to that feast. She couldn't keep it to herself.

This is one of the most important, joyous, and scary callings we have—to bring the Good News to weary friends. That day, my friend could have remained silent out of fear. But in her own way, with a frothy coffee from the corner shop, she brought hope to my doorstep. I'll never be the same.

Then they said to each other, "We're not doing what is right.
Today is a day of good news. If we are silent and wait until morning light,
our sin will catch up with us. Let's go tell the king's household."
II KINGS 7:9

What You Say Really Matters

I was in second grade, excited to be attending another Brownie meeting. Our troop leader—an imposing woman with a commanding voice—stood and began barking instructions. Something she said seemed unclear, so I raised my hand. She rolled her eyes, clearly annoyed. "Would you please put your hand down, Donna? You always have a question. Sometimes I'd like to flush you down the toilet!"

Well, that was a mean thing to say, I thought. In retrospect, my childlike assessment was an understatement. Her words were downright rotten. My Brownie leader's words remain etched in my brain to this day, but all these years later, I'm grateful her cruel comments didn't cause permanent damage. Looking back now, I realize why. Often—daily, in fact—I heard words of life-giving affirmation from the lips of my parents.

Words like . . . *I love you. We're proud of you. Thanks for being so kind.*

Words of consistent blessing build more than confidence or courage: they build a wall of protection, preventing permanent wounding from hurtful, discouraging, or critical words. Not everyone grows up with parents who build like this. My mother didn't. But despite her upbringing, she took the words of Ephesians to heart. And by doing so, she protected mine.

_No foul language is to come from your mouth, but only what is good for
building up someone in need, so that it gives grace to those who hear._
EPHESIANS 4:29

The Gifting and Lifting of Grief

When my fourth child was born, my body struggled to make milk for her. The hormonal peaks and valleys of that process seemed to switch a lever in my brain. I became depressed. I had so many reasons to be happy, but depression sucked all emotion from my mind and filled the emptiness with anxiety. I can remember sitting in my comfortable, soft rocking chair, holding my baby, and trying to remember why I had once cared about babies or repairing old farmhouses or ordering seeds for the spring garden or anything at all. I could no longer remember why it mattered if any of us ever got out of bed.

When I stopped trying to nurse my baby and the last of my milk dried up, the depression lifted. A severe mercy. It meant that I knew happiness again. It meant that I knew sadness again. Healing looked like a renewed capacity for both joy and sorrow. When I read the words from Psalm 105, I remember what happened to me after my daughter's birth and that I have a song of praise. And I give thanks.

Give thanks to Yahweh, call on His name; proclaim His deeds among the peoples.
Sing to Him, sing praise to Him; tell about all His wonderful works!
PSALM 105:1–2

When Someone Hits the Pause Button on Your Life

Years ago my daughter needed surgery on her spine to repair a broken neck. The neurosurgeon explained that there were two options for treatment. One was a more secure way by inserting a pin into the bone on each side of her vertebrae. This meant wearing a neck brace in post-op. But if her bones were too small and he had to use a less-secure treatment, she would have to wear a halo—a more restrictive headgear that keeps the head and neck completely still. Obviously, we prayed she'd be able to wear the neck brace.

During surgery, my husband and I sat in the waiting room and fidgeted. Even as we clung to hope, that morning felt like a held breath, like someone hit the pause button on our lives. Finally, the nurse told us that the doctor was able to insert a pin on one side, so our girl could wear the neck brace during recovery.

When I think back, the waiting we endured wasn't long in the grand scheme of things. But waiting can feel long when you don't know what the outcome will be. It's in those times, when you find yourself holding your breath, that hope is the reason to keep going, to keep trusting, and, yes, keep breathing.

And when the chief Shepherd appears,
you will receive the unfading crown of glory.
1 PETER 5:4

To Work Quietly with My Hands

I've been learning to crochet. And in the process, I've found that I like the idea of staying a beginner. This is because I like moving my hands in a predictable rhythm to make nothing in particular except maybe some space and time for my soul to breathe. I like the absence of pressure, the complete lack of temptation to show off a piece that's finished.

This week, as I imperfectly practice this new craft, I'm discovering the spiritual discipline hidden beneath the uneven rows of yarn. Sometimes I need to engage in an activity for the single purpose of disengaging from productivity.

There's an invisible world that lives inside our bodies, the inner world of the soul. And this inner world needs our attention, but it doesn't respond to programs, agendas, or hustle. The soul responds to space, silence, and Jesus.

I'm discovering Christ in everyday, ordinary moments . . . in both the visible world I can see and the invisible one that lives within me. And sometimes I need to actively do things I'm not good at in order to remember how desperately I need Him.

Lord, my heart is not proud; my eyes are not haughty. I do not get involved with things too great or too difficult for me. Instead, I have calmed and quieted myself . . .

PSALM 131:1–2

Practicing True Hospitality

We live near the airport and some friends had a morning flight, so it was a great excuse for them to sleep over. We sat in the kitchen, talked until midnight, and shared crackers right out of the bag. Their room had clean sheets—and an avalanche lay in wait behind the closet door. The dirty dishes in the kitchen were overflowing, and I wasn't even home when they arrived!

A couple weeks earlier I heard someone say, "True hospitality is when your guests leave your home feeling better about themselves, not feeling better about you." Those words hit home. Too often I'm a hot mess before guests arrive. I whirl around the house cleaning, arranging, and planning the meal. I snap at my husband and plunk the kids in front of the TV so they're not in my way. But not this time.

The condition of my house was less than ideal, but it was real. We were in the middle of a busy week, and they stepped right into the thick of it. The thing is, I didn't bat an eyelash and neither did they. The mess didn't matter because in that moment, being together mattered more.

If people don't feel welcome in our homes, they won't feel welcome in our hearts.

Be hospitable to one another without complaining.
1 PETER 4:9

Seeing the Greatness of Who He Is

*B*e *still,* I told myself. Slices of sunshine found their way through the branches to kiss the path in front of me. I knew at once that time in His creation would refill my soul.

I took a deep breath of air. Spring was still a few weeks away, but nature was clamoring to find expression for her Creator. I paused to take it in. Yet my breathing began to shallow as my mind focused on to-do lists and the voices declaring I was not enough. My spirit chilled at the invitation to be self-absorbed amidst His glory. I felt ashamed for losing my view of His splendor.

Suddenly I noticed two deer in the woods nearby. Together they walked until one froze as my shuffle caused a startle. The front deer slowed cautiously but did not stop. The halted deer then followed in step and joined the increasing pace of the one who led.

This allowed my heart to skirt away from its inward focus. My God will lead me. I will freeze and falter, but just as the deer found their way, I will also be led toward safety and life. My heart is learning to see Him. He will teach me to trust. Let everything that has breath and beauty testify.

But ask the animals, and they will instruct you; ask the birds of the sky, and they will tell you. Or speak to the earth, and it will instruct you; let the fish of the sea inform you. Which of all these does not know that the hand of the Lord has done this? The life of every living thing is in His hand, as well as the breath of all mankind.

JOB 12:7–10

Against All Odds

Iplanted it more than a decade ago—a lavender plant in a four-inch pot that held a tiny dream.

I'd moved to the country from our suburban neighborhood, and I imagined that someday I'd have a beautiful lavender farm. I knew it wouldn't be easy. People told me I didn't have a chance. But I chopped the rocky soil and planted the seed anyway.

Then life got tough. The economy tanked and I worked hard to make ends meet. I abandoned the lavender-farm dream and went into survival mode. The little plant was forgotten in the years that followed, but somehow it hung on through blistering heat, record-setting drought, ice storms, and torrential rains.

Not once did it flower. It just *survived*—as though its strength was used up to simply stay alive and there wasn't a single drop left over for something as frivolous as a bloom. I understood, only too well. Sometimes, just *staying alive* is the best we can do. Surviving is victory.

Then one morning, my breath escaped in an awestruck sigh. Fresh purple blooms floated above the green mound like a tiara. I sank in front of it and couldn't contain a smile. *Just look at you. You made it.*

The wilderness and the dry land will be glad; the desert will rejoice and blossom like a rose. It will blossom abundantly and will also rejoice with joy and singing. The glory of Lebanon will be given to it, the splendor of Carmel and Sharon. They will see the glory of the Lord, the splendor of our God.
ISAIAH 35:1–2

When You Need to Step Away

A growing restlessness in my soul, coupled with the prompting of the Holy Spirit, whispered to my heart that I needed to pull way back from the unending chatter of the internet. God had stepped into my thoughts and invited me to a secret space—a sacred space, alone. With Him.

I liken this kind of stepping away to therapy. It's like stepping into God's office to dump out all my emotional garbage and let Him help me sort it. When I stop focusing on God and start listening to others' stories, I quickly forget that, just hours before, God was working out some of the kinks in my own.

This time, however, I stepped fully and quietly into that secret place with Him and endured the month-long unwinding of a great many knots in my heart. Instead of anxiety, I experienced relief. I came to God dirt-dry and found revival in His presence alone.

Surely, there is a time for testimony. We are called to tell of His goodness and grace to all who will listen. But, also, we are called to the quiet, tucked-away place alone with Him, where uncomfortable-but-necessary healing and growing happens. Alone with the Almighty, we taste the sweetness of grace that cannot be experienced anywhere else.

The one who lives under the protection of the Most High dwells in the shadow of the Almighty.
PSALM 91:1

Welcome In

Our family lives in an impoverished part of town where mamas work odd jobs and daddies are absent from homes. Hunger is as real as the drugs being pushed down the street. You could call our home a community center because it is the hub of neighborhood activity. Life whirls around in the middle of what some would call the badlands. The yard and everything in it belongs to all of us, and all of us come to the table as equally needy family members.

But this gathering together as a family didn't happen overnight. It has taken five years of living among those in the margins of life and intentionally inviting the poor, the addicted, and the abused to our table. It has taken five years of residing in a lowly place for us to find acceptance here. And it has taken five years of continually opening our hands wide enough to let the superabundance of kingdom resources flow through our fingers for God to remind us that we simply get to steward what He graciously gives us.

Jesus promises that our hospitality to the poor will be repaid at the resurrection of the righteous. But, friends, we can reap the blessings now. Let's open our homes and invite the poor to our tables.

When you host a banquet, invite those who are poor, maimed, lame, or blind. And you will be blessed, because they cannot repay you; for you will be repaid at the resurrection of the righteous.
LUKE 14:13–14

JANUARY 26
The Things We Say Yes To

We'd been waiting for a gentle and quiet time in life. We'd been waiting for our own space, and for silence. We just didn't know how to find it until I learned how many nos it would take to make a yes.

I said yes to quiet. I now drive in silence. I come home and tell the boys to read. I sit on the patio and watch doves fly up from the harvested corn and the seasons take their course.

I relish silence as much as a burst of loud laughter and wrestling. I have peace in a dish-stacked kitchen with no dishwasher and four hall drawers to fit what used to go in an entire room.

When we said yes to scaling, slowing, and quieting down, it wasn't really saying yes to less work. We said yes to better work. I said yes to picking squash and researching how to harvest hazelnuts. These are things I love. I said yes to the work of closeness, the children always within the reach of a whisper.

These are little things to which we'll look back and remember. I said yes to living small. I said yes to which I call a beautiful life, and it surprises me. Work boots and scrub gloves on, I can hear God in this place.

But let your word "yes" be "yes," and your "no" be "no."
Anything more than this is from the evil one.
MATTHEW 5:37

JANUARY 27
A Sympathetic Heart

I learned that firsthand knowledge of pain grows empathy. Years ago, we visited an out-of-state family with our new baby boy. Another family member was there who had recently miscarried. I knew she was happy for us, but I also realized that being around our son reminded her of the baby she lost. As much as I wanted to comfort her, I didn't know how, so I remained silent.

The next year I experienced a miscarriage. I will not ever forget the range of emotions I felt: overwhelming sadness, followed by guilt over the lack of excitement I experienced when I found out I was pregnant (our baby had just turned one).

I will never again remain silent when a woman I know miscarries a child. Not only do I sympathize, I empathize. I truly understand how it feels. I know what to expect emotionally in the days and weeks following a miscarriage and how something as innocent as a baby food commercial can hit like a punch in the gut.

Sympathy mingled with firsthand knowledge is a powerful combination. When we empathize, we can act with compassion, speak with wisdom, and listen with understanding. The lessons we learn in hard times can become holy gifts to other women, like beauty raised from ashes.

For we do not have a high priest who is unable to sympathize with our weaknesses, but One who has been tested in every way as we are, yet without sin. Therefore let us approach the throne of grace with boldness, so that we may receive mercy and find grace to help us at the proper time.
HEBREWS 4:15–16

A New Morning Routine

My breath fogs up the mirror as I swipe another coat of mascara onto my lashes. *Thank You that my skin hasn't broken out today.* I step back to examine my attempt at dreamy eyes. *Thank You that my hair doesn't look strange, even with all the humidity. Thank You for my dear friends. Thank You for sending them my way.*

I check my phone for the time. *Thank You for sound sleep last night with no bad dreams. And the opportunity to serve You today. Oh, and that new opportunity that You brought out of the blue. Thank You, Lord.*

My morning routine has changed. Not with a new loofah or hairbrush, but with how I dress my mind. Instead of waking up and asking for things with rapid gunfire prayers toward heaven, I turn my heart toward gratefulness. I acknowledge the small things that can break my day or make my attitude.

My goal is simple—to give God glory. And I love when He reveals to me how to do the desire of my heart. The one He planted there long ago. Not blood, sweat, or try-hard sacrifice, but thankfulness. A thankful heart for the big and most definitely the very small. That's all Jesus wants from me.

Sacrifice a thank offering to God, and pay your vows to the Most High. Call on Me in a day of trouble; I will rescue you, and you will honor Me.
PSALM 50:14–15

Evidence of Beauty

I think they were surprised at my response. After all, I am a makeup artist and hairstylist. The bride and her bridesmaids had been saying for a good half hour how "mouth parentheses" and crow's feet around the eyes were so ugly, and since we have medical means to "erase" those signs of aging, it only made sense to use them. Then they asked me, "Don't you think so, too?"

I smiled, my own lines showing, "Well, I don't have a traditional view on wrinkles or beauty due to my mom. She was always smiling at me. She read that it was important for kids to see the smile on your face when they entered the room to communicate that you were happy to see them, that you treasure their presence. It would have been sad if she had erased all the beautiful evidence of her love for me."

Then the mother of the bride's smile settled softly in its familiar lines.

"And," I added, "I've begun noticing that expression lines have started on my face, too, but I pray that my daughters will mainly remember me smiling at them. Beauty is from the inside. When I do makeup and style hair, I'm just putting a personalized frame on the masterpiece that you already are."

*A joyful heart makes a face cheerful, but a sad heart produces
a broken spirit. A discerning mind seeks knowledge.*
PROVERBS 15:13–14

From East to West

The look on their faces said it all. I was mad and they knew it. I made my way to the restroom, shut the door, and, with tears streaming down my face, said, "Lord, what is the matter with me?" Slowly it all poured out, every hurt feeling and overreaction. Jesus, as patient as ever, received every last drop of my confession and whispered: *"Loved, my daughter."*

Maybe you can relate. Like me, you have one of those no-good, horrible, bad days. And you blow it. You yell at your kids. Or lie to a friend or speak hurtfulness to your spouse. And in the midst of it, you are shocked. Embarrassed. Angry. You don't like you right now. So you withdraw and hide and hope no one notices.

But Jesus does. And while you are swimming in a sea of guilt and shame, He is tenderly speaking truth from His Word to your heart. . .*I've removed your sin as far as the east is to the west. I took it away so there would be nothing between us.* And somewhere in the middle of the mess, you start to believe it.

Your sin is not greater than His power of forgiveness. You could try to measure it, but east to west will get you every time.

As far as the east is from the west,
so far has He removed our transgressions from us.
PSALM 103:12

JANUARY 31
Growing Confident

During lunch with a dear friend, the lightheartedness changed when a sticky topic came up. Immediately, I felt the atmosphere shift with an undertone of tension. When I asked if she was okay, she said "Of course." But on her drive home, she called to say how she was really doing—our conversation had hit an "insecurity button." She was gracious, humble, loving, and open— open to God's healing in her life and open to walking in true confidence. And her phone call resulted in a newfound freedom in our friendship.

In similar situations, instead of being real, I've said "I'm fine" when really I was dying inside. Maybe I was too scared to be honest. Or maybe I wasn't sure how to express my feelings. But my friend's example set me on a path to freedom.

Growing into a woman of true confidence means we'll risk doing real life with real people. I know from experience that it's hard to find friends who are trustworthy, safe, and caring. But it's so much better to do life with people than alone. It's what we were made for. When we pursue wholeness in Christ, we pave the way for others to follow and find freedom for themselves. That's what my friend did for me.

Do not fear, for I am with you; do not be afraid, for I am your God.
ISAIAH 41:10

When God Says No

I was excited for this big opportunity. I was going to be used by God for something magnificent, something meaningful. I could feel it . . . until the phone rang and I heard, "There has been a change of plans." Have you ever received one of those calls? The type that bursts your bubble of joy?

I was asked to hand over my dream to another woman. I didn't want to, but I relented. I felt like kicking and screaming, but part of me trusted God to use this to speak to my heart. So I listened. And I was reminded that we cannot fathom the things God has prepared for those who love Him, so He had plans for us both.

It's in moments like these that we can choose to wallow in the idea of limited opportunity or choose to see our unlimited God.

Not too long after, I got word that the other woman was diagnosed with cancer. She noted how vital that event was in her life. How God had carved it out just for her soul. To her, it was a cherished honor she would hold through hard times. She received her "something magnificent, something meaningful," but so did I. He made my sacrifice count for her. And that is worth something.

But as it is written: What eye did not see and ear did not hear, and what never entered the human mind— God prepared this for those who love Him.
1 CORINTHIANS 2:9

Small-Home Hospitality

We have a small home. Any time we have more than a handful of people over, our guests sit on the stairs when the couches and chairs are full.

A couple of years ago we hosted a small group that grew to nearly thirty people. So I prayed that God would literally make physical space for every person who came into our house. And He did. It was tight. Each stair doubled as a seat and many people sat on the floor. And it was hot, even when the air conditioner blew on high. But we read the Bible, sang, and prayed together, and people came back—and brought friends. And no one complained. No one told us they thought our home was hindering what God was doing. That's when I quit apologizing for our home. That's when I stopped letting my hospitality button get pushed by what we didn't have and what I couldn't control.

I realized that if God could fit thirty people into our little house and that all those squished people could encounter His truth and His goodness there, the square footage didn't matter. It wasn't holding Him back. So until God moves us, this home is the one we have and I will be grateful for it.

Share with the saints in their needs; pursue hospitality.

ROMANS 12:13

When It's Time to Move

Moving means change—and change brings conflicting emotions and sometimes chaos. But God is never surprised by any of it. In fact, He's been in the business of moving people since the beginning of creation. Adam and Eve were evicted from the Garden of Eden—a consequence of their sin. Noah and his family were moved by torrents of rain and landed without any prospect of neighbors. Abram was told not only to move, but also to change his name. He went to a foreign land without knowing a single person.

Without knowing what the future held, they all lived by faith when they moved, and they lived by faith when they died. They knew they were aliens and strangers on earth, yet every one of them remembered God's faithfulness in the past and that He promised them hope and a future.

Whether we're in the midst of a move or not, remember how God has been faithful in the past and that He will be every bit as faithful in the future. He promises that Jesus is coming back one day. Until then, we can live with our hands open—going where He goes, staying where He stays.

These all died in faith without having received the promises,
but they saw them from a distance, greeted them, and confessed
that they were foreigners and temporary residents on the earth.
HEBREWS 11:13

The Gift of Our Words

At the grocery store, my five-year-old was in full-on extrovert mode. She was literally dancing through the aisles.

Well, I was exhausted. I had been up with the baby all night, and I was doing my best to stay patient as I reminded my daughter that people did not view the produce aisle as her personal stage.

Then I turned to see an elderly woman smiling. She said, "I was watching you with this one. I can see she's a wild one, but you are such a good mama. You're so patient with her, and I know you must be tired with this little boy here. But I can tell your kids are well-kept and well-loved."

She went on to tell me about the son she lost to cancer when he was thirteen years old. "So you just keep being grateful for your babies," she told me.

When I got home, I ugly-cried. That morning my heart was discouraged. But the kind woman saw me weary and noticed that I was doing my best. She spoke encouragement into my life. She was sweetness to my soul.

That interaction touched me so deeply that I determined to speak encouragement aloud as much possible. I want to say something uplifting to everyone I pass.

A word spoken at the right time is like gold apples on a silver tray.
PROVERBS 25:11

The Mediator in My Mess

From the moment my feet hit the floor, I knew it wasn't going to be a banner day. I'd overslept. We were out of coffee. And both my husband and my daughter seemed determined to get on my last nerve. By 8:30 that morning, I was ready to throw in the towel (or at least run away from home for a day or two).

Even as I sat down with my Bible and journal, the enemy whispered through my head: *You're not good enough, not godly enough.* And I nodded in assent, because I knew those things were true.

I opened my Bible to be reminded of a beautiful truth: Christ is my Mediator. He is ever standing before the Father, interceding on my behalf, pleading my cause and claiming His blood over my sin. Of course I'm not good or godly enough. Most days I'm just a hot mess trying to manage the chaos of life and hoping I don't ruin anything.

But there is Jesus, leaning in to the Father saying: *"She's mine. That one, with all the fears and anxieties, all the falling and fumbling, My blood was shed for her."*

Jesus isn't in that borrowed tomb anymore! He is standing now before the throne, interceding on our behalf, mediating for us.

For there is one God and one mediator between God and humanity, Christ Jesus, Himself human...
I TIMOTHY 2:5–6

The Fellowship of His Sufferings

I had cried myself into a mess during the prayer time of our Bible study. The sorrow over my irreparably damaged marriage left my emotions raw and easily triggered. As the prayer ended, I opened my eyes and realized an older woman had come to sit by me. "It's not fair," I sobbed. "I'm a Christian and I prayed for God to restore my marriage, but it ended in divorce anyway."

The older woman listened, then asked, "Can you praise God even if He never tells you why?" I stared at her, unable to answer. For years I have mulled over this question as sorrows came, trying to leach the happiness from my life.

Praising Christ in the pain seems, at first, to increase my pain. But when I rejoice in who He is more than the sorrows I mourn, something wonderful happens. Clarity comes.

Suffering is never easy. But there's a fellowship that comes when we go through difficulties with Christ. We might not ever know why, but we know who is with us—Jesus Christ, our Friend. It isn't until we are further down the road that we look up from our tears and realize His arm was around us the whole time.

My goal is to know Him and the power of His resurrection and the fellowship of His sufferings, being conformed to His death...
PHILIPPIANS 3:10

FEBRUARY 7
Purpose in a Quiet Life

"She's going to change the world." Those were the words I read on my seminary recommendation letter, the words I had heard growing up. I was meant for greater things. I knew it, and others affirmed it. To me, *greater* meant glory. But it wasn't for His glory; it was for mine.

Though I planned my life for bigger and more, God wanted small and quiet. He dismantled my dreams so He could bring His kingdom through me. Instead of sending me off to unreached people, He sent me back to the middle of suburbia, where I stay at home investing in the little ones He's set in front of me.

It's here that God works out the faith He's started in me, transforming me toward Christlikeness. It's here that my faith is being matured, that my character is being honed into holiness.

I once despised the small, quiet life because it felt beneath me, but now I see its purpose. All the opportunities and all the platforms will amount to nothing if Christ in me can't be seen. So I stay grounded in the seemingly insignificant responsibilities, because in His kingdom, success and reward are found in the faithfulness of the small and quiet.

Seek to lead a quiet life, to mind your own business, and to work with your own hands, as we commanded you.
I THESSALONIANS 4:11

Roadblocks and Signposts

While attending a graduation party for a friend's son, I was struck by the prayer said by his grandfather. He gave thanks for the roadblocks that kept his grandson from sin and the signposts that led the way. The grandfather prayed for more of both in the young man's journey.

I thought about the roadblocks God had used in my life. The party I couldn't go to when I was younger. The unhealthy relationship that ended. And the termination of a job that wasn't good for my family.

There were signposts too. A friend that encouraged me to hunger for more of Christ. My small group's challenge to serve and share the love of Jesus. My family's constant support.

In the same way, we can be a roadblock or a signpost for others. I can share about the dangers of sin and the consequences that have happened in my life as a roadblock. For signposts, I can challenge my family and friends to pursue holiness. I can speak of God's grace, forgiveness, and unfailing love.

I'm thankful for that grandfather's prayer. I pray that God will use my life as a roadblock and a signpost for His glory, and that my actions will point others to Jesus and His gift of grace for us all.

*How happy is the man who does not follow the advice of the wicked
or take the path of sinners or join a group of mockers!*
PSALM 1:1

Embracing the Imperfections

I just noticed a new, growing hole in my sofa. I love this sofa, but all of its edges are starting to wear dangerously thin. My sofa has holes and stains and is starting to fade in all the wrong places. Then I got teary-eyed, knowing that we can't afford a new one anytime soon.

Somewhere deep in my twisted thoughts I realized that there is a good side to having a not-so-perfect sofa. Toddlers can eat melty chocolate chip cookies on it and no one will gasp when a chip falls onto the fabric. And when one of my boys has an upset stomach, they can rest on it without fear that it will be ruined. If my husband's greasy popcorn hands touch the arm of the sofa, there's no threat of me giving a disapproving look.

Then it dawned on me. There is something worse than a falling-apart, used-up sofa: a perfectly unused five-year-old sofa. What a tragedy if my old sofa were in mint condition. We are actually so much freer to enjoy it because of its imperfections. And I am thankful for the daily reminder that something doesn't have to be perfect to be beautiful.

[Be] hospitable, loving what is good, sensible, righteous, holy, self-controlled.
TITUS 1:8

Do It Afraid

Years ago, when I was a young mom, I was afraid. Afraid I'd never get motherhood right. Afraid that I had been so damaged that, like a banged-up old suitcase, I'd carry the clutter of my chaotic childhood into the lives of my babies. There were times I sat on the floor with a child in my arms and prayed: *Lord, how can I be a good mom if no one showed me how? I'm so afraid I'll mess this up.*

One day these words whispered deep in response: *"Do it afraid, Suzie."* Looking back, I believe that God wasn't asking me to embrace my fears, but to trust that He could use this ill-equipped, work-in-progress woman to love and shape three human beings. It meant that it was okay to say that I didn't have all the answers all the time. It meant that on those hard days when I felt like I didn't have a clue, when my knees hit the carpet, I was met with mercy and a fresh start for the next day.

And every time I did it while afraid, the layers of the past peeled back to reveal who I was today, separate from my childhood. At some point, fear shifted to quiet assurance. And somehow His presence was enough.

The Lord is for me; I will not be afraid. What can man do to me?
PSALM 118:6

FEBRUARY 11
The Difference Our Words Make

She came to our first meeting prepared, with a half dozen legal pages full of notes. It was clear she had taken a lot of time to ready herself for this meeting. She was always going the extra mile, making calls and doing additional research to make us better. So before going home, I went to her cubicle and thanked her, saying she was appreciated and made a difference.

The next day we arrived at work at the same time and she said, "You know, I was thinking about what you said to me last night." Did you catch that? She went home that night, hours after I spoke to her, and thought about my words. They were still on her heart, while I had not thought of them since.

Caring words are a balm for our souls, but too often I miss opportunities to extend them. My colleague's response reminded me that all it takes is a few seconds to say "Thank you; you matter. You helped me; you made a difference."

Now I look for opportunities to say encouraging words and verbally acknowledge someone's good work, what they mean to me, or even just how they look. Today, let's all make someone's day and share a kind word.

A timely word—how good that is!
PROVERBS 15:23

The Key to Giving in to Rest

My friend's five-month-old is in a stage where he fights the inevitable nap. Once he begins to get sleepy, no amount of rocking, swaddling, or bouncing will convince him to lay down, especially if there's a conversation going on around him. He doesn't want to miss a thing.

He doesn't understand that sleep is the best thing for him—that rest is what helps him grow so he can experience even more of the world around him.

I tend to be a fighter of rest too. I don't want to miss out on opportunities or experiences with people who fascinate me. But like the five-month-old, I sometimes lack the perspective needed for giving in to rest.

The beginning of Psalm 46:10 is also translated "Be still" (NKJV) and "Cease striving" (NASB). These are difficult tasks for an achiever. I like to be busy climbing ladders and completing my checklist. Waiting and resting are not my strong suit.

The command, however, is not simply to "stop your fighting," it is also to "know that I am God." This is the key to giving in to rest. He has a good, abundant, and specific plan for my life. Amid all my activity, I can trust in Him enough to include a rhythm of rest within my busy days.

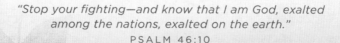

*"Stop your fighting—and know that I am God, exalted
among the nations, exalted on the earth."*
PSALM 46:10

FEBRUARY 13
Unloading the Stones

I've always had a thing for stones. They bring to mind one of my favorite places on earth—this sliver of a beach nestled along the north shore of Long Island. Oh, the countless evenings I spent on that stony beach, watching the sun go down while my children splashed out on the sandbar. There I sat, thinking and pondering, as I'd scoop up the stones in my hand and admire their uniqueness and their story. Soft and smooth. Hard and impermeable. Dark and light. Speckled and spotted.

Each stone was a poignant reminder of life. Because we, too, can be soft and smooth while also being hard and impermeable. We may long to reflect the light of Christ, but we've been dulled by the downbeat of storms.

I confess my heart was hardened, even after a decade of knowing Jesus. I was lugging around guilt, shame, and anger. But once I got honest with God and gave Him access to my heart, He moved in and emptied out all the stony parts formed by wounds.

God turned my heart of stone to flesh. He made my heart His dwelling place as He wrote a new story upon the stones of my life. And He wants to do that in you.

I will give you a new heart and put a new spirit within you;
I will remove your heart of stone and give you a heart of flesh.
EZEKIEL 36:26

Toward Transparency

Hello, my name is Mei and I'm a recovering perfectionist. Left to my own devices, my pantry would be color-coded, labeled, and organized by height, expiration date, and food group.

But I'm really a fraud. I tried to emulate the home-decorating magazines, but trying to maintain this facade was exhausting and led to a pit of depression. I was in bondage to a lie—that my value and self-worth were tied to how beautiful and immaculate my home was.

Jesus criticized the religious leaders of His day for being more concerned about the appearance of righteousness than being internally transformed by the love of God. The religious leaders were more interested in outward appearances, from handwashing ceremonies to tithing the smallest amounts from their herb gardens.

We can try to hide our messiness behind doors of self-righteousness, but God sees our inner self—our motives and desires. And He wants to do an inward work, conforming our hearts into the image of Christ. It's His grace poured into us that will ultimately produce the outward manifestation of a beautiful heart, a heart that exalts our Creator. And by His grace, we are allowed to open a few cabinet doors and permit others to see the messiness of our broken lives.

There is nothing covered that won't be uncovered,
nothing hidden that won't be made known.
LUKE 12:2

The One Thing That's Impossible to Lose

I don't know how I could have lost my wallet, but I did. When I got home from shopping, I couldn't find it—a pink wristlet that was a special birthday gift from a friend. An hour later, after zooming back to the store, looking in all the shopping carts and turning my car inside out, I had to accept the truth: my wallet was gone.

There are moments in life when we may be at a loss for what to do or say. But God's wisdom is always there in the midst of the unexpected. Our names are written on His heart and He desires to meet us in the midst of our challenges, disappointments, and losses.

God's love for us never fades. And He understands our needs better than we do. When we're uncertain about our next steps, we can be certain that God's not letting go.

Let's choose God's love and seek His wisdom this week. Let's choose to be still and listen. God is called Emmanuel, God with us, because He *really is with us*. As is. We are close to His heart.

For wisdom is better than jewels, and nothing desirable can compare with it.
PROVERBS 8:11

A Place of Your Own

I remember a season of life where I felt really down and discouraged. I needed to connect with God and sense His presence. So one morning I stepped into my yard and started a garden. You know what? God met me there. I had set everything else aside to be alone and make time to hear from Him.

Do you have a place to be alone, a place where you can shut out the world and hear God's voice? A quiet place where you look forward to meeting God and where He is invited in to meet you?

It's easy to slip into only meeting God at church on Sundays. But to really grow and get to know Him, we need to set aside a time and place of our own—a place where we are intentional about being with Him in our day-to-day life. It may be a special chair or a corner booth at a local coffee shop—it really doesn't matter where that "place" is. The important thing is that we're deliberate in our intent to meet Him somewhere regularly. And then once we do, we can know He's there, waiting for us to show up and invite Him in.

*I will meet with you there above the mercy seat, between the two
cherubim that are over the ark of the testimony; I will speak with you
from there about all that I command you regarding the Israelites.*

EXODUS 25:22

Freedom from Perfection

As I turn my face toward the glow of the alarm clock, I will myself not to look at the time, not wanting to know the limited hours until sunrise. Instead of counting sheep, I talk to the Shepherd, but my thoughts are jumbled.

The laundry sits piled in the basket. My to-do list of projects grows. Why can't I pull it together? Christ came so that I could have freedom, but I'm not free—I'm trapped in an unending chaos of everyday life.

Then, in the stillness of the morning, I hear the faint whisper of the Spirit: *"Come to Me and rest."* I reluctantly oblige. And when I open my Bible, my guilt collides with truth. God's grace is sufficient for me. God never intended for me to be perfect.

Freedom in Christ comes when I relinquish my need for perfection and instead rest in Him. When I let Him fill my shortcomings with the glory that is His and only His, I find rest. Sweet, soul-quenching rest.

So today, I'm making a promise to myself: not to be burdened with the yoke of perfection. If I could attain this lofty standard, Christ would never have come. For the sake of weary perfectionists everywhere, I'm so glad He did.

Christ has liberated us to be free.
Stand firm then and don't submit again to a yoke of slavery.
GALATIANS 5:1

The Little Foxes We Find

One Saturday we woke up to a sunny kitchen crawling with black ants. We hadn't been in our new house long, but we knew that moving back to the Deep South, after years away, would mean dealing with bugs. They started in the kitchen and then popped up on the second floor in our bathroom. I was discouraged. Somehow, the ants had spoiled our new-house excitement.

The little things can really get you down sometimes. Like little foxes spoiling a vineyard, life's trials—even petty annoyances—can prevent us from resting in Jesus. Simple, everyday struggles can squash the perfect fruit of relationship with Him. They are like little foxes, threatening to steal the fruit of joy, hope, and peace that Jesus says is already ours.

How easily I forget that instead of dwelling on the little foxes, we can rejoice, knowing that in spite of the mess swirling around us, we are chosen to be a light in the world. And these earthly struggles are reminders that Jesus came to give us peace with God. He can and will accomplish His purpose in your life and in mine. He is the reason we have joy and hope and peace. And there isn't a fox anywhere that can steal that.

Catch the foxes for us—the little foxes that ruin the vineyards—for our vineyards are in bloom.
SONG OF SONGS 2:15

Fit for Glory

When I think about a treasure, I think of things secretly stored in a locked chest and hidden safely away. What doesn't come to mind is a fragile jar of clay.

Treasures are typically placed in strong containers so they are able to protect what they contain. Yet God chose to place the treasure of the gospel in weak, fragile "clay jars." In us.

At first, this seems counterintuitive, as if maybe God didn't think this plan through. But He wasn't being careless. He had a definite purpose in His decision to entrust the treasure of the gospel in us—so the source of the gospel's power would be clear and God's glory would be revealed in our weakness. We are fragile by design! I am weak, cracked, broken, and sorely lacking in any inherent strength. But it's right in the middle of that humble reality that I am most fit to reveal God's glory.

I used to despise my weaknesses and tried to hide my flaws. But rather than being places of shame and frustration, my liabilities have the potential to draw me into the security and safety found only in deep dependence on God. And that sweet place is where I can reveal His glory best.

Now we have this treasure in clay jars, so that this extraordinary power may be from God and not from us.
II CORINTHIANS 4:7

Chosen by God

Istared outside the restaurant window in silence while the rest of the table talked law, politics, and business ventures.

The waiter slipped in and out with a fresh basket of bread with such ease, it appeared as if the table magically replenished itself. He made himself invisible, and as I sat surrounded by my husband's colleagues, I faded into the shadows too. I wondered what I would say if anyone asked about my work—the quotidian tasks of raising small people and tidying up. No one ever asked.

As we parted ways and everyone said their goodbyes, I hooked my hand around my husband's arm and tried not to cry. On the drive home, I remained silent. While it hurts to feel invisible to the movers and shakers of this world, I'm learning to let go of my need for their validation. Like Hagar wandering in the wilderness, I serve a God who sees what others don't see. In my smallness, I remain His chosen.

As with the disciples, God glories in choosing the unexpected to do the work of His kingdom. Jesus chose radicals and zealots, doubters and unknowns. And despite this, they embodied the message of the gospel. Like the disciples, I am an ambassador of the Good News. Chosen, cherished, and wholly known.

Instead, God has chosen what is foolish in the world to shame the wise,
and God has chosen what is weak in the world to shame the strong.
I CORINTHIANS 1:27

Held by God

I remember when my kids were young and they wanted to hold my hand when they were unsure of their next step. Looking at me with their sweet, round eyes, they'd reach up with their chubby fingers and wait for my hand to grasp onto theirs.

Once they felt my hand, they happily and confidently took their next step forward because they knew I was there. They knew I wouldn't let go. That is how God is with us. He's always there, waiting for us to reach up and grab hold of His hand. He's there to guide us through the unknown future.

I've always been the girl who begged God for a sign, when all I really needed was to draw close and take the hand that's waiting. In the silence. In the whisper. That's when I sense His presence. That's when I know. It doesn't matter what the future holds or whether I'm on the right track. He's right there with me.

Being close to the One who holds my heart—who has named the stars and counted my hairs—is what really matters in life. And so I take His hand and my breathing slows. My heart fills with knowing. I am held. And I can trust that He won't let go of me.

He reached down from heaven and took hold of me;
He pulled me out of deep waters.
PSALM 18:16

Be Astonished

The MRI hummed and whirred. A fetal MRI is a delicate and lengthy procedure. It requires lying still long enough that sweat drips onto your pillow and your hair becomes clumped at the nape of your neck. But it's worth it to see a miracle of life.

Surely this technology is the kind of astounding event that the prophet talks about. And surely this unborn child would be our miracle . . .

God brought my family into the bright, new world of parenting our son Jack. Then God brought us into the bright, astonishing goodness of Jack's first smile with his wide cleft palate and the second smile with the tiniest ghost of a scar on his upper lip. The results of Jack's surgery astonished me, astounded me. Another astonishing miracle.

Through these experiences, I've learned to spend less time trapped in my own tunnel of imagination and, instead, trust that God can do immeasurably more than I can imagine.

Look at the nations and observe—be utterly astounded!
For something is taking place in your days
that you will not believe when you hear about it.
HABAKKUK 1:5

Because a Little Goes a Long Way

The house smelled amazing as all the ladies arrived to pray for our children's school. I opened the oven to remove the banana bread, excited to have made a treat served warm from the oven. It looked odd, though. The entire middle was sunken inward.

I jiggled the pan and realized that something was terribly wrong. It was mushy and gooey, but not the kind that makes something more delicious.

Oh, mercy! I forgot the eggs! Those eggs would have risen the entire batch to spongy perfection, but as it was, leaving them out impacted every crumb. And so it goes . . . when we leave out the right ingredients, the entire batch can end up completely impacted and often inedible.

It's much the same when we place our faith in Christ. He gives us a new identity. When we do things our own old way, or when we leave out the fresh new ingredients that we have been given in Him, the whole lot is affected. In Christ, we have a new recipe to live fully in the very best life. So let us learn to live for Him, and with Him, and in Him—to cast off the old ways and, instead, operate with the ingredients of His goodness and truth.

Your boasting is not good. Don't you know that a little yeast permeates the whole batch of dough? Clean out the old yeast so that you may be a new batch. You are indeed unleavened, for Christ our Passover has been sacrificed. Therefore, let us observe the feast, not with old yeast or with the yeast of malice and evil but with the unleavened bread of sincerity and truth.
1 CORINTHIANS 5:6–8

The Only Way

My biggest obstacle in this life journey has not been giving my life to Christ—it's been submitting my will to His.

I remember adults asking me throughout my youth what I wanted to do when I grew up. They said to follow my heart when it came to where I'd go to college or what career I'd pursue or who I'd marry. And for so long I got stuck trying to follow my heart and my dreams. When I prayed, it wasn't "Thy will be done"; it was always, "Lord, please let my will be done."

But His will is often not what we have in mind—or worse, an undisclosed will requires us to wait and simply trust in His plan. Ick.

Yet God asks us to release our plans, and sometimes it takes something major to get our attention and do it. Then He presents His will as an alternative to the "path of me."

I realize now that there is only ever one way: His way. All other roads are a distraction. His will is where I can rest in the knowledge that I am walking in the good deeds He set in advance for me to do. Daily praying, "Your kingdom come, Your will be done."

Your kingdom come. Your will be done.
MATTHEW 6:10

The Day I Stopped Believing

After seventeen months of praying, the woman I called "Momma" lost to a faceless, cruel disease that didn't care that she had fourteen- and seventeen-year-old daughters who still needed her. Cancer didn't care. And on that day, I decided that God didn't either. I kept up the facade. I still attended church. I even went on to seminary.

I believed in God, but I didn't trust Him. I believed He was able and that He could; I simply didn't believe He would—for me. Sure, He loved me enough to let me into heaven after believing in His Son. But did He care enough to answer the prayers of my heart on earth? So I stopped believing in prayer, its purpose, and its power. Why pray when God is going to do what He wants anyway?

Eventually I'd meet the man who would become my husband—and the supporter, encourager, and cheerleader that my mom never got to be. Together, in times of joblessness and homelessness, with bills and babies, we learned that God is a faithful provider. And together we learned to pray more, cling tighter, and trust harder. God has provided just enough light to keep us on His path. And He'll do the same for you.

Answer me quickly, Lord; my spirit fails.
Don't hide Your face from me,
or I will be like those going down to the Pit.
PSALM 143:7

Because We All Need Somewhere to Belong

There were hundreds of pigeons, everywhere. I tiptoed among them when suddenly dozens of them flew into the sky at once, as if on cue. But no sooner had they taken off, then they landed right back on the spot where they began. They did this over and over. This place was their community.

I'm longing for community like that. To find our people and hang together. To fly together when we hear threatening "footsteps" coming. To stick together and return again to "our place."

But sometimes it's just easier to leave the flock when surroundings become threatening. We compare and measure ourselves short. We quit risking. We leave everyone behind to be alone. Except *alone* won't work—we need each other.

Community needs the one who's perched in the tree and the one whose view is from the ground. We need the older one and the younger one. Everyone has something unique to offer. And what would community be if there were no diversity?

Few things are as lovely as pulling together and cheering each other on. Few things are as wonderful as giving our strengths and receiving from others what we lack. Few things are as sacred as protecting, trusting, and caring for one another...building a community where we all belong.

And let us be concerned about one another in order to promote love and good works, not staying away from our worship meetings, as some habitually do, but encouraging each other, and all the more as you see the day drawing near.
HEBREWS 10:24-25

On the Other Side of Impossible

I never believed I would make it to this place. They announced my name and handed me a diploma. I can hardly hold back the tears. So many times, I almost gave up.

Six years ago I dropped out of high school. College seemed too good for a girl like me. That's where the smart people went—the ones with parents who believed in them.

By God's grace I finished high school and went to a community college. I felt so different and stupid compared to the other students. And some days school and work collided. But I continued and pushed forward, looking toward the finish line.

At age twenty-one, I was adopted. Now I have parents cheering me on. They never let me give up. They encouraged me all the way to the finish line.

Now wearing cap and gown, with bachelor's degree in hand, I am so thankful the Lord took a broken girl and did the impossible. He saw something in her that she didn't. He pursued her and reminded her that His ways are no limit to her circumstances. Most of all, He showed her that she is worthy because her worthiness is found in Christ alone. Everything that was taken from her, God in His gracious love has redeemed.

A man who endures trials is blessed, because when he passes the test he will receive the crown of life that God has promised to those who love Him.

JAMES 1:12

Starting Small

I have an embarrassing confession to make: I used to want to be famous. I thought that if I could plan that huge event, speak on a gigantic stage, or write that best-selling book, I'd somehow make God happy.

But then I had kids and devoted years doing the not-so-glamorous work of laundry, diaper changing, and runny-nose wiping. Unfortunately, I also spent a lot of time resenting the mundane work, thinking this wasn't the "it" God had planned for me.

One day, sitting amid scattered toys and clambering children, I cried out and confessed that I didn't like who I had become—a whiny, resentful, complaining mother who was unsatisfied with God's provision. God heard my cry and began to show me that this life was shaping my character and helping me become the woman He wanted me to be.

And so through small, new beginnings, God helped me see that it's not what I do that pleases Him, but who I am.

I wouldn't trade those early years with my daughters for anything, not just because of the fun we had together or the joy I experienced watching them grow into adulthood, but because of what God did in me during those years. He patiently took a miserable, frustrated young woman and pointed her to grace.

For who scorns the day of small things?
ZECHARIAH 4:10

The Friend I Didn't Know I Needed

While standing in the rain, my friend handed me a small square painting with yellow-orange bursts of flowers. We had just finished a hike; our shoes and pants were splattered with mud, our faces dripping with water.

"I made this for you," she said.

The week before, after another muddy hike, she had played me a song on her phone as we sat in the front seat of her car. It was a song of longing and healing—of faith and knowing that God is near. Each word spoke straight to my heart.

I received the painting and the song, the conversations and the time together, as the gifts they were: God pursuing me in the flesh. She was a dear friend who loved with wide-open generosity and bold vulnerability. I had never met a person with which to show honor, respect, and love. It's risky to give without reservation so that another person feels valued and seen.

On the back of her painting my friend wrote, "For His Flower." She knew my heart for God and that He was wooing me to Himself through her. The actions we take in esteeming the people in our lives show the face of God. And I want to see that face more than anything.

_____

_____

_____

_____

_____

_____

_____

_____

Show family affection to one another with brotherly love.
Outdo one another in showing honor.
ROMANS 12:10

When God Turns Your Kicking and Screaming into Beauty

I live in a sleepy town with one stoplight to its name. It would be an understatement to say that I did not want to move here. So, at age fifteen, I kicked and screamed. The kicking is metaphorical. The screaming? Well, that is literal. I threw a lot of teenage tantrums. I holed up in my room, wrote letters to people who were gone, and I cried a lot. And I refused to paint my bedroom walls until there was a ring on my mother's finger.

But then came summer . . . a time of pausing, reflecting, and growing. Then came a ring, and then a beautiful wedding.

I look back and can see how God turned all my kicking and screaming into beauty. I didn't think I would find beauty or comfort or peace in a one-stop town, but I did. I didn't think I would learn about humility or hard work on a smelly farm, but I did. I didn't think I would watch a sunlit sky with golden hues and savor the feeling of home and a stable family, but I do. And I think that speaks to a God who hides beauty in the most unexpected of places when we trust Him.

He has sent Me to heal the brokenhearted, to proclaim liberty to the captives and freedom to the prisoners; to proclaim the year of the LORD's favor, and the day of our God's vengeance; to comfort all who mourn, to provide for those who mourn in Zion; to give them a crown of beauty instead of ashes, festive oil instead of mourning, and splendid clothes instead of despair.

ISAIAH 61:1–3

Deep Roots

The flower bulb wouldn't survive the coming fall season without careful planting. I lined a pot with soil and inserted the bulb, then put another handful of soil on each side. It appeared to be a project completed, but it had only just begun.

Each morning I slowly watered around the bulb. At first just a few drops were needed—the bulb had yet to settle in to the soil. Day after day, I faithfully watered the soil.

It wasn't long before a few drops were not enough. The bulb took root, and after several weeks, I woke to a green shoot emerging from the soil. It wasn't much to look at, but I cheered and clapped so loudly you would have thought I won the lottery. Weeks later the green shoot grew several feet high. And then, seemingly overnight, the flowers bloomed big and bright. The natural result of careful watering was new life, steady growth, and incomparable beauty.

The brilliance of unfurling petals was unmistakable, but the incremental growth was too miniscule for my human eyes to see. Our personal growth often feels the same way. Yet as we stay close to the Source, and as He is faithful to water and tend, our roots sink into Him as our lives grow upward and outward.

The man who trusts in the Lord, whose confidence indeed is the Lord, is blessed. He will be like a tree planted by water: it sends its roots out toward a stream, it doesn't fear when heat comes, and its foliage remains green. It will not worry in a year of drought or cease producing fruit.

JEREMIAH 17:7–8

The Gratitude Train

When I visited the Virginia War Museum with my family, I was delighted when my son said, "Mom, look, there's the Gratitude Train. It was given to the US by the French and filled with gifts to say thank-you for sending aid in World War I." Coming home, I thought how nice it would be to have a gratitude train in our daily lives.

Scripture tells us to live with hearts of gratitude, but sometimes we forget. We may forget war battles of the past, which purchased our freedom in America. But when we remember the courage of the soldiers and their families, gratitude comes. In our homes, we remember the wrongs committed against us, but what about the rights?

So whenever I'm not feeling grateful for my spouse (he snores!) or for my kids (they're on my last nerve!), I picture a Gratitude Train rolling right through my family room. Not the Little Engine That Could or Thomas the Tank Engine. The full-size Gratitude Train! And inside each boxcar are treasures to remember. Like the day I met Christ. Or the job offer that came just in time.

Today, let's take time to remember the goodness of God through the years; then we won't ever run out of things to say thank-you for.

Let us enter His presence with thanksgiving; let us shout triumphantly to Him in song. For the LORD is a great God, a great King above all gods.
PSALM 95:2-3

Steadfast and Sure

"Nobody loves me!" she cried, hot tears spilling from her little-girl heart. Of course her words weren't true, but her perception became what she believed. I know this has been true of me. We're all hungry for acceptance and approval. Our feelings often lie, telling us we're unloved or unlovable, but the truth never changes—you and I *are* loved by God.

How deeply are you loved? You are loved with the same intensity and consistency that God loves Jesus. No matter how you feel, you are loved completely, profoundly, unwaveringly! Nothing can separate you from His love! But here lies the crux: Jesus instructs us to *remain* in His love by keeping His commandments. That means to love God with all our hearts and souls and minds and to love our neighbor as ourselves. Will we?

Jesus doesn't ask us to do anything He hasn't already done. His life is characterized by serving, praying, giving, obeying—even unto death. Are we willing to live like Jesus? Will we follow His example of surrender and sacrifice?

May we remain in Him, resting our lives on the love of Christ, so we can authentically give our lives away to love Him and love others well.

As the Father has loved Me, I have also loved you.
Remain in My love. If you keep My commands you will remain in My love,
just as I have kept my Father's commands and remain in His love.
JOHN 15:9–10

MARCH 6
When All Isn't Calm

I'm an anxious person. And I hate to admit that I have anxiety. Feeling weak and ashamed, my mind screams, "Keep that curtain closed!" I hate for people to know that my husband is married to an anxious wife.

I don't want people to know that my kids have an anxious mom. I hate for my friends to know that I am anxious.

The anxiety hits me out of the blue. But over the years, I found what calms me down: writing, walking, listening to music, deep breathing, reciting verses or song lyrics. Eventually, all is calm again. But this year, instead of coming suddenly, the anxiety began to slowly seep in. Regaining calm and suppressing the anxiety became more difficult.

And here's the hard truth: the only way I can breathe freely is to admit that I'm anxious and know I don't have to face it and suppress it alone. When the attacks threaten to seep in, I face them by trusting in God's promises and listening to words of encouragement from family and friends.

If you are facing an anxious moment (or moments) and you need to breathe freely again, join me in the trusting, embracing, clinging, cherishing, and listening.

I will listen to what God will say; surely the Lord will
declare peace to His people, His godly ones.
PSALM 85:8

MARCH 7
Singing for Joy

I grew up with two girls who became my best friends. We share a lot of memories, but there's one that stands out more than the rest.

We were about six years old and had just discovered our gorgeous singing voices. Crowding around the piano while their older sister played, we belted out the song, "Let There Be Peace on Earth" for the entire neighborhood to hear. Believe me when I say there was no peace on earth that day! Our singing turned almost to screaming as we each tried to outdo the others.

But for all the screechy loudness that took place, we sang with joy . . . overflowing amounts of it. My own six-year-old daughter is the same way. She'll sing a tune and dance around the house, exploding with joy for absolutely no reason other than she loves life and she loves Jesus. That inspires me . . . not only in the singing or the dancing of my days, but also in how I live.

Regardless of the day's challenges or life's circumstances, there's always a reason for joy. The singing kind. The dancing kind. The living-it-out-because-I've-got-Jesus kind. So if you catch me doing a little dance or singing a silly opera tune with my girl, well, that's why.

You are my helper; I will rejoice in the shadow of Your wings.
PSALM 63:7

He Calls the Broken

Every Sunday I step onto the stage with our church's worship team. While I love leading worship, the stage part terrifies me. But I do it because I love entering God's presence by singing His praises.

I used to believe I had to have my life all together before I had the "right" to be on stage. I was a hypocrite and a sinner, and God only calls the perfect, right? That's what the enemy whispered to me, and for a long time I believed it. Finally I heard someone say: God doesn't call the perfect; He perfects the called. Oh, what sweet music to this girl's heart.

I don't have to have it all together—I have a lot of growing and refining to do. But knowing I am called me to a specific purpose, and knowing that God will equip me along the way gives me the courage to say yes to being a part of something that is for His glory and not my own.

I don't know what your past looks like. I don't know what secrets the enemy is using to convince you of your limitations. But it is through Him and by Him we are redeemed. And God uses the redeemed. That means you and me!

Falling to the ground, he heard a voice saying to him, "Saul, Saul, why are you persecuting Me?" "Who are you, Lord?" he said. "I am Jesus, the One you are persecuting," He replied. "But get up and go into the city, and you will be told what you must do."

ACTS 9:4–6

She Scares Me

"She scares me," the young lady said as she pointed to a name on the sign-up sheet. I burst out laughing, because the name belonged to a dear friend. This "scary" friend is bold in spirit but has a heart the size of Texas. I could see how the young lady might be intimidated by my friend's larger-than-life persona. But then I started thinking about all the times we miss out on friendship opportunities because we perceive someone as different than reality.

The beautiful lady dressed to the hilt with all the diamonds might be the most humble person in the room. The super-chatty girl might not be as bad once you get to know her and realize her infectious zeal for life. The quiet girl who looks away when you catch her eye may be drowning in grief or depression. The truth is, we all come to the table with our own personalities and hang-ups.

But while people look at outward appearances, God looks at the heart. And we should do the same. Let's take time to get to know the hearts belonging to all the faces around us. We just never know what God has waiting for us on the other side of a friendly conversation.

But the Lord said to Samuel, "Do not look at his appearance or his stature, because I have rejected him. Man does not see what the Lord sees, for man sees what is visible, but the Lord sees the heart."
I SAMUEL 16:7

For When You're the New Girl

We had just moved to Atlanta, so I was the new girl. I met new people quickly—something I normally enjoy—but it felt exhausting.

I was afraid of saying something silly or laughing when it wasn't intended to be funny. Afraid of my outfit coming across too loose or not age-appropriate. Afraid of not meeting expectations or not knowing the Scripture reference. Afraid of . . . rejection.

Fear needs approval, but love needs you. Love agrees with God that He is sovereign and will orchestrate our relationships no matter how casual or deep.

Fear says I cannot be my true self, but love says I want you to know the true me. When I walk in love for others, I can open myself up to people—flaws and all. And I can love others by being a safe place for them to be who they are.

Fear is self-focused, but love is others-focused. When we walk in fear we are thinking too much about ourselves. And when I spend too much time in my own head, I don't love others well—because I'm not thinking about them.

But love listens and focuses on getting to know others. With God's grace, I'm clinging to love and investing in the relationships I'm building.

_Do nothing out of rivalry or conceit, but in humility consider
others as more important than yourselves._
PHILIPPIANS 2:3

God's Word Is Our Compass

Growing up in the country meant that most car drives became geography, genealogy, and directional lessons. So as an adult, my sense of direction is well-developed.

But when we recently went to Washington, DC, my internal compass was broken. I had to trust that our daughter knew the way since she was a sophisticated city driver.

Similarly, Joshua finds himself in new territory, uncertain of the direction to take. The people of Israel had been making inroads in Canaan, defeating the nations, and the Gibeonites were next. So they used their wits to save their tribe. They brought moldy bread and worn-out sandals to persuade Joshua that they had come a far distance. Joshua wasn't to make treaties with anyone living close by, but since the Gibeonites appeared to live far away, Joshua made a treaty with them. He neglected to ask God for wisdom in this situation.

When we're tempted to take action without consulting God, we're wise to remember that our wits, though sharp, and our hearts, though set to follow after Christ, can be fooled. Being grounded in God's Word is so vital. God's Word guides us and leads us in the way of His wisdom and grace.

Then the men of Israel took some of their provisions,
but did not seek the LORD's counsel.
JOSHUA 9:14

True Rest

It was just another day—from changing diapers and shuttling kids to scanning unread e-mails and prepping for an event.

My to-do list, home, and work responsibilities overwhelmed me. Everywhere, voices seemed to shout: *You can't do this. There's not enough time. Just give up. You're such a failure. You're such a bad mom. Bad wife. Bad friend.*

I jumped on Amazon to buy new shoes for my kids. Their current holey ones—not to be confused with "holy," because shoes and kids are far from it—give the appearance of homelessness. Just sayin'.

One click from purchasing I noticed eight other unplanned items in my cart! How'd that happen? Hmm. Scanning them, I justify the need even though I know I shouldn't. But it's too easy. *Click.*

When life feels overwhelming, why do we settle for temporary relief in the form of shopping, Instagram . . . you fill in the blank. While these things may not be inherently bad, the provided solace is fleeting. In fact, they often leave us aching even more. If you're feeling weary and empty, His Word is clear. Jesus will give us rest. Seek Jesus. Pray to Him, right now. He is the peace and rest your soul is longing for.

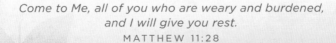

Come to Me, all of you who are weary and burdened,
and I will give you rest.
MATTHEW 11:28

Finding God in a Deserted Heart

My son wouldn't be born for several months; still, I labored through a different kind of pain. The God I'd loved as a child had become distant, demanded too much. He wanted me to love Him—and Him alone. He wanted my heart committed to Him fully.

I longed for a man to love me and never leave me. Nothing worked. Me—a broke, single mother with a second child on the way.

I thought of my sister who had shared a poem with me; it spoke of surrender and satisfaction in God alone. Not what I wanted to hear, but what I needed to experience. He spoke to my heart tenderly, though I recoiled.

Eventually, the Spirit nudged me into one honest step forward. "God, I confess I don't truly want You. Help me to want to want You." More tears came and my struggling turned into surrender. This crisis of faith sent grasping hands in search of His loving grip.

Wrestling in this wasteland led me to know God in a deeper way. I came to trust the kind of love which never fails and never leaves. And this same love is yours in Christ too. God is faithful to grow a new love in us—a love that never fails and never leaves.

This is what the Lord says: They found favor in the wilderness— the people who survived the sword. When Israel went to find rest, the Lord appeared to him from far away. I have loved you with an everlasting love; therefore, I have continued to extend faithful love to you.
JEREMIAH 31:2–3

When God Fills the Gap

I have a biological father, but there isn't much to tell about him. He and my mother never married. When I was nine, he gave me a purple-and-white bike with matching colored streamers on the handle bars. He died before I turned ten. That is the sum of what I know. My mother never talked about him, and I never asked. Welcome to my family.

Rather than mourning the loss of my father, I mourn the loss of what should have been—a lifetime of memories together. He should have played a significant role in my life.

Growing up fatherless stirs up a well of insecurities that has been an underlying motivation in many of the decisions I've made. It hasn't been easy, but I know that God has been with me. He has been ever so faithful to extend His grace to me at times when I've been unaware of Him or even when I've been far from Him.

I haven't had any spiritual fathers in my life. Maybe God decided to fill that gap, which floods my soul with hope, peace, and joy. He chose me—just as He chose you—to be His beloved daughter. There is no end to His love and grace toward us.

_Even if my father and mother abandon me, the L_ORD _cares for me._
PSALM 27:10

When It Appears That All Is Lost

My friend is a painter, and we happened into a conversation about her process. She showed me her canvas and spoke of the "underpainting." First she painted the basic images in terms of lights and darks. It looked like a sketch in a sepia filter. She said the painting would emerge out of these initial details, but that it's easy to give up in this phase. As she spoke, God was stirring in my heart to pay close attention to her words.

You see, in the middle of my hardest seasons, I've looked at the canvas of my life and felt like God skipped over me. I want to see a finished work, but I get discouraged when my canvas is seemingly colorless.

For a vivid picture to emerge, lights and darks are needed. They add tone value to the painting. My "dark" seasons are the first I want to dismiss or hide. But God desires to use them to point to His work as the Creator. He uses the darks and lights to create an image of Himself in those who call Him *Lord*.

God is painting on the canvas of my life . . . and yours. Let's choose to trust the Artist. Because the picture is still in process.

We know that all things work together for the good of those who love God: those who are called according to His purpose.
ROMANS 8:28

Lavished with Grace

When I got married, I remember feeling very blessed, in part because of the multitude of gifts lavished upon us. Over time, however, those gifts ceased working or they outgrew their usefulness. In contrast, God blesses us with spiritual blessings, including His mercy and grace, which are eternal.

I especially love the word choice here in Ephesians. God didn't just give us His grace, He richly poured, or lavished, His grace upon us. His grace simply doesn't run out. Never do we have to worry that His grace will dry up. When we think we've used up our allotment, there will still be grace to spare.

Picture yourself standing under a rushing, roaring waterfall—with all of His grace pouring down upon you, completely soaking you. God, in His great love for us, drenches us in His grace. Unlike human gifts that will eventually turn to dust, the gift of His grace will carry us from here to eternity.

In order for us to live free from the bondage of our sin, God paid a huge price—death upon a cross. If giving One's life is not the ultimate act of grace, I don't know what is! He did this specifically for you and for me. And His grace will never, ever run out.

We have redemption in Him through His blood,
the forgiveness of our trespasses, according to the riches of His grace
that He lavished on us with all wisdom and understanding.
EPHESIANS 1:7–8

Facedown and in Need of Forgiveness

"**Y**ou and you are out of here! Follow me!" I bellowed as I flung the classroom door open, leaving my students in my angry wake.

As I tromped down the hallway toward the office, leading these two young men to their doom, I had a moment of clarity. What was I doing? I knew my tantrum wasn't really going to fix anything. In my attempts to get the class back on track, I grasped for control the only remaining way I knew how. I yelled, and anyone who disagreed could just get out.

I cried in shame on the drive home from work. How could I have let things get so out of control? Didn't I know better? Apparently on this day, I didn't. I needed forgiveness for stepping onto the easier path that I knew to be wrong.

When we're facedown in a mess, it's hard to remember that the failure we feel is not the failure we are. Quite the opposite. Repentance is a sign of God's deep goodness within us—this "made in the image of God" part of us that can't be eclipsed.

These facedown moments are also weirdly comforting. I am reminded that it's not my job to have everything together. God's got that covered. And for that, I say thanks.

I will make known the LORD's faithful love and the LORD's praiseworthy acts, because of all the LORD has done for us—even the many good things He has done for the house of Israel and has done for them based on His compassion and the abundance of His faithful love.
ISAIAH 63:7

Rooted and Grounded

While working in the yard, I saw a young crape myrtle shoot sticking out of a flower bed. I tried to yank it out, but as soon as I started pulling, I realized it was going to take more than a hard tug. I grabbed my hand ax and started digging around the base. This revealed a surprisingly hefty root system. Before I knew it, I was pulling up dirt and grass along a seemingly endless path.

I stared. That little shoot seemed utterly unimpressive on its own. But its root system was substantial.

It made me realize that we too often judge others by what we can see and measure. Impatience, addiction, a bad temper...these troublesome "shoots" are remnants of an old root system in the process of being discarded. The system must be displaced by a new one.

We get distracted from this reality when we focus solely on fixing problems we see aboveground. Every problem stems from an unhealthy, unseen root system. But a strong, fruitful tree will develop naturally from a healthy one.

We are to be rooted in the love of Christ. As we drink from the infinite well of His love, our roots grow stronger, healthier, and more established. We, in turn, become rooted, grounded, and, ultimately, transformed.

I pray that He may grant you, according to the riches of His glory, to be strengthened with power in the inner man through His Spirit.
EPHESIANS 3:16

For the Love of God and Place

I didn't want to be here. I wanted my home, friends, and community back. I wanted the way things were before people wrecked both our community and our workplace—before friends and coworkers were forced to move away.

I gazed out the window as portions of Psalm 137 came to mind: "By the rivers of Babylon—there we sat down and wept when we remembered Zion. . . . How can we sing the LORD's song on foreign soil?" (vv 1, 4). I was a foreigner here, weeping—with no friends, no church, and no community.

I had to forgive those who had wrecked our community, I had to do it while wounded and left for dead. How does one escape such profound sadness and creeping bitterness?

Slowly and painfully I forced my gaze off myself and onto Jesus. I trained my eyes on this verse in Jeremiah, trusting that I'd eventually move through my grief as I sought this city's welfare.

Perhaps you don't want to be where you are today. Maybe you feel unknown, alone, and out of context. Yet while you're here, why not ask the Lord how you can seek the welfare of this place? Soon you'll find it's wrapped up in the welfare of the people who are right around you, right here.

Seek the welfare of the city I have deported you to.
Pray to the LORD on its behalf, for when it has prosperity, you will prosper.
JEREMIAH 29:7

Your Gifts Revealed

Several years ago I enrolled in a "Discovering Your Purpose" class. It involved learning the spiritual gifts described in Romans 12. I identified with the gift of teaching, but there also was the potential of coming across as a know-it-all.

After our instructor explained this, I hesitantly said, "I'm a teacher, but I try hard not to come across as a know-it-all. I learned a long time ago how to keep my mouth shut." Her first response was, "What happened?" Then she said, "Who squashed your gift?"

Immediately, the Holy Spirit brought to mind a memory from the third grade. I was an excellent student, but I usually received a poor grade in "Conduct" because I couldn't stop talking. I learned that in order to be seen as good, I needed to keep my mouth shut. Eventually my "Conduct" grade improved, but I didn't learn how to harness my gift; I only learned to suppress it.

I realized that experience held me back from the plans God had for me in the present. Likewise, you also may have untapped gifts inside because of a well-meaning teacher, friend, or family member. Like Daniel, ask God to reveal your gifts to fully live out His purpose for your life and give Him praise for what He reveals.

He reveals the deep and hidden things . . .
DANIEL 2:22

MARCH 21
Hope Falling

At first glance, an unexpected bother has sabotaged my momentum. I'm stopped and irritated. But then I listen. I lean in to hear the falling snow. Hope is free-falling to earth.

As winter white blankets earth, I let the snow fall. I don't stop it, adjust it, or grieve it. I let it change everything—to script a new plan for today. Because I sense Him saying: Let My grace not be an interruption, but a divine appointment. Let hope fall all around you today.

Finding hope has become my soul's desperation, begging for something to rise from the ashes that have made me crumble. The lonely, the poured out, the caregivers, the risk-takers, the dreamers . . . with souls sore, and yet, God is always enough. This truth is a yielding, an attempt to take one more step, one more act of faith, with little guarantee that this act will provide the results we desire.

And here, today, I sense His quiet encouragement for all of us. To keep hoping for that job of your dreams. To keep hoping that loving others counts. To keep hoping that each deposit made in this life has eternal significance.

Snow finds us in the quiet as He finds our hearts and whispers hope.

Purify me with hyssop, and I will be clean; wash me, and I will be whiter than snow.
PSALM 51:7

When All You Want to Do Is Eat a Cheeseburger and Cry

Out of desperation I call my husband at work. But I hear his voicemail instead. Here I am, at home with two screaming babies while he's in a quiet conference room with other adults. So I don't say anything—I record the shrill cries of two infants.

I hang up and try everything to soothe the shrieking cherubs. I feed them, bathe them, and dress them. I swaddle and bounce, sway and burble. Still, nothing. Finally, I buckle them into their car seats and drive around the neighborhood. Then I have a brilliant idea.

I find the nearest drive-through and whisper "Thank you" to the girl who hands me a bag with my cheeseburger and fries. I pull into a nearby parking space, and with both babies finally asleep, I eat my happy meal and cry.

Several years have passed and even now, whenever I feel down, guess where I'm tempted to go? Not to my knees. Not to God's Word. But to the nearest drive-through altar.

But I want to hunger and thirst for righteousness more than a cheeseburger—because only God can fill a hungry heart. Only when we come to the banquet of the King and dine in His presence, feasting on the goodness of His Word, are we truly filled.

Those who hunger and thirst for righteousness are blessed,
for they will be filled.
MATTHEW 5:6

When You Feel Unusable

"Thank you," she whispered through her tears. I squeezed her hand and smiled, my own tears falling to my lap. I didn't know her, but I saw the loneliness, the sorrow, in her eyes. When we bowed our heads to pray, I wrapped my arms around her.

She told me the story of a husband's betrayal, of losing what she'd thought was forever. She hadn't shared the weight of her loss, her brokenness with anyone. But that day, the dam broke open. I told her the one thing I knew was absolutely true: God loves her and nothing in her story rendered her less precious to the God of all creation.

I wish I'd had time that day to share about the women in Jesus's genealogy: Tamar. Rahab. Ruth. Bathsheba. Mary. These women, the ones named in the ancestry of Christ, were each broken, imperfect.

I don't know your story—the parts of your past that make you feel unusable by God. But I know this: the very same truth I shared with my friend is true for you as well. The God who chose to include these five women in the family tree of His Son looks at you and sees potential, possibility, and promise. And His plan for you is good, very good.

The historical record of Jesus Christ, the Son of David, the Son of Abraham: Abraham fathered Isaac . . . Judah fathered Perez and Zerah by Tamar . . . Salmon fathered Boaz by Rahab, Boaz fathered Obed by Ruth, Obed fathered Jesse, and Jesse fathered King David. David fathered Solomon by Uriah's wife.

MATTHEW 1:1–6

Taking Care of Each Other

When I turned the key to our front door, what I found surprised me. My house was cleaner than I'd left it! I opened a card on the table and discovered why: my friend had cleaned my house, left dinner in the fridge, and placed notes all around to remind me of my value in Christ and His love for me.

Her thoughtfulness overwhelmed me—I felt taken care of. Most of my days are spent taking care of others. You're probably caring for others too. As women, we're used to being the ones who take care of others. But how often do we let others take care of us?

It feels foreign and vulnerable to be taken care of by others. When my friend came over and cleaned, she saw things I didn't want anyone to see. And she learned how unorganized I am. But if she had asked if she could help, my knee-jerk reaction would have been to say no.

Instead, my friend loved me by taking care of me before I asked. She relieved stress from my life. And I experienced Christ's love through her that day. Taking care of each other is one of the sweetest gifts we can give. But that might mean taking care of someone before asking permission.

I give you a new command: Love one another.
Just as I have loved you, you are also to love one another.
JOHN 13:34

The Very Best Kind of Rest

"I've been trying to rest," I say to my husband, "and I don't think it's working." He looks at me. "Maybe your idea of rest isn't really rest." I nod. When I felt I needed to slow down, I took that literally. I spent more time lounging. I completed my to-do list. And I felt worse.

I'm coming to see that when God asked me to rest, it was actually more about my heart. Trusting instead of striving. Enjoying rather than pushing. Focusing on the moment instead of on results. This verse in Song of Songs is a call to arise . . . to come away with Him. It's an intimate invitation not to step away from life but to embrace the Giver of it.

I read once that the word *rest* is closely related to the word *celebration*. What if God's invitation to rest is really an invitation to joy—to experience life to the full?

I felt hope seep back into my bones and peace find its way to my soul again. What if we think about rest not as simply the absence of work, but instead as the presence of a Person? To be with the One who made us, who formed our hearts, and who places dreams within us.

My love calls to me: Arise, my darling. Come away, my beautiful one.
SONG OF SONGS 2:10

Making Old Things New

We have this old dresser. I've thought about getting rid of it but decided to try painting it instead. I bought the cheapest paintbrush and drop cloth and picked out some new hardware for the drawers. And then . . . I cranked up the music. I barely sanded. I just went to work. It was ridiculous how much fun it was. And sister! It's ridiculous how proud I am of myself.

I wasn't paranoid about perfection. I just focused on the fun of making something old new again. I wasn't sure if it needed a second coat, so I texted a friend. Her response made me laugh because, of course, there are no paint police. "Paint it till you like it," she said. Isn't that just the best advice? Sand it till you like it. Paint it till you like it. Our homes should be safe places. Why do we allow them to boss us around? No, ma'am. Make like this newbie decorator and move it, paint it, or redecorate it till you like it.

And I like it, very much. It's so pretty. I keep walking over to pet it and admire it from different angles in the room. My only regret is that I didn't try this a decade ago.

For I will create a new heaven and a new earth . . .
ISAIAH 65:17

When That Thing Is Too Hard

Today I feel like Moses. I am swallowed up in my inability. Tomorrow morning, I will stand behind a cross of wood and honor my beautiful friend, Jennifer, who now lives in heaven. And the only thing I'm sure of is, I can't do it.

I can't speak words that will adequately cover the vastness of her life. I can't paint the love and soul and passion of this woman in vivid enough colors. I can't not become a blubbery mess, since what I most want to do is curl up in a corner, doing the ugly cry, while mourning my own sense of loss. I can't pretend I feel worthy of the honor to speak when so many other people loved her too. I can't say the right thing. I can't say enough. I can't say anything, at all. I can't. It will have to be Him.

I do not care what all the inspirational books in the world say about the vast abilities of humans to create life-changing moments for ourselves. It's simply not true. All those good, lasting, important, inspiring, not-a-train-wreck, not-about-ourselves moments in life won't come from you or me. When the too-big thing that is not able to be humanly done is in front of us, it will only be Him.

But Moses replied to the Lord, "Please, Lord, I have never been eloquent . . ." Yahweh said to him, "Who made the human mouth? Who makes him mute or deaf, seeing or blind? Is it not I, Yahweh? Now go! I will help you speak and I will teach you what to say."
EXODUS 4:10-12

The Truth about Comparison

As I opened my Care Bears lunch box, my mind dreamed of the possibilities. I'm not sure why, since I knew exactly what it held—a peanut-butter-and -jelly sandwich with a side of banana. My usual.

I peered from lunch box to lunch box. What did they get? Pudding? Oreos? Is a banana tradeable? Do they think I'm lame because I have nothing to trade? Who notices that I eat the same thing every day?

Underneath the questions around my sandwich, I was really asking something much deeper: do I measure up? I was looking for confirmation of my worth. I was looking to see if others counted me less valuable because I didn't have what they had. I was looking to feel special.

Even if we aren't comparing ourselves to others, don't we all desire to feel valuable, worthy, appreciated, admired, acknowledged? These desires are not intrinsically wrong. But God has more for us than jealous eyes that size up what's in a lunch box. He wants us to see more. To live greater. To discover life in a richer sense.

God wants us to live abundantly in the identity He has uniquely given us— not in one set by the standard of others.

For we don't dare classify or compare ourselves with some who commend themselves. But in measuring themselves by themselves and comparing themselves to themselves, they lack understanding.
II CORINTHIANS 10:12

The Truth Is, I Am Tired

We sit on barstools, waiting for the hostess to clear a table. My friend asks how I'm doing, and I know I can tell her without her eyebrows knitting together.

The truth is, I'm tired. My need gapes wide, and I've not the strength to pretend anything less. I've filled my need with lesser things, always to be more ravenous than before. Yet I find the most beautiful presence of God when I am the most wretched. His presence feels like nourishment, amazing grace. I am not without hope.

Sometimes obedience is exhausting. Sometimes following His call doesn't mean things work out. Sometimes in the failing we longed for a tiny taste of our own glory, and it dies bitter on our tongues like the poison it is.

"I am tired, but well," I tell her, and I mean it. I smile wide, and it spreads through my cheeks up into my eyes. My circumstances haven't changed, but I feel hope that God is at work.

I may be tossed ragged but am not unanchored. I am tethered to the grace that lets me breathe under the weight of the tempest. I stretch my limbs like deep roots and inhale freedom. It is the blossom of hope unfurling toward the light. And it is enough.

I said, "If only I had wings like a dove! I would fly away and find rest.
How far away I would flee; I would stay in the wilderness. Selah.
I would hurry to my shelter from the raging wind and the storm."

PSALM 55:6–8

That Hidden Place

Years ago I stood in Vienna outside a church from the 16th century. Some people stood with cameras, angling for beautiful shots of the Gothic architecture. Others lined up to see the painted ceilings.

But right next to the front doors a man sat cross-legged. His face, downcast. His feet, dirty. His clothes, ragged. He held his palms up hoping for alms. But no one saw him. He was lost in the crush of the crowd, at their feet, to the side. My heart became heavy with the irony. We were surrounded by beauty and a symbol of the Ancient of Days, and a hungry man was lost in the tradition and adoration of a building.

Sometimes we find ourselves in that very place—surrounded by the beautiful exterior trappings of our faith but failing to see the poverty of our own need, living in hidden spiritual poverty. So how do we fill the emptiness inside? His presence. We go to God and empty ourselves—of fear and striving, comparison and worry.

It's a bold move in a sense, but one that Scripture teaches. Because of Christ, we can now come boldly and confidently into God's presence.

So I ask myself: if my palms were held up, what would Jesus pour into them today?

In Him we have boldness and confident access through faith in Him.
EPHESIANS 3:12

MARCH 31

How It Feels to Be Held by God

We pulled up in our driveway, exhausted. Our unplanned trip to my sister-in-law's bedside and subsequent funeral left our little family emotionally empty. Raw. Familiar cars parked in front of our house. They quietly filled in the gaps our journey left, doing what needed to be done. As I dropped bags of dirty laundry in the laundry room, I saw bags of groceries on the countertop. Ten minutes home and there was dinner at the front door. The mailbox held condolence cards, the phone had messages. Family and friends, neighbors and community, all holding us.

The first Sunday back at church we heard whispers of condolence and knowing looks. Compassion. I believe this dinner-serving, grocery-giving, and burden-bearing is what Jesus had in mind when He said we should love one another. We wonder how to change the world, how to leave a mark, move the hand of God? We change the world when we simply meet the needs of another, when we love others more than ourselves, not expecting anything in return.

Because no matter the troubled road we journey (and we all walk it at some point), life goes on. Laundry piles up and bellies need to be fed. When we rake the yard of one who can't, we see God. That is love.

And whoever gives just a cup of cold water to one of these little ones because he is a disciple—I assure you: He will never lose his reward!
MATTHEW 10:42

When You're Waiting on God in a Lonely Season

From my spot on the front porch, my eyes bounced from my laptop to the white car driving by, and I immediately recognized the two friends inside. I sprang up and waved so hard, I nearly took flight right off the porch. When the car rounded the corner out of sight, tears came out of nowhere.

Once again I found myself in a season of changing friendships, and it had been too long since I had solid, in-person girlfriend time.

A few months ago, one of my friends went to work full-time. Soon after, two other friends moved away. It felt as if our family had moved again, even though we hadn't gone anywhere. I mulled this over and whispered, "Lord, whomever I'm meant to be friends with, please just work it out."

As the words of my prayer soar upward, I trust He'll catch them. You can trust He'll catch your prayers too. And please know this: every component of your life—including your need for friendship—is tucked inside God's care.

Yes, God is a God of follow-through and finishes, and I'm learning to live in each friendship season with hope-filled contentment. We don't yet see things clearly. But it won't be long before the weather clears and the sun shines bright.

For now we see indistinctly, as in a mirror, but then face to face. Now I know in part, but then I will know fully, as I am fully known.
1 CORINTHIANS 13:12

On Prayers That Permeate His Heart

I've found that my most important conversations happen in the most mundane places. Even the bathroom. My preschool-age son is super proud that he is potty-trained. Now he prefers that I wait behind the closed door while he does his business, and we often talk through the door. One day he said, "Jesus lives in my heart. God lives in the sky. And sometimes God cannot hear us when we pray."

Let me tell you . . . a good long door-between-us heart-to-heart ensued. Even at three years old, I want him to know that God always hears us. In the every-moment chatter. In the impassioned and pleading tear-filled prayers. In the muttered-under-our-breath asks for patience. In the silent moments when the Spirit intercedes for us. In the joyful praises. In the desperate pleas for a swift answer. He hears them all.

I was once taught that there are three answers to prayer: yes, no, and not yet. This may be theologically simplistic, but it brings me peace to know that "unheard" isn't an option. No matter where we pray or how we pray—the eloquence of our words notwithstanding—He hears. Our words don't fall on emptiness but go right to the throne room, rising like incense.

Now this is the confidence we have before Him: Whenever we ask anything according to His will, He hears us. And if we know that He hears whatever we ask, we know that we have what we have asked Him for.
I JOHN 5:14–15

When It Feels Like You're Wilting

These past few weeks I haven't been praying. *I'm just so busy right now,* I told myself. I haven't been reading my Bible either. It sits on my nightstand but is covered up—by glasses of water, notebooks, textbooks . . . my laptop. I have a list of reasons why I wasn't praying or spending time with Jesus. I just had surgery, my second art show is approaching, and the amount of college schoolwork is somewhat shocking to me. As legitimate as these reasons are, without spending time with Jesus, all these things empty me.

I sat on my bed and started crying. "I can't do this anymore, Jesus," I told Him. "I'm too tired. I'm too overwhelmed. I said yes to too many things. I feel like I'm drowning. No, not even drowning. I feel like I'm shriveling right up."

If I was a flower, I was a wilted one. I was trying to fill up on people. I would talk to people about how I was feeling, but no human was satisfying enough for me.

Jesus is the One who takes my shriveled-up self and breathes life into me. Without Him, I am empty. Only when I give Him my worries and fears and anxieties can I finally be full.

The Lord is just; He is my rock, and there is no unrighteousness in Him.
PSALM 92:15

APRIL 4
The Lord Is Our Defender

As I tiptoed into the kitchen, I overheard my parents in the living room, interceding in prayer on behalf of a horrible man. A man bent on ruining my father's reputation and lying to restore his own financial success. I stood eavesdropping, all the while becoming more upset. "We pray blessing over their family . . . reconciliation . . . harmony . . . forgiveness." How could they pray for our enemy? How could my parents not be outraged?

My justice-oriented nature wanted to gather the troops and defend at all cost—and my mother's simple retort rocked my world, "The Lord is the defender of our reputation." *But this isn't fair. Let's gather the assembly. Let's tell them what he's done. We can create a community with a common adversary.*

It took me years to understand that their choice was not done out of weakness, but with strong conviction and strength of character. And I'll be honest, I don't always get this right.

In painful situations, I'm reminded of my parents' early morning intercession. For years they offered their blessing to an enemy. I've come to realize how futile it is to worry about a reputation. As my kids would say, "God's got my back." And, friend, He's got yours too.

The Lord will fight for you; you must be quiet.
EXODUS 14:14

Don't Give Up on That Girl

"Go ahead, I dare you." Like venom, those words struck poison right into my heart. I held the razor blade and sobbed. I couldn't do it. Mom dared me to plunge those razors into my wrist after I threatened I could. My whole teenage spirit hurt desperately; I only wanted her to stop me, to plead for my life, to tell me I was worth more, to show me she loved me.

Alone in my awkward adolescent world, I got pregnant. I had an abortion. Life hurt and felt out of control. I eventually moved back in with my dad and tried to regain "normal."

When I think back on that time, it seems like another life, one completely foreign. I'm now sitting in my nice suburban home, with my good husband, and three much-loved babes. We live "normal."

But I was "that" girl. She was hurting and desperate and just wanted to be loved. She just wanted to be held and comforted. She just wanted the me that is here now. And she wants you. She needs you. If you see her in your child's school or in your neighborhood, talk to her. Show her love and grace. Show her the Savior. Don't give up on her. She just might have something worth saying one day.

[You took] off your former way of life, the old self that is corrupted by deceitful desires; you are being renewed in the spirit of your minds; you put on the new self, the one created according to God's likeness in righteousness and purity of the truth.
EPHESIANS 4:22–24

You Don't Have to Hide Your Scars

I have a scar on my left leg, a souvenir from a head-on car collision. The insurance company offered to pay for plastic surgery, but I declined. I wanted to remember what I'd been saved from. The stitched wound was in the shape of a Y. To me, the letter stood for *Yahweh*. I felt as if I'd been marked by God's first initial.

I know it's not healthy to live in the past, but I think every once in a while, Jesus wants us to remember. We see this in the Gospel of Mark. Some friends bring a buddy to the feet of Jesus, and after healing him, Jesus tells him to pick up his mat and go home. Imagine the condition of that ratty, dirty mat. Yet Jesus tells him to take the mat, like a wretched souvenir. That man's mat is like a scar. It's a reminder of who he had been and what he was rescued from.

Friend, your mats—your scars—they're part of your story. Someday you will cross paths with someone with the same kind of wound. They'll need to know your story. You might shake a little when you show them your scar, but don't be afraid. It doesn't mean you failed. It means you were healed.

I tell you: get up, pick up your mat, and go home.
MARK 2:11

We Are Carried

The *bing-bong* revealed a friend reaching out for prayer. I paused in my morning hustle and prayed, then texted back, "Ask Jesus who He says you are."

Soon my phone flashed. "Carried. Jesus says I am carried." I smiled and gave thanks in my heart for such a poignant word gifted to my friend who carries a very heavy load. Yes, she is carried.

My day bustled forward with tasks big and small as I buckled my four-year-old into his car seat and picked up his brothers from school—it was dentist day. I smiled walking into the brightly painted office, and what happened next left me sorely disappointed.

My youngest son became heels-dug-in defiant. The next hour was a battle of the wills. After much pleading, FaceTiming with Daddy, and help from a fantastic staff, I'm relieved to say that he got his teeth cleaned. But back in the minivan, relief spilled over in angry, embarrassed tears.

I felt totally defeated. Hadn't we moved past this stage? Then I reread my friend's message. "Jesus says I am carried."

I realized that as mad as I felt, God had empowered me to act with love, patience, and gentleness. I hadn't lost my cool nor given into my son's defiance. The Spirit whispered to my heart, *I carried you.*

He redeemed them because of His love and compassion;
He lifted them up and carried them all the days of the past.
ISAIAH 63:9

Hope for the Rejected

My great-grandmother was a young maid for a wealthy farm owner, and she got pregnant before she was married. That baby was my grandmother. She was gorgeous and had a wit and beauty that snagged a handsome country boy. Together they had my mama and my aunt, but he didn't stay.

Something in every one of us has felt the sting of rejection. Some of us hold back our beauty for fear of coming under the shame of rejection. I know my grandmother did.

I knew that I was supposed to go into all the world and share the gospel, but something within held me back. I asked for God's kingdom to come, but then it terrified me—I knew I was hindered in my walk. So I began to work through all the things that kept me from loving others.

My world then began to crumble when I finally realized I had a spirit of fear and rejection. I finally named it, called it an idol, and saw what lies it had fed me. And I ran in the opposite direction. The walls I've built are now crumbling. Sometimes we just haven't yet believed how much we are loved. What I'm finding in this freedom is completely new. I am full-on running toward hope.

This hope will not disappoint us, because God's love has been poured out in our hearts through the Holy Spirit who was given to us.
ROMANS 5:5

The Kingdom of Heaven Is Like a Mustard Seed

One year I bought my husband a Meyer lemon tree. It's the first time I've attempted to keep any plant alive. Not surprisingly, my patience wore thin early, despite my promises to the woman in the greenhouse where I bought it. She warned me that the tree needs time and care—that it can be years before they blossom with fruit and that the care should not waver. But mine did.

One morning I read Matthew 13:31–32, where Jesus said the kingdom of heaven is like a mustard seed. I once thought His point was to look for the kingdom of heaven in the small, unexpected things. But on this morning, I heard differently.

I sensed Jesus telling me to look at the tree. The kingdom of heaven is the care that a seed requires. The kingdom of heaven is working in the company of the unseen, watering when you see no flowers and pruning when you see no fruit.

In this life, we won't always see the fruits of our labor. We're making investments that impact eternity. Like the care for the tree, we care for what the Lord has put in front of us, knowing that it honors Him and honors others. And we trust there will be fruit whether we see it or not.

He presented another parable to them: "The kingdom of heaven is like a mustard seed that a man took and sowed in his field. It's the smallest of all the seeds, but when grown, it's taller than the vegetables and becomes a tree, so that the birds of the sky come and nest in its branches."
MATTHEW 13:31–32

When You Have to Say the Hard Thing

My palms were a little bit sweaty as I sat at the coffee shop. A friend had hurt my feelings and we needed to talk about it. To be fair, I had hurt hers as well.

She and I are great friends. And because I value the friendship, I wasn't willing to sweep my feelings, or hers, under the rug. But hard conversations are still hard, even if there's lots of love in the mix.

For years I thought that if I loved my friends, I should keep my hurt or sadness to myself and move on. My personality tends to lean toward "Let's have a great time!" not "Let's have a hard conversation!"

But the older I get, the more I recognize that the hard conversations are actually what make for the great time. Not in the moment, but later, when voices have been heard and feelings have been shared.

So there we sat, and we said the things that hurt. It wasn't easy. I cried. She did too. We both said what hurt, we both apologized, and we both walked away a little wounded and a little healed.

Truth in love leads to health and life. Truth in love doesn't kill; it resurrects. Truth in love may hurt, but it will also heal.

But speaking the truth in love, let us grow in every
way into Him who is the head—Christ.
EPHESIANS 4:15

Margin of Error

My pastor used a term in a completely different way than I'd heard before—I scrambled to open my notebook and write down exactly what he'd said. He defined patience as having margin in your heart for other people's errors.

For a brief time in college I majored in psychology. And it took exactly one semester of required math and science to cure me of that career option, but that doesn't mean I didn't learn anything. One concept was the margin of error, or, in my nonscientific mind, wiggle room. That phrase was more about research studies, sample sizes, and credible, scientific results. But this was about the way God calls us to love others, of the way He loves us.

Through much of my life, I've struggled with perfectionism. And I've held my friends and family to exacting standards as well. At the first sign of weakness, I've become devastated by their inability to live up to my unrealistic expectations.

God has shown me over time how this tendency is hurtful, both to me and to the ones I love. But this encouragement to allow margin for other people's errors—to save some wiggle room for my people to be human—showed me how to live (and love) differently.

Be kind and compassionate to one another, forgiving one another, just as God also forgave you in Christ.
EPHESIANS 4:32

You'll Never Be Perfect

(and That's a Good Thing)

An e-mail filled with criticism had slipped into my in-box that week and it hurt my feelings . . . for days. It set off a storm of self-doubting emotions. It's amazing what one person's criticism can do. Ten people could say something nice to or about me, but what I remember most is that one person's criticism.

I called a friend to process the harsh e-mail and my emotions. With wisdom she told me, "Renee, you'll never be perfect. And if you ever get to where you are perfect, you will be all alone!" She was right! I'll never be perfect, and I'm thankful because I don't want to be all alone.

Sweet friend, Jesus was the only perfect Person to walk this earth, yet He was constantly criticized. But guess what? Nowhere does Scripture say that Jesus ever doubted Himself. He stayed secure in His purpose and confident in His calling.

What His Father said was all that mattered. And that is what He wants for us too. He is there in the midst of our less-than-perfect lives, when disappointments and failures leave us empty and make us doubt our worth and purpose. He sees us, and He's pursuing us with the gift of His perfect love.

She opens her mouth with wisdom and loving instruction is on her tongue.
PROVERBS 31:26

Sandpaper People

As a young mom, I was struggling with a strong-willed child. I read all the parenting books and plumbed the depths of Scripture for wisdom. But then my father-in-law posed an inflammatory question: "What if this is about you?"

How dare he suggest that my son's behavior was my fault! I hurled a half dozen recent incidents to illustrate how wrong he was. But he gently continued, "I didn't say how he's acting is your fault. Maybe God is allowing the dynamics with your son to do a refining work in your life."

A few days later, his words still lingering, I was strolling down a toy aisle, and I came across a rock tumbler set. This set could take a bag of ordinary rocks and transform them into extraordinary polished stones by adding water and grit and spinning them for a few weeks.

I suddenly understood what my father-in-law had been saying. Different kinds of grit produce different results, and all are necessary to produce a polished stone.

Like rocks, a person changes over time when external forces rub up against them. This "rub" forever changed the way I viewed my son. My perspective realigned to what God might be teaching me, and I began to ask, "What does God have for me in this?"

Pursue peace with everyone, and holiness—without it no one will see the Lord.
HEBREWS 12:14

Fancy's Feathers

We'd lived on our farm for only a few months when I had to take one of our hens, Fancy, to the vet. She ate ravenously, but she kept getting thinner and was losing her feathers. We came to find out that she was being picked on.

We didn't understand the signs, but chickens establish rank, and everyone wants to be over someone else. The other chickens had been pecking on the back of her neck, pulling out her feathers. But on her stomach, she was pulling out her *own* feathers. Fancy was down to three pounds, because she had stopped fighting back.

At this point, the other chickens didn't have to convince Fancy that she didn't deserve the same as the others. She believed what they dished out and had turned on herself. So we rehabilitated her with time away from the flock and extra nutrition.

How many of us have felt the same? Beat up. Worn out. And needing a safe place to heal and recover. Let's stop pulling out our own feathers, believing the lies that the enemy spews about us. Let's replace each lie with the truth of God's immeasurable love and grace for each of us.

Rest in God alone, my soul, for my hope comes from Him.
He alone is my rock and my salvation, my stronghold; I will not be shaken.
PSALM 62:5–6

It's Not Always Easy for Nice Girls to Be Nice

I was tired and hot—definitely in no mood to be put on hold by customer service. By the time the rep answered the line, I'd heard their elevator music for so long that my last nerve was shot. I was snippy, even a bit rude. And, honestly, I didn't care. I was weary of the incompetent service I'd gotten and ready to give a piece of my mind. I expected my issue to be met with justifications, which is what happened the last time I called.

But I detected something different in this young man's voice. Could it be kindness? Even so, it wasn't going to deter me from my rant. This company needed to know I was very dissatisfied. But the longer I ranted, the nicer he got.

Soon I couldn't justify my behavior any longer. His kindness melted my harshness until I found myself awash in a pool of humility. While my intent had been to change his company's actions, his actions changed mine.

First Peter 3:9 says, "You were called for this"; what an apt picture of a customer service rep's daily routine! And I'm reminded, ultimately, that God is the One who calls us to kindness. Blessing others is to be part of our daily routine, even—or maybe especially—when others do not.

All of you should be like-minded and sympathetic, should love believers, and be compassionate and humble, not paying back evil for evil or insult for insult but, on the contrary, giving a blessing, since you were called for this, so that you can inherit a blessing.

I PETER 3:8–9

The Spiritual Gift of Cheerleading

In high school, I was a cheerleader. Even though cheerleading wasn't considered a sport, it is every bit as athletic as running the 400-meter relay. Each summer, just like the soccer team, we rose early to rehearse. We worked hard. We invested in the success of our football team as if we were holding the line ourselves. When they won, we celebrated. And when they lost, we carried the burden, right along with the players.

Today I'm still a cheerleader. I take great pleasure in watching the dreams of my family and friends come true. It's as though their dreams take up residence in my heart.

What about you? Do you find pleasure in cheering on others? Or maybe you are frustrated with a role considered a non-sport. You wonder why God has called you to the sidelines instead of the main stage. In God's great manuscript, there is no such thing as "sidelines." Every role, every season, every assignment matters and has great significance in His kingdom.

Like Moses, everyone needs an Aaron and a Hur. Sometimes we get to be Moses, and other times we get to be—yes, *get* to be—the ones who help carry the load. There is nothing quite like being a cheerleader in the body of Christ.

When Moses' hands grew heavy, they took a stone and put it under him, and he sat down on it. Then Aaron and Hur supported his hands, one on one side and one on the other so that his hands remained steady until the sun went down.
EXODUS 17:12

APRIL 17
Waiting for God's Gifts

I gather the tiny pieces into a freezer bag. Barbie shoes and Matchbox wheels, Lincoln Logs and fairy wings. This "piece bag" is a coveted thing around our house. The kids climb on chairs and pull at the cabinet. "Can we please look in it?"

I say no often because I *know* what happens when they look into the bag. They begin to covet—they long for things they're not yet ready for. I know—many things have remained out of my reach, not suitable for my handling, *or mishandling.*

As I tuck my middle boy into bed, he asks for something he cannot yet have. I smile weakly because I empathize with and understand the challenge of waiting. I remind him about the piece bag in the cupboard. We talk about how God has a "piece bag" for each of us, and though the one in our cupboard contains hazardous items, God's "piece bag" is a treasure chest with gifts that He will hand down in His perfect timing.

Then my child asks, "Does God really have special gifts for me?" Without hesitation I choke out, "Yes, my sweet boy, with only your name on it." He rolls over and closes his eyes, but his hand finds mine.

"I'm really happy now," he says.

Take delight in the Lord, and He will give you your heart's desires.
Commit your way to the Lord; trust in Him, and He will act.
PSALM 37:4–5

APRIL 18
He's Never Too Busy for Me

My brothers and I were home alone after school and all day long during the summers. I was the baby of the family—and the resident snitch. My mom worked, and I would call her every day, multiple times, to tattle on my brothers. You can imagine how much it must have thrilled her to receive those calls.

One day I called one too many times. The next thing we knew she was walking through the door in the middle of the day. She'd had it and told us to get into the car. She took us back to work with her so we couldn't bug her anymore. We sat in the car in the parking lot of her job, all of us too angry with each other to speak.

It's now a funny story we tell about our youth, but what I can appreciate about it now, especially with my own kids who call me multiple times a day, is that our Father is a God who never gets tired of us or is too busy for us. He loves for us to share all the things, big or small, on our hearts. He waits for us and vows to hear us when we call, to listen while we're speaking, and to respond to our prayers.

Even before they call, I will answer;
while they are still speaking, I will hear.
ISAIAH 65:24

Removing the Remnants

With a grumbling heart, I pulled into the parking lot . . . the heat of the day pressing down. An abandoned lot ridden with weeds is the project before me. I was given a service mission to cultivate humility: one full hour of pulling weeds. Just God, the weeds, the heat, and me.

As I pulled one dead weed after another, it amazed me that although they were dead, they had deep and stubborn roots. And some that looked dead still had life in the deepest part of their root.

Amid my grumbling, a message for my heart came straight from God's: These dead weeds are like the sin we've allowed to creep into the soil of the heart. Our past can be ridden with weeds that appear to be dead, but their roots still contain life. To really heal from past sin, we must go back and remove their stubborn roots once and for all.

As the hour ended, I looked back on the cleared stretch of soil and felt satisfied. The soil was ready for something new that wouldn't be choked out by the ugliness of dead weeds.

Driving away I gave thanks—remembering that in spite the wretchedness of my attitude, God met me. In my service, I was changed.

For we know that our old self was crucified with Him
in order that sin's dominion over the body may be abolished,
so that we may no longer be enslaved to sin.
ROMANS 6:6

APRIL 20
Choosing Change

I struggle most when I wrestle with the season in which God has placed me. I find myself making poor decisions out of a fearful and reactionary heart. I choose self over others, distraction over commitment, or my desires over God's desires for me.

In 2 Samuel, King David chose to stay behind in the city when kings were called to battle. Rather than leading his people, defending his land, and conquering old boundaries, he remained in Jerusalem. There, he fought an even greater battle against his own flesh.

In the latter part of 2 Samuel 11, David is awakened to a desire in his heart that eventually led down a path of adultery and murder. His experience reminds us to be focused on the still, small voice of our Father. If we refuse the direction of this season because it is painful or wounding or it strains against our own desires, where will it lead us?

God continually calls us forward into new seasons of growth. The Christian life is ever changing, ever growing. When we refuse to fight new battles, we become deaf to the voice of victory calling to us from the future.

Let's learn how to embrace every hard and holy moment we find in it.

In the spring when kings march out to war, David sent Joab with his officers and all Israel. They destroyed the Ammonites and besieged Rabbah, but David remained in Jerusalem.
II SAMUEL 11:1

Building Bridges with Our Stories

Sometimes God asks us to turn the page of our life, but occasionally we get to look back. Recently I returned to the hospital where I had brain surgery. I'm tempted to look the other way as I pass where I pushed my legs to walk again. But these pages in my story are the moments when God proved Himself faithful and strong.

You have a story, you know. And God is weaving a tapestry of beauty that will tell of His faithfulness when generations to come read the pages of your life.

Inviting someone into your story is not easy—it means you'll need to reveal a few scars. But Jesus said if people keep quiet, the stones will cry out in praise (Luke 19:40). But there's no need for the rocks to cry out when we share our stories with each other.

Tell me of your mess; I will feel less alone. Allow me to hold your hand as you share bad news. Call me and we'll have a dance party, from miles away, because He's opened another door to your dream.

Share your story with those around you. Let's be a community that shares our stories, gives Him the glory, and remembers that He is still writing. The story isn't over yet.

_____

_____

_____

_____

_____

_____

He comforts us in all our affliction, so that we may be able to comfort those who are in any kind of affliction, through the comfort we ourselves receive from God.
II CORINTHIANS 1:4

APRIL 22
How to Measure the Size of the Waves

My grandchildren stand at the water's edge where waves bigger than life pound at their feet, but they have no fear, not as long as Granddaddy is near. We stand to the side, far enough to allow them a sporty adventure, yet close enough to pick them up should the adventure make sport of them. Their souls live free because they trust us. They don't know about bacteria or sharks. Fear is foreign to them. They simply know the joy of discovery and play.

As we grow older and hear news of tragedy, we build walls to protect ourselves and our families. We build as if salvation, protection, and provision are ours alone to fight for and achieve. We try to hide from danger and fear instead of facing it, knowing we are held in God's right hand.

The truth is, we sacrifice our freedom on the altar of fear when we measure the size of the waves instead of the size of His hands. When we measure the waves by God's Word, we discover fear's impact is little more than a ripple in the water. I step into the cool of the water's edge all the way up to my waist, and I begin to allow the waves to push me higher.

Jesus said, "Leave the children alone, and don't try to keep them from coming to Me, because the kingdom of heaven is made up of people like this."
MATTHEW 19:14

Now or Never

We're in the middle of a series at church about living a life filled with intention. Our pastor asked what we'd do if we had a week left to live and suggested we do those things now. Not to wait.

As an illustration, he had our congregation text anyone we felt lead to reach out to. So I texted an old friend:

Just wanted to tell you how much your friendship means to me. Your encouragement, laugh, and ability to truly listen are such gifts. Though we don't talk often, when we do I leave feeling filled up. You truly are one of the greatest blessings of my college experience. Love you.

She responded: *These words reached the depth of my heart! Thanks so much, Jess, for taking the time to say this. Means the world.*

A few days later I called her, and she said, "Thanks for that text. I don't know what prompted it, but it meant a lot to me." She made me think about others who need a word of encouragement.

So once a week I plan to write cards to friends to let them know they matter. My messages won't be long, but they'll be heartfelt. My prayer is that each simple card will be like honey to the souls.

Pleasant words are a honeycomb: sweet to the taste and health to the body.
PROVERBS 16:24

At the End

Growing up, my last name began with a "W," so I was always at the end of roll call. And often I'd enter a bathroom only to find a toilet paper roll with six or fewer remaining squares. Somehow I regularly find myself standing in front of the company watercooler as the bottle reaches its end.

This isn't just a physical occurrence, either. I tend to be at the end of my proverbial rope, too. Why am I always at the end of things, situations, and supplies? Perhaps I need to get to the end of myself.

What does it mean to get to the end of oneself? To say, "Enough!" to one's self? Where do I even begin? My unique personality seems too perfectly positioned to feed the me-monster.

Graciously, I've been given heaping doses of humility, but still the me-monster will not die. So . . . I must rise daily to slay the me-monster. But that me-monster continues to resurrect itself. It's a constant battle—a constant death to self. I should be discouraged, but I relish in the truth that God's compassion never fails. His mercy is new every morning. The me-monster is not going down without a fight. But Christ in me wins in the end.

So he answered me, "This is the word of the Lord to Zerubbabel: 'Not by strength or by might, but by My Spirit,' says the Lord of Hosts."
ZECHARIAH 4:6

He Just Keeps Giving

My son asked me whether God had ever given me a gift. I gleamed and said, "Yes, He gave me you and your brother."

He responded, "Mom, He gave you Jesus." Well, there you have it, schooled by a seven-year-old on the greatest gift of God ever.

Yeah, it was even tweet-worthy, but afterward, with a little more introspection, came the conviction and the searing question: Do I genuinely see Jesus as the gift He is? The gift for my soul salvation every single day?

When that same son is faced with difficult interactions with peers at school, God reminds me that He is sovereign over my son's challenges.

When friends are busy and there's no one with which to verbally process, I have the gift of prayer and a listening ear that's always available. He also gives us grace when we fail to turn to Him first. He keeps on giving of Himself throughout the day, the week, and eventually the years.

I count my kids, friends, house, and the food on my table as blessings—all gifts from God's hand and worthy of my thanks. But no gift is as precious as Jesus Himself. He is my treasure; He has gone before me and will be my eternal inheritance.

I pray that the God of our Lord Jesus Christ, the glorious Father, would give you a spirit of wisdom and revelation in the knowledge of Him. I pray that the perception of your mind may be enlightened so you may know what is the hope of His calling, what are the glorious riches of His inheritance among the saints...
EPHESIANS 1:17–18

The Way It's Supposed to Be

One morning I drove to the hospital, parked, carried my suitcase, and checked in, alone. My husband was deployed and it was time to have my baby. Motherhood wasn't supposed to be this lonely.

Later, another "birth"—the completion of a project I'd worked tirelessly on. I was exhausted and thrilled, and when I shared my little treasure with a friend, she seemed to like it. Then she turned sharply, saying, "But don't forget, there's nothing new under the sun." Her motive might have been good—to keep me humble—but the words seemed out of place and mean-spirited. Friendship wasn't supposed to feel so raw.

Then there is the birth of sickness. One dear friend has rheumatoid arthritis and another has multiple sclerosis. My husband has Crohn's disease.

We live in a broken world. Some days, family can't, or won't, be there for us. Friends disappoint us. Our bodies fail us. Everyone and everything on earth will let us down but God. He never does.

In Hebrews, God's faithful love is called *hesed*. Today, we know this as grace. God pours out *hesed* through Jesus, whom He sent to rescue, redeem, and renew us. Jesus is living proof of God's faithful love. He is God's promise to us, made flesh.

My lips will glorify You because Your faithful love is better than life.
So I will praise You as long as I live; at Your name, I will lift up my hands.
PSALM 63:3–4

The Marching of Time

A large maple tree in the middle of my backyard, which has probably stood as long as our house, is being removed. Problem is, the trunk is half dead.

I also just learned that one of our favorite restaurants closed. An unassuming place with cheesy decor, twinkling lights, oilcloth covering the tables, yet the food was amazing. Years of family celebrations took place at that little restaurant. Now it's gone, memories never again to be made there.

Our youngest just graduated from high school. Family drove and flew in from across the country. The weekend was grand and fun, but it was also another closing, as we will never again have a child in school here. The empty nest is looming.

Sometimes I'd like to hold on to those "good old days" when everything seemed simpler and sweeter, but that's not possible. Time marches on. Trees are cut down. Favorite chefs retire. Our children move on. Yet our hearts are forever tied to those memories, those places, those experiences.

I admit there are days when I struggle just a little with putting the past behind me. But I know the days ahead will be just fine because I know my life is more than the past. I've been promised a future. And so have you.

The boundary lines have fallen for me in pleasant places; indeed, I have a beautiful inheritance.

PSALM 16:6

When You Feel Like You're the Only One with Yuck

Standing hand in hand, with India's heat sweltering us both, she whispers, "Thank you for making me know I am not alone." Earlier I had shared with a group of women how God turns our mess into His masterpiece. No matter what we've been through, we are chosen, forgiven, and holy daughters of the king. I shared my yuck—my insecurities and how I sometimes lose my temper, and, well, I don't always like my job as a mother.

At one point my translator asked, "How do you translate 'yuck'?" With deep spiritual and theological insight, I made a gagging noise with my throat, and soon we had over fifty women gagging to explain what it meant.

Yuck started way back in the garden with Adam and Eve. They gave up the beauty of the garden and a pure relationship with God for selfish pride. But when we let go of our yuck, God replaces it with a crown of beauty.

It's okay to have a past you'd rather forget. Real beauty isn't found in looking perfect or being perfect; real beauty is found in the romance of being loved by a perfect God. In spite our yuck, *God* calls us His beloved. We are wanted, chosen, and so dearly loved.

_____

_____

_____

_____

_____

_____

_____

_____

But you are a chosen race, a royal priesthood, a holy nation, a people for His possession, so that you may proclaim the praises of the One who called you out of darkness into His marvelous light.
I PETER 2:9

You May Never Know

I've had six jobs in the past ten years. Why can't I find the thing I'm made for and stick with it? Why wasn't I one of those girls who knew she was a teacher from the moment she played school with her dolls? Why can't my résumé be simpler and show a sense of commitment?

A friend's words recently stopped me short in a discussion about call and vocation. "Well, you may never know," she said. "Think of all the people in the Bible who came to the end of their lives not having any sense of whether their ministry truly made a difference."

This thought had never occurred to me. Somewhere in my search for vocation, I got the message that this was all figure-out-able if I just tried hard enough.

What if, instead of striving and searching and worrying about the thing I was made to do, I look around for a thing that needs doing today? While I might not know my one true calling, I do know I am called to follow the way of Christ. What would it look like to answer the small calls of my life wholeheartedly? What if that is enough? What if it is more than enough?

Humble yourselves, therefore, under the mighty hand of God,
so that He may exalt you at the proper time,
casting all your care on Him, because He cares about you.
I PETER 5:6–7

When It's Hard to Take a Family Photo

Two years ago my twenty-nine-year-old brother, James, died. My husband and I frantically packed our family of five and left for home the next morning. *This can't be real. He's really not dead. He'll be there when we get home. He will.* It felt completely surreal.

I stood shaking in the funeral-room parlor with my mom and dad, brother and sister. We sobbed as we said our final goodbyes. My eyes played tricks on me—his chest seemed to raise and lower. But it couldn't be. He'd been dead for days. My hand touched his cold face and I kissed his forehead.

Goodbye, James.

To this day, I expect him to walk around the corner and make his appearance. There's a place in my heart that will continually long for him to pull up in the driveway, to join us for dinner. But he never does. He never will.

As a family, we are completely incomplete without James. We have yet to take any new pictures together. It's not that we've made a pact not to. It just doesn't seem natural anymore; it doesn't seem right with one of us missing.

Maybe we'll be able to this year. Maybe.

Death, where is your victory? Death, where is your sting?
I CORINTHIANS 15:55

The Rhythm of Thanksgiving

As my child was born I fought against nature and attempted to hold her in. I was supposed to work with the contraction, breathing out and letting my baby deliver. Instead I gripped bed rails and held every breath attempting to stop her from slipping away from me, in both body and spirit.

They took her anyway, through an incision. At twenty-five weeks gestation she was born near Thanksgiving rather than Valentine's Day. Many thanksgivings have left my lips but none so full of truth than the day I saw her heartbeats on a monitor. I counted every one.

Thank You, Lord. Another heartbeat. *Thank You, Lord. She forgot to breathe. Please breathe.* She took a breath. *Thank You, Lord.* I don't need a calendar for Thanksgiving now, all orange and brown, marked by apple cider and falling leaves. When she rolled over, it was Thanksgiving. When she spoke a syllable, it was Thanksgiving. When she took shaky steps toward us, it was Thanksgiving.

I'm still counting the Thanksgivings with heartbeats, a new rhythm of life where the smallest things really do call for rejoicing. And at night, when I feel her chest rise and pulse of a heartbeat underneath my hand, I can see it in the flesh. *Thank You, Lord.*

Rejoice always! Pray constantly. Give thanks in everything, for this is God's will for you in Christ Jesus.
I THESSALONIANS 5:16–18

The Friends Who Pursue Us

"I could hang out with you." My new friend seemed so confident in our budding relationship. But a month later I was thrown into the world of the unfamiliar—I had an emergency C-section, then learned my grandmother died. I tried to care for my newborn, mourn, and take care of myself, but I sank into a depression I thought would never end.

I rarely left our home as I navigated my new roles as a wife and mother. One day I heard a knock at our door. My new friend stood there holding a bag of treats—not going to leave until I let her inside. She fed the baby while I rested, then insisted we go for a walk outside in the brisk air. I drank it in.

Sometimes it's only in hindsight that we can look back and see the mercies of God through a friend reaching out and a word of encouragement received. Even though I continued to be a recluse, she kept showing up. She introduced me to other moms of littles, and she brought me to Bible study. She didn't give up on me.

Little by little I came out of the darkness and embraced the Light. Through those moments, when we embrace the real, God reaches down and says, "I'm here."

He reached down from heaven and took hold of me;
He pulled me out of deep waters.
2 SAMUEL 22:17

Spiritual Daughters

The elementary children had picked fresh strawberries and made pies for a fund-raiser for Mother's Day. "Can we buy the ones I made?" my son asked.

Immediately Mrs. Sizemore's face popped into my mind. I thought: *We can buy the pies and take them to her.* Shortly after I accepted Christ, God brought her into my life. We'd only shared a few brief conversations at church but there was something about her kindness I felt drawn to.

"Happy Mother's Day!" we beamed as we gave her the pie. She started to cry. I didn't know she and her husband didn't have any children. This was the beginning of a special relationship between us. She taught me all things Southern, including homemade butter pecan ice cream. Above all, she showed me how she loved Jesus. So when my son's school had Grandparents' Day, it seemed apropos to invite Mrs. Sizemore and her husband.

One day, she said, "You are like a daughter to me!" This time, I cried.

Recently, I was asked to help lead a senior high girls' small group. These precious girls have become my spiritual daughters, much like Mrs. Sizemore has been a spiritual mother to me.

God knows our deepest longings, and sometimes He fills them in completely unexpected ways.

Shepherd God's flock among you, not overseeing out of compulsion but freely, according to God's will; not for the money but eagerly; not lording it over those entrusted to you, but being examples to the flock.
1 PETER 5:2–3

Embracing Life Change

During a kitchen renovation, we pulled up the fake-brick linoleum only to discover a flowery pattern. Below that was a darker version, and below that, a lighter one. The former owners swung from one extreme to the other, much like we do when we make vows about our future.

I was guilty of making vows about how my grown-up life would look different than my childhood. When I put my faith in Jesus Christ, those vows changed and morphed into new ones. I vowed that anger, worry, and fear wouldn't ruin my testimony, but praying and going to church didn't fix my temper or mind-set.

I was so intent on my "top layer" that I couldn't see what was happening below the surface. By God's grace, a dear friend challenged me to get help to deal with the "bottom layer" issues.

Getting honest with God is like removing the old linoleum to build upon a solid foundation for the future. Through that process, I learned how to walk in His truth, and His truth is what changed me at the core of my thinking and thereby my living.

Embracing life change isn't about waking up one morning and being totally different. It's about inviting God to transform us over the long haul, one belief at a time.

I, Yahweh, examine the mind, I test the heart to give to each according to his way, according to what his actions deserve.
JEREMIAH 17:10

When the Door Closes

Over the years, I've prayed a number of prayers—both answered and unanswered. And there are times when I've celebrated because God not only provided what I was asking, but did so in ways far beyond my dreams and expectations. Other times, I've been so devastated by His "No" that I struggled to believe Him, or believe in Him and His goodness, deciding I would never ask Him for anything else.

The years have taught me, however, that oftentimes a closed door is a blessing. That job that I didn't get? There was another one better suited for my personality. That closed door to the city I wanted to move to? It would take another ten years before the door opened, and this time I was better suited to thrive and commit to the calling God has given me. That man I didn't marry? It's not because he wasn't a good guy. He just wasn't the best for me. After almost ten years of marriage, I know that to be true. But God knew the whole time . . . and He provided.

Closed doors. They're painful. But I am often reminded God doesn't promise that all things will feel good, but He does promise to bless beyond anything we could ever imagine.

*To Him be glory in the church and in Christ Jesus to
all generations, forever and ever. Amen.*
EPHESIANS 3:21

MAY 6
Friendship Is Worth the Fight

Recently a woman waved me to her table in a crowded mall food court when she saw I couldn't find a place to sit. I then enjoyed forty-five minutes of conversation with her and her friend. I heard words that I needed to hear and shared a lovely lunch with two ladies I'll probably never see again. God was aware that I needed connection more than solitude.

Some women possess a gift for encouraging others to open up more than they would otherwise. Sometimes you must gently probe to take a relationship beyond shallow waters. I want to be that girl. My awareness of boundaries and personal privacy sometimes keeps people at a distance. But I want to be that friend who's not afraid to ask hard questions and lean in close. I want to be the kind of friend who inspires trust, encourages truth, and welcomes honesty.

Perhaps you're in a season where friendships are abundant. Or maybe they seem scarce. Maybe you're new to your area or you're tangled in toddlers. You work long hours or you're self-sufficient and keep to yourself. But we all need community. And the effort it takes to grow a friendship is always, always worth it.

Two are better than one because they have a good reward for their efforts.
ECCLESIASTES 4:9

Lost in the Details

As we walked through the crowded church foyer, our youngest barreled his way through a sea of knees, a good five steps ahead of us.

Then he smacked right into a pair of legs. He looked up and immediately realized he was not with his parents. In an instant, doubt and fear overwhelmed him and he began sobbing. His daddy, with eyes set on him, reached in and scooped him up and quieted his fears.

We never lost sight of him because our vantage point was higher than his. He saw knees, we saw him. He felt lost and couldn't make sense of his surroundings, yet we were only a few steps away.

Doubt. It is the hesitation to believe, and doubt's travel companion is usually fear. When I defer to doubt and fear, asking "How?" becomes my guiding principle. Unfortunately, getting lost in the details of "how" leaves me with "faith paralysis."

Faith is the assurance of things I cannot see. When I rely on my nearsightedness, the details I can see leave me swallowed in doubt and paralyzed by fear. Circumstances won't always make sense, but my confidence is in my Father, whose eyes see me when I can't see Him and who is assuredly working in ways I cannot see.

"How can I know this?" Zechariah asked the angel. "For I am an old man, and my wife is well along in years."
LUKE 1:18

But God

"But God." Two simple yet powerful words found in Ephesians are a sweet reminder that God is gracious.

His grace continually steers us back to light and life. If anyone understood this, it was Paul. He was a man who spent years persecuting believers of Jesus. A man who didn't deserve the kind of scandalous grace that God offers.

But God. A generous reminder that the best of my best is but dirty rags to Him. And yet, despite all my failings, He loves me. Most days I can't wrap my head around this kind of love. Even when I was so deep in my sin, He wanted life for me.

But God. He knew the witness Paul would become. Paul's conversion story is a powerful reminder that even when we fail or run from God, He can and will use us for His purposes.

In the book of Ephesians, Paul is in prison, yet his response was to write a letter to encourage other believers. He obviously understood, in a deep way, the immense grace that only God could give, and he wanted us to understand it as well.

God's gift of grace is undeserved but always a balm to our over-striving, weary hearts. We don't have to be perfect. We are perfected because of Him.

But God, who is rich in mercy, because of His great love that He had for us, made us alive with the Messiah even though we were dead in trespasses. You are saved by grace!
EPHESIANS 2:4–5

Finding Joy

For much of my life, the word *joy* was like a dangling carrot I could never grasp. Joy seemed elusive.

In the Psalms, David expresses anger, fear, hurt, and sadness—all emotions I relate to. In Psalm 30:5 he also says joy comes in the morning.

So I've often wondered, *When will it be morning?* Or, more specifically, *When will it be my morning?*

I cried out about what I felt deep in my heart—abandoned. Even so, I knew God wanted more for me. And that joy is hard to find when you can't see Jesus.

The more honest I became, I knew I needed Him. In the darkest places, I found Him tending to me. Caring for my hurts and speaking life into dead places. I've learned that joy doesn't come and go with circumstances—it can be experienced despite them. Because joy comes in knowing Jesus and experiencing His presence. Joy comes when we fall more in love with the One who loves us most.

God often uses the hard things to refine us. To transform us to be more like Christ. And as absurd as it may sound, God allows the hard things to make us more holy. Christ is the hope ever before us, ever behind us, and ever with us.

For His anger lasts only a moment, but His favor, a lifetime.
Weeping may spend the night, but there is joy in the morning.
PSALM 30:5

All for One

This verse and its directive comes to us in the context of Paul's comparison of the followers of Christ to a body. Paul makes it personal, and its effect is profound—every Christian is a member of one body. And when one part of a body hurts, the entire body does what it can to relieve and care for the hurting member.

Our youngest son was born premature and very ill. Fast-forward a few years, and Sam began to have dental issues. We couldn't understand why he'd have teeth troubles, but the dentist explained that during Sam's early days the energy that would have normally gone to forming strong teeth was diverted to fighting illness and literally saving his life. His body "rearranged" its priorities to care for the weak, sick, and suffering parts at the expense of another "member."

In these days of increasing conflict in the church, this principle can help us avoid division and reunite the body of Christ. I may not understand why you hurt. My perspective as one member of the body is limited. But the fact that you hurt is reason enough for me to care and do what I can to relieve your pain. We're a body, and that's what a body does.

So if one member suffers, all the members suffer with it; if one member is honored, all the members rejoice with it.
I CORINTHIANS 12:26

The Gift of Spiritual Hunger

One of the most formative things I learned at a very young age was the power of spiritual hunger. I'm talking about having an undeniable hunger for more of God—a desire for God that releases heaven's fullness to overflow into your life. God honors and blesses spiritual hunger.

Here are three keys to understanding spiritual hunger:

1. Spiritual hunger is a gift. When we sense a tugging to know God more, to read the Bible, to ask questions about Him, to be near people who know Him, it's not a random emotion. It's the drawing of the Holy Spirit.

2. Hunger must be acted upon. If we feed the hunger, it will grow. If we ignore the hunger, it will fade.

3. Hunger begets hunger. The more we taste, the more we want. The less spiritually hungry we are, the less we'll desire God and be filled.

God loves to stir within us a desire that takes us into a lifestyle of walking with Him as our source of fulfillment. My prayer for us . . . that our hearts would be consumed with a hunger for more of Him. That our awareness of Him would increase. And that we would come to Him and be filled. Again and again.

Taste and see that the Lord is good.
How happy is the man who takes refuge in Him!
PSALM 34:8

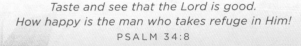

Every Step of the Way

The thing about the words "run your own race" is that I hate running. Walking, however, I can do. Tennis shoes laced, earbuds in, and a trail through the trees encouraging me onward. Step after step, one and then another, steady and sure. I just keep going, walking at my own pace, showing up.

Joshua did the same. Before leading the Israelites into battle, God instructed him to tell the people to walk—not "fight" or "get ready" or "bring a sacrifice." So for six days, thousands of Israelites walked in obedience. And stayed with it. Yet from their perspective, there was no progress, no result to show for the time put in.

Life feels this way sometimes. We walk through joys and struggles, heartache and confusion. And although we know God is with us, nothing seems to be happening around us. But I imagine God's words echoing inside, playing in their ears: be strong and courageous.

Even when it doesn't make sense and the road is long. Even when we can't see past the next step. We carry the truth with us and, eventually, day seven arrives and the walls fall. We walk, and He wins. Step after step, one and then another, steady and sure.

Haven't I commanded you: be strong and courageous?
Do not be afraid or discouraged,
for the Lord your God is with you wherever you go.
JOSHUA 1:9

The Stories We Live

I retreat to the living room and sit with a book that gets me thinking about story—about the impact of another person's life on our own. Stories are more than just words. They're the choices we make and the experiences that shape us.

We take in each other's stories just by living our own. Our experiences with others shape the way we live out our own story. Sometimes we learn stories through books, and sometimes we learn them from others. But for a story to be truly taken in by another person, it needs to be shared, through the sharing of a life by living alongside one another. For how we live—what we say and don't say, what we do and don't do—is telling a story that shapes the listener too.

Consider the story you write with your life. It is part of the story of the body of Christ—part of the larger story God is telling. Let us walk alongside others and live our unique stories with the stamp of the Holy Spirit. For that's the story we want written, the story the community around us needs to read. *Help us, God, to tell a good story this day.*

They conquered him by the blood of the Lamb and by the word of their testimony, for they did not love their lives in the face of death.
REVELATION 12:11

The Gift of Quiet

Growing up, we had a family friend who always teased me about being quiet. He would come up to me and say, "No talking." He was teasing in the nicest way and simply pointing out the obvious: I was a quiet girl. As an adult looking back, I believe it was one of my strengths.

It took me years to embrace my quiet—maybe because I was usually surrounded by loud. The loud get attention. The loud get noticed. The loud get picked first. The quiet are quickly forgotten.

As I've gotten older, I've learned it's okay to be quiet. Quiet wants to spend time with you. Quiet wants you to take a few deep breaths and sit awhile. Quiet wants you to lean in and listen. Step away from the computer screen, put down your mobile device, and turn off the television. Quiet wants you to pay attention. Quiet gives permission to say, "No talking."

What's the quiet saying to you? Because when you've taken the time to listen—truly listen—you'll have a better idea of what you're supposed to say.

There is an occasion for everything . . . a time to be silent and a time to speak.
ECCLESIASTES 3:1, 7

On Being a Soft Place to Land

I asked my friend how she was doing. Her child had been very sick and I could only imagine how scared she must have felt.

She told me that she was okay, although not good. She admitted that when answering other friends who'd asked her the same question, they looked at her blankly. As if they'd never felt a little crazy themselves. I hugged her and said, "If someone says they've never felt a little crazy, they're either lying or boring." She laughed and thanked me for understanding.

When I think about my various friends and the crises we've endured together—or watched each other face—I can't help but think of the body of Christ. We are all one, but we each have a different part to play. I have friends who will offer to watch other friends' kids anytime a difficult situation comes up. I have friends who are handy and can fix things. I have friends who are great listeners and, when asked, can offer sound advice. I have friends who make great casseroles and fold laundry without feeling awkward.

I'm not like those friends. Those aren't my gifts. But if you need someone who will understand when you feel a little crazy? I'm your girl.

For as many of you as have been baptized into Christ have put on Christ like a garment. There is no Jew or Greek, slave or free, male or female; for you are all one in Christ Jesus.
GALATIANS 3:27–28

Choosing Joy

Before I was married, I reluctantly went mountain biking with the man who is now my husband. I didn't know how to ride a mountain bike, so he had to keep me from crashing into the poles—on both sides of the dirt trail. He taught me about steering in five words: *You go where you focus.* I needed to keep my eyes on the path, not on the poles. "Focus," he said, "on where you want to go. Don't focus on the obstacles."

Fast-forward a few years, and, well, since we've had kids, there hasn't been a whole lot of mountain biking. But earlier this month we were in New York City, staying with his brother and sister-in-law, who happen to be hard-core mountain bikers. So there I was, back on a mountain bike after a long hiatus. As the trail got narrower and switched back and forth, I had to stop before wiping out. I hissed to James (if you can picture me hissing), "I hate this!"

You see, the first five minutes of the ride happened to be the most challenging. I thought, *If the whole trail is like this, I'll never make it!* To my relief, it opened up a bit and wasn't as difficult. I did okay. But before you're too impressed . . . it was a beginner loop.

There were parts of the trail that led between two really big tree trunks. As I approached the trees, I thought, *Oh no! I'm going to hit that tree trunk!* But then I'd remember James's advice: you go where you focus. So I forced myself to look straight at the trail and not at the trees. And you know what? I made it through, every time.

Let your eyes look forward; fix your gaze straight ahead.
PROVERBS 4:25

The Days We Doubt

One morning my daughter said, "Sometimes I don't know if God is real. I want to, but sometimes I just don't know." The truth is, I've doubted sometimes too.

I've whispered, "God help me believe; increase my faith" more times than I can count. There were nights I've read my kids a Bible story and thought . . . *Did this really happen? How can I teach them, when I feel so uncertain?* Many times I've felt like an Israelite begging for a sign.

Thankfully, God heard my cry. He didn't zap me with a ton of faith overnight; instead, He allowed me to walk through some long, dark valleys. It was in those valley moments that He revealed himself the most.

Two years ago our home in Alabama wouldn't sell. Then a tornado ripped through town, destroying everything in its path except my neighborhood. Another family needed a home and ours was available. It's as if God had kept our house on hold just for them.

It's hard explaining to a twelve-year-old that sometimes we see God best when trials—or even tornados—come our way. He reveals Himself in the most unexpected ways.

Now without faith it is impossible to please God, since the one who draws near to Him must believe that He exists and rewards those who seek Him.
HEBREWS 11:6

May We Wrestle and May We Overcome

Right before I began my fifth year of university, I felt paralyzed. Every time someone asked me, "What are your plans after school?" I would avoid eye contact and say, "I don't know." Part of me thought that, after five years, God's calling would have been revealed to me. It was not.

I knew I had options for life after graduation, but there was this constant whisper in my heart that said, "Hannah, not this." So like any mature twenty-two-year-old, I began to fight. I fought what everyone told me I should do. I fought against the tugs of different passions. I fought the God-whispers in my heart, telling me I needed to do something uncomfortable.

Eventually, I grew tired of fighting. So I went to a favorite park, ready to give up the fight. I sat under a tall tree on a red fleece blanket, took out my journal, and said, "Okay, God, we're doing this. I'm done fighting with everyone, and I'm done fighting with You."

We can wrestle. We can meet God in the desert and fight all night long, but at some point, we have to stop the fighting, listen to the whispers, receive the blessing, and receive a new name and a renewed calling.

Your name will no longer be Jacob," He said. "It will be Israel because you have struggled with God and with men and have prevailed.
GENESIS 32:28

The Delight in Her Eyes

"I'll call a taxi," Grandma said. And so we were off. First we went to Brooksie's Diner. Being seven, I ordered a grilled cheese sandwich and a vanilla cola.

After lunch, we walked to the five-and-dime. "You can pick out anything you like," Grandma said.

"Anything?" I knew what I wanted. A white baby doll seat, with a floral print cushion. I smiled and squealed, "Thank you, Grandma!"

"Is that all you want?"

I was stunned. "I can get more than one thing?"

"Yes," she said, "whatever you want."

An hour later I climbed back into that taxi holding all my new finds, but what I remember most was the look in her eyes—they smiled *with delight*. Now grown, I would love one more afternoon with my grandma.

As great as that would be, I have something even better . . . a Father in heaven who loves to give good gifts. And I'm not talking about stuff from the five-and-dime. His gifts are good. But the best part? *The Giver does not change.* He's the same God who gave us the stars in the sky to light our way and His Son on Calvary to purchase our freedom. Do you see His eyes? They are smiling with delight. And His delight is for eternity.

Every generous act and every perfect gift is from above,
coming down from the Father of lights;
with Him there is no variation or shadow cast by turning.
JAMES 1:17

MAY 20
How Beautiful You Are

The other day I asked my husband to come into our backyard to help with a project. As he walked behind me, I cringed that I was still wearing the old pair of jeans that weren't a good fit. I've always been self-conscious about my curves, so I wished I had a long sweater to cover an unflattering fit.

With every step I took, I imagined that my husband was thinking the same thing that I was thinking about myself.

Then he said, "You have such a cute little walk." What? I made him repeat himself to make sure I heard him right. "You have such a cute little walk." He wasn't assessing my faults like I was in my own head; he was simply appreciating something he saw in me as he walked with me.

The example of love he set that day inspired me. Through all the curves and ups and downs we've navigated over nearly three decades together, I see his daily decisions to choose to love me as a reflection of his ultimate commitment to live and love like Christ.

A commitment to pursue love in spite of imperfections can help refine us and inspire others when they see Christ working in us.

How beautiful you are, my darling. How very beautiful!
Behind your veil, your eyes are doves.
SONG OF SONGS 4:1

MAY 21
To Linger at the Table

Nine lives living under one roof—with six kids, two parents, and now a houseguest. It was enough to make my head spin. Our home was feeling the weight of one more person.

I realized that doing for our new guest was inhibiting my ability to truly see her. That is, until I got the wild idea to treat her to lunch at my favorite restaurant.

After a long day in court and one dismissed charge against her, we ate guacamole and fish tacos and celebrated like old friends. And somewhere between the chips and salsa and mutual vulnerability and closeness at the table, I caught sight of the person. She looked like Jesus.

The cost of hospitality, the death to self to give to another life, only serves to pave the way to real encounters with Jesus, who is the Bread of Life. May we choose to be with our neighbors and linger at the table long enough to see the image of Jesus reflected to us.

It was as He reclined at the table with them that He took the bread, blessed and broke it, and gave it to them. Then their eyes were opened.
LUKE 24:30–31

Radical Hospitality, Extravagant Love

"What punishment do you think the young man deserves?" the officer asked my mother-in-law. A troubled teenage boy had broken into her car and stolen her purse.

"I think he should be required to come to my house for Sunday dinner," she said. The police officer was shocked. Radical hospitality extended.

Sunday dinners were always interesting at my in-laws. You never knew who would be there; neither did she. If she knew of anyone eating alone or someone who just needed to be loved on—including a young transgressor— she'd invite them to dinner. When we openly welcome strangers, outcasts, and the neglected, we're showing them their value and worth in Christ. This is the heart of true hospitality.

My mother-in-law lived the gospel until her final breath. I know that one day we'll be reunited again, around another table for supper—at the great heavenly banquet, the glorious feast with our Redeemer, the wedding supper of the Lamb. It will be a joyous celebration of His divine kingdom, a new heaven and a new earth. There will be no more death, no more tears, and no more suffering. Together we will gaze upon the Bridegroom and behold the full radiance of His glory.

Then hesaid to me, "Write: Those invited to the marriage feast of the Lamb are fortunate!" He also said to me, "These words of God are true."
REVELATION 19:9

The Everyday Woman

Our culture is consumed with having it all. Oftentimes I buy into this lie. I begin to believe I can be Superwoman. I can show everyone online how I am living the dream. When in reality, I'm a mess.

I get into trouble when I try to be everything. The toxic "I'm not enough" thoughts, the oppressive "I ought to" expectations, and the constant pressure of my "I should" ideals squeeze every ounce of joy from me. But in Christ we are promised abundant living. Not paralyzed living. Not terrified living. Not guilt-ridden living. *Abundant living.*

Everyday Christian living isn't meant to be confusing and crippling.

Rather, we can direct our efforts toward Spirit-led obedience in simple everyday moments: working and watching, cooking and cleaning, teaching and training, sleeping and stirring. Because the promised abundant life is cultivated best when we are living out the everyday life God has planned specifically for each of us to live.

Every woman is an extraordinary masterpiece with layers of beauty and strength. We're each a piece in a God-sized puzzle, and our unique everyday pieces fit together to display the image of Christ to the world around us.

A thief comes only to steal and to kill and to destroy.
I have come so that they may have life and have it in abundance.
JOHN 10:10

Why Rest Takes Courage

"Prison is starting to sound really good." My friend was so tired that even the idea of prison didn't repel her if it meant laying on a mattress and reading a book alone. We laughed, shaking our heads at ourselves.

When a desert island, a hospital, or prison start to sound like a vacation, you know you need to take a rest on purpose.

Taking regular time off means taking a day to open your hands toward heaven and acknowledge that you don't make the world go round.

Maybe a break means a time to listen without the pressure to hear something profound; a time to read without the pressure to learn something interesting; a time to receive without the pressure to turn the gift into something more useful.

But just because you take a break from something doesn't mean you're resting. And what I need even more than a break is rest—the kind that sticks around even after all the sand and chlorine is washed out of my bathing suit, the kind that softens the shadows of my soul even after I return to the dishes, the kind that comforts and sings in the midst of the same old routines. What I need, what we all need, is to find rest for our souls.

I am at rest in God alone; my salvation comes from Him.
PSALM 62:1

The Blessing of Endurance

I want to run a marathon. The spiritual connection, the life lessons, the crossing it off my bucket list. Yes! I pump myself up with these thoughts, lace up my running shoes, and start jogging.

But I barely finish a lap around the track before I'm sweating from every pore, my legs are burning, and my face is red. I lose all motivation, and my jog slows to a defeated walk.

I get like this with everything. Whenever something gets hard, I want to run away. I'm scared to fail *and* scared to succeed. If I fail, there's shame, but if I succeed, there's pressure to go to the next success. It's easier to stay low and avoid the work I need to do for my soul's good.

To endure means being in it for the long haul—even when it gets boring or you feel like quitting. It's taking the next step, whether it's running a marathon or walking in obedience. And maybe that's the point, because easy doesn't grow us.

I tell myself this when I want to quit doing any hard thing. When I take the next step, I lay the foundation to the path ahead and discover life in ways I never could've foreseen.

Therefore, since we also have such a large cloud of witnesses surrounding us, let us lay aside every weight and the sin that so easily ensnares us. Let us run with endurance the race that lies before us, keeping our eyes on Jesus, the source and perfecter of our faith, who for the joy that lay before Him endured a cross and despised the shame and has sat down at the right hand of God's throne.
HEBREWS 12:1–2

MAY 26
The Woman in the Mirror

I returned from the women's conference refreshed, but most of the sessions were filled with strategies, charts, and procedures that I never got around to doing.

Sometimes I don't even want to get up early to read my Bible—I want to stay in bed a few more minutes, one more snooze, and one more dream. Basically, I want my own way.

The Bible says that when we listen to the Word but don't do what it says, we are like the person in this verse. It's what I do, except I'll take it a step further: I'll put on glossy lipstick, sparkly eye shadow, and a touch of plum blush. Then I'll forget what I look like.

The fact is, without the power of the Holy Spirit encouraging us and changing us, we would never want to do what God's Word says. It's by His amazing grace that He gives us the desire to grow and hunger for His Word, and when we abide in His Word, He gives us the strength we need—not just to read about change, but to actually experience change. Then we'll no longer be mere hearers of the Word, but also doers.

Because if anyone is a hearer of the word and not a doer,
he is like a man looking at his own face in a mirror.
For he looks at himself, goes away, and immediately
forgets what kind of man he was.
JAMES 1:23–24

MAY 27

It Starts with a Yes

When my husband Peter and I bought our first house, we prepared two guest bedrooms for out-of-town visitors. Once we felt settled, we started having people over for dinner.

Although we're both introverts, we shared a desire to steward our resources well and to learn how to practice biblical hospitality. We prayed, "Lord, help us be a blessing to others through what You've given us."

Soon after, a missionary we knew returned home when she couldn't get her visa renewed. We invited her to live with us as she figured out her next steps. A few months later, we took in a young mother and her son for three weeks as they worked through a family crisis. Our guests required more than clean sheets and towels, so we learned how to be advocates and provide emotional and spiritual presence.

Peter and I have hosted more people over the years, and each time we've said yes, God has tested and stretched our limits. But He has also given us glimpses of His heart for the poor, the orphaned, and the widows while expanding our hearts in ways we couldn't have imagined.

Biblical hospitality looks different for all of us, but it starts with a yes. God then takes our yeses and transforms them into unimagined possibilities.

_____

_____

_____

_____

_____

_____

_____

_____

Don't neglect to do what is good and to share, for
God is pleased with such sacrifices.
HEBREWS 13:16

MAY 28
Waiting for Someday

I was knee-deep in financial worries and sleep deprivation, living in a state of minute-to-minute dependence on God and dreaming of those mythical "somedays" ahead. You know the ones. Someday we'll have company more often. Someday I'll have quiet devotions before anyone else wakes up. Someday I'll take a class on graphic design and create the ideas floating in my head.

Do you wait for "somedays"? What do yours look like? Someday we'll have a house that's big enough for entertaining. Someday I'll have children. Someday the kids will be grown and I'll do all those things I've kept in a holding pattern.

Planning ahead isn't a bad thing—even God has plans for us. But even so, I don't think we're supposed to wait for those "somedays" before we dive in and do the work He's put in front of us today. God has given us today—right here, right now—for us to use for His glory.

Since man's days are determined and the number of his months depends on You,
and since You have set limits he cannot pass,
look away from him and let him rest so that he can enjoy his day...
JOB 14:5–6

A Cure for "If Only"

I was in the attic going through boxes of books when I heard some arguments downstairs taking place with my adult children. Hearing this had me wondering: *If only I had done something different, perhaps things would be different now.* I was plagued with "If only this . . ." or "If only that . . ."

As I sorted through the books, a sheet of paper fell out of one of them. Tears welled up in my eyes as I looked at my father's words written in block print. He had passed away years earlier, yet his handwriting revealed an answer to my mulling in some sermon notes from years before titled, "A Cure for If Only."

With his words, my father reminded me that, indeed, God is at work fulfilling His plan through the failure and regret. Just as Joseph's hardships eventually brought him to a place where he could serve an entire nation, God has a plan and He's in control.

No matter how badly I screw up, no matter how many mistakes I make, no matter how many "if onlys" I have, God can redeem them. Our mistakes can never thwart the sovereign will of God. And in this we find great hope and deep peace.

But Joseph said to them, "Don't be afraid. Am I in the place of God?
You planned evil against me; God planned it for good to bring
about the present result—the survival of many people."
GENESIS 50:19–20

A Season of Waiting

I'm currently in a season of waiting. I'd describe it as a holding pattern of sorts, as if God broadcasted over the speaker of my life: *Delay ahead. Grab a snack and settle in for that movie. All those things you planned for at your destination? Forget them for the foreseeable future. We're holding.*

This season of waiting squeezes uncomfortably tight on a heart that wants room to land, room to stretch, room to run wild and free. It's caused me to step back and revisit my decisions, to dig deeper into my motives, to question my plans, and to lean harder into my prayers. I sense very little in the way of divine intervention, and it seems as if the connection's gone silent. While waiting I wonder if it holds any meaning.

As I wait, I place my hope in the fact that this holding pattern is in itself a destination. Every decision made led to this place here, and I remain confident that regardless of how long it takes, I have seen the goodness of the Lord in the land of the living. Even when He's silent, I know more goodness lies ahead.

I am certain that I will see the Lord's goodness in the land of the living.
PSALM 27:13

Giving Out of Excess Isn't Equivalent to Sacrifice

We gathered in a circle to pray over the women who would be the recipients of donations collected. The prayers offered were thoughtful and heartfelt, but as the time of prayer tarried, I had a growing conviction: *What we're doing isn't heroic.* We had gone to our closets, which were overrun with excess, and plucked out a few items we really didn't like anyway. As I glanced at the piles, I saw items pruned from the "has no value" section. We didn't pull out our favorite sweaters or best handbags for the women. This wasn't a sacrifice.

Giving out of excess isn't sacrificial giving. Sacrifice is the act of surrendering something prized. Our "giving" wasn't an act of courage or bravery.

Conviction and tears welled up. When it was my turn to pray, I spoke the words God had placed on my heart: "Forgive me for giving out of my abundance and then getting puffed up in arrogance about my good work. This act is not heroic. Refine me, Lord. Help me learn to give sacrificially."

That moment will not escape my memory. I am still truly grateful for the conviction I experienced that day. I pray that moment of refining lasts a lifetime. *Please, Lord, continue to draw out the impurities in me.*

Each person should do as he has decided in his heart—
not reluctantly or out of necessity, for God loves a cheerful giver.
II CORINTHIANS 9:7

JUNE 1
Making Room for More

My wedding was supposed to be a small affair. Partly because we had a tiny budget and partly because the venue said "We can comfortably seat about fifty people." So I sent out exactly fifty invitations. If you've ever planned a shindig, you see my mistake here. I assumed fifty invitations equaled fifty people. but I ended up with one hundred people on my RSVP guest list. My groom-to-be then explained to me how multiplication works.

In the end, it all worked out. I mean, I had to cut almost my entire flower budget, return my fancy shoes, and hand-make my wedding programs in order to afford the extra food. But what I remember the most about that day isn't the things I cut, but how much love filled that room.

I remember dancing with our guests under garlands strung with lights. I remember clasping hands with family and friends who came to witness the start of our new life together. I remember that our love was multiplied by the gift of their presence.

That is my hope for all of us, not just on special occasions, but every day—that we measure our moments not with finite numbers, but with the love we share. Because that is the best kind of multiplication.

And may the Lord cause you to increase and overflow with love for one another and for everyone, just as we also do for you.
1 THESSALONIANS 3:12

Kingdom Ways

When I log on to social media, I am quickly reminded how much I'm polarized by politics and theology. My instinct is to jump in and either defend or attack depending on the situation. It's as if God's commandments for how we're to lovingly treat one another don't apply to our political and theological differences. I don't want my theo-political allegiances to override my neighborly obligations. But how?

First John 4:20 says, "If anyone says, 'I love God,' yet hates his brother, he is a liar." Not having a hateful or disagreeable posture makes me wonder how on earth Jesus's twelve disciples loved one another given the likelihood of different political views. I have a hunch that through the power of the Holy Spirit, fellowship with one another, suffering together, observing Jesus's life, and by personally experiencing Christ's love, they saw that their obligation to love one another was more important than their political disagreements.

As they spent time with Jesus, they discovered that the nature of the kingdom is not centered on political and theological tribalism, one-upping one another, or constant division. Instead, as Paul says in Romans 14:17, the kingdom of God is characterized by "righteousness, peace, and joy in the Holy Spirit"—what they saw in Jesus.

For the kingdom of God is not eating and drinking,
but righteousness, peace, and joy in the Holy Spirit.
ROMANS 14:17

All In

The first time I used the expression "all in" was during a card game called Tripoley. As the game unfolds, it's common to reach a point where you push all your chips to the center and declare "All in" as your strategic move to win the game.

Every time I've gone "all in" in Tripoley, I've experienced a conviction in my spirit. While I might risk "all in" in a card game, was I living my life "all in" for God's glory? Do my "moves" demonstrate a wholehearted commitment to God? Am I totally invested in obeying God's Word and living for His glory? Does God have access to all of me? Or am I devoted to someone or something else more than God?

There have been too many times when my "moves" convey that I've made an idol out of a relationship or a responsibility, a pursuit or a project, a title or an award. I've fallen in to the trap of loving "the created thing" more than my God who created me!

As awesome as it is to win a game of Tripoley with an "all in" move, how much more rewarding will it be when I'm face-to-face with God and can confidently say to Him, "Lord, I was 'all in' for You."

Love the Lord your God with all your heart, with all your soul, and with all your strength.
DEUTERONOMY 6:5

The Sisterhood of Messy Hearts

If we look closely enough at our sisters in Christ, we'll see a lot of women with stoic faces who actually have holes in their hearts. We carry the weight of secrets, heartaches, and betrayals. Wary of trust, walls go up, separating us from one another. So what's the solution for repairing that separation? What can we do? Scripture says we should put others first, thinking of their needs ahead of our own. It also means taking the lead in loving a sister first . . . before she loves me.

What if we put away all unfavorable perceptions and choose to think only the best? What if we forget previous clashes and choose to start with a clean slate? What if we keep confidences in perfect trust and choose to speak only positively about her? And when we fail, what if we humbly ask for forgiveness and choose to forgive when hurts come our way?

In order for this sisterhood of messy hearts to flourish in Christ, grace must go both ways. Beauty is found in grace. Hope is exchanged in love. Redemption is mined from humility. And the meekness of a messy sisterhood can be a beautiful tapestry of merciful grace . . . if only we'll take the lead to love first.

For by the grace given to me, I tell everyone among you not to think of himself more highly than he should think. Instead, think sensibly, as God has distributed a measure of faith to each one.

ROMANS 12:3

To Be Brought Near

My four-year-old and I found ourselves in the midst of a duel. At first I calmly answered his questions, but then he began spewing disrespectful words. I was ready to spew some back when suddenly he flung himself into my arms for a massive embrace with tears flowing. I wrapped my arms around him and brought him in near with my embrace.

Looking at my son's sin, I am reminded of my own. The wrestle—fighting a strong desire to do what I want versus obeying what God has said. I sometimes still try to make my own decisions apart from God. There are days I battle with Him over why I don't understand His answer or why I don't understand His plan.

But soon after demanding my own way, I run home to the arms of the One who shed His blood for me, the One who gives me true worth. My son reminded of that when he threw himself into my arms. When I was once far off and dead in my sin, I was brought near. And I am still brought near today.

But now in Christ Jesus, you who were far away have
been brought near by the blood of the Messiah.
EPHESIANS 2:13

He Stood in Silence

When I read about Jesus being on trial, I'm struck by how He stood silently, not answering His accusers. He was put on trial, first before Pilate, then to Herod, then back to Pilate. Because Pilate bowed to the angry crowd, he ordered Jesus to be flogged and killed. And the whole time, Jesus stood silently, not saying a word to defend Himself.

I think about how quickly I jump to defend myself, especially when I feel backed into a corner. But if anyone was backed into a corner, it was Jesus. False accusations flew all around Him, yet He did not respond in any retaliatory way.

Why did He just stand there and take it? Why didn't He bring the temple crashing down on them all? Why didn't He at least laugh at them and tell them their day was coming? Humility . . . love . . . and Jesus knew this was His time. He knew He was the only One who could save the world.

When I think of Jesus's hands and their scars and the death He endured, not just for the world, but for me personally, I close my eyes and whisper, "Thank You." And the next time I'm falsely accused of something, I will remember His example.

The chief priests and the scribes stood by, vehemently accusing Him.
LUKE 23:10

JUNE 7
He Goes with You

Passport, check. Bag, check. Deep breath, check. A few months earlier I'd joined a team of college students headed to the Amazon jungles of Peru. It was a long flight to a faraway place, and someone kept mentioning anacondas . . . I whispered a prayer and off we flew.

Once we landed, we hit the ground running. We spent our first days hanging out with street kids, holding baby alligators, practicing our Spanish, and getting ready to lead Vacation Bible School.

Then we climbed onto a houseboat for a two-week adventure down the Amazon. We should have been nervous, but we knew God was with us every step of the way.

He was there the night we led a church service without electricity and the day we climbed off the boat into knee-deep mud. He was there when we visited the leper colony, giving hope to those with little of it. He was there when the sweet woman in that tiny village prayed to ask Jesus into her life.

Every single little part . . . He was there. And if He was there for all of that, then He's there for all our moments here, too, no matter how ordinary the day may seem. Take a deep breath, friend. He goes with you.

The Lord is the One who will go before you. He will be with you; He will not leave you or forsake you. Do not be afraid or discouraged.
DEUTERONOMY 31:8

Connecting the Dots

"You are only a dot on a dot," I was told. Compared to the solar system, the size of the earth is but a dot. And me on the earth? A dot on a dot. The universe does not revolve around my dot, and yet, my dot, my life—your life—matters.

Consider a child's dot-to-dot puzzle, the picture the connected dots make, and a person's life. For example, twenty years ago, a mentor suggested I attend seminary . . . (connecting) . . . I then found a seminary in another city I had visited years earlier and relocated. I befriended many wonderful people—more dots—who impacted my life. One of those "dots" suggested an organization for me to work . . . (connecting) . . . I ended up there and met my husband. Ten years, three children, and three states later, we've connected many more dots.

None of us will ever know how our dot will impact someone else. Our actions matter. Our words matter. How we raise our children, treat our friends and random strangers on the street . . . it all matters.

So as you go through your day, week, month, life, remember your significance to the dots around you.

_Therefore encourage one another and build
each other up as you are already doing._
I THESSALONIANS 5:11

JUNE 9
Can I Just Have a Normal Life?

Recently, I shared several hard things happening in my life with a friend. Then I blurted out, "Ugh! Can I just have a normal life?" I took a deep breath and immediately said, "Does anyone really have a normal life?" We both laughed.

Maybe you've had these thoughts too. When life hits hard and you wonder why it isn't like so-and-so's life, do you ever want to burst out with a similar plea?

Chronic illness. Financial blows. Parenting challenges. Deep loneliness. The list is seemingly endless. So what is normal anyway? I tend to think of normal as a life free of long-standing challenges. This kind of normal says there will always be money to pay the bills. No one is sick. Nothing breaks down. People get along.

But you know what? If normal is what's common to all people, then normal is the reality of living in a world where sin, decay, and a prowling enemy surround us.

Our current normal changes because life ebbs and flows. The only One who stays the same is Jesus. He is our constant. He is the source of knowing how to navigate whatever our current normal is. And in our normal living, we find a God who is anything but.

*For the L*ORD *your God is the God of gods and Lord of lords, the great, mighty, and awesome God, showing no partiality and taking no bribe.*
DEUTERONOMY 10:17

JUNE 10
Loving-Kindness Poured Down

The windshield intersected the raindrops as the wipers cleared the remnants in a steady, rhythmic strumming sound. Amid their mesmerizing cadence, my thoughts were filled with all I needed to accomplish that day. In the drizzling rain, I bolted out the car door to get the mail, and little did I know that the cold metal mailbox held a priceless gift—a treasure that's rare in these cyber-heavy days. A note card, hand-addressed to me!

The sweet words of a friend poured down like rain on my parched and cracked soul, soaking in deep. And they brought the rain of flowing tears.

Overwhelmed by her kindness, I found myself actually enjoying the rain. Then my phone chimed with a random text: *Have a wonderful day!* I paused, my heart full from the goodness of it all. This wet day was a gift to me, straight from the Father's heart to mine—from my Abba to me. He sent His nourishing, reviving water to me this day, through the kindness of friends. They responded to His promptings and became His hands and feet to me, bringing an affirming message of His heart . . . *"You, my child, are loved."* And the loving-kindness of our God overwhelms.

The tongue of the wise brings healing.
PROVERBS 12:18

The Good News: This Is Only the Beginning

Last Saturday, my husband looked down and started murmuring about the floor. "Would now be a good time to pull out the steam mop?" he said.

Loving wife that I am, I shrieked, looked up, and said, "No! Now would be a good time to get out the paint can!"

He sees the tiny crumbs and dirt; I see the large unpainted walls. In our house, someone always has their eye on the details and someone else on the big picture. So when each Saturday of projects comes around, I often repeat the words, "This is only the beginning." These words remind me that something good is starting. That, in the grander scheme of God's story, the best is *always* yet to come.

This is as true for the newborn as it is for an aging parent—we're all at the beginning of something. Each day is a beginning where we experience the work, play, rest, and worship we will enjoy *forever*.

I think "the beginning" matters because it means we are moving toward renewal. That means the petty annoyances, the illnesses, the losses, and even the tragedies we suffer are ending. The sin and evil and general brokenness that leave us breathless with fear and anger? They have already been defeated.

They are on the way out.

Then the One seated on the throne said, "Look, I am making everything new."
REVELATION 21:5

JUNE 12
Because Hope Wins

A canopy of heaven stretched over the snowy floor. Colors and splays of nature beautifully enveloped me. Yet depression clung to my every step. It seeped into my pores and crisscrossed my face. Life did not wait for me; no, it created a tide of expectations and a current of must-dos. I parceled out my energy to see others, to meet requirements, to do right by a career, family, friends, and a future. My smile, real enough to some and the shallow clear to others.

But as sorrow lies near—I live. To love. To teach. To lead. To write. To whisper. I do not know who will follow or who will listen, but my steady foundation of faith and the formation of friends and family remind me, to be me to the world. Who I am, whether small and in a ball, tired from the day, or strong and tall, knowing my purpose, I am alive.

One more day, friends. To tasks and talents, give what you can. Allow others to lend you hope when yours is low and depression is real. Let's walk together. Another day, yes, the light still shines.

Now this is what the Lord says—the One who created you, Jacob,
and the One who formed you, Israel—"Do not fear, for I have
redeemed you; I have called you by your name; you are Mine."
ISAIAH 43:1

Living with Less While Giving More

Over lunch my friend tells me that she's challenging herself to limit her spending on groceries. She wants to simplify, to cut the excess. To me, her actions seem like a burden, but her enthusiasm spurs me to consider my own spending habits. And I determine not to enter a store unless I've planned my purchase and hold myself to it.

Months later, I'm surprised by how much this has impacted my life, from the daily task of sorting mail to the time I used to spend dillydallying in a store.

This discipline of intentional frugality has also helped me realize how often I purchased an item for its beauty, even when I had no use for it nor a place for it.

By finding ways to simplify our lives, we make room for God to use us as channels of His good. We are stewards of the wealth He gives us. He wants us to be like a river, our wealth flowing in and flowing out, not like the Dead Sea, accumulating salty mineral deposits, choking out life. When we choose to live more simply, with less to care for, we open the opportunity to give more generously.

Give to him, and don't have a stingy heart when you give, and because of this the Lord your God will bless you in all your work and in everything you do.
DEUTERONOMY 15:10

When God's Faithfulness Sounds like Silence

A recent flood in Baton Rouge has had me wondering how I'll replace my belongings, how I'll replace my vehicle, and then, most recently, how I'll find a new place to live. These thoughts have crept into my rest, keeping me awake at night. I'm at a loss as to what step to take next or even which direction to move toward. But I rest in the fact that God can handle my worries and my fears. Because He is God.

So when life feels like a flood that you might not survive, here are three things I've learned to do:

1. Lean on what I know to be true. *Nothing* comes as a surprise to God. He is a provider for *every* need. He holds us.

2. Surround myself with faithful friends. God has blessed me with an abundance of friends who have sat with me, cried with me, and prayed for me. That is what a spiritual family does.

3. Choose to believe God's best for my life. I've decided to start believing that He will bring about good from my circumstances. He's been faithful in the past, and He'll be faithful in my present and future. This is a truth we can stand on today.

_____

_____

_____

_____

_____

_____

_____

_____

God is my helper; the Lord is the sustainer of my life.

PSALM 54:4

JUNE 15
Living the In-Between

My students are writing their names on my marker board during study hall, all wound up after state and unit testing. Ten minutes to the bell, and I don't have the energy to remind them one more time to sit down. But as long as it is today, this hour, I remind myself that I am living a day that matters.

Sometimes that's hard to remember as I anticipate plans in my future—weddings, grandchildren, or the end of the school year. But these days of waiting, these daily in-between days, I am tempted to rush things, to jump from one activity to the next. And if I'm not mindful, I may miss truly living and experiencing the richness God has planned for me in the moment.

So live this day, not some far-off day in the future when you're finally rich enough, free enough, good enough, or graduated enough. Live right here, right now where you are, already enough in the eyes of God.

Even now, in a crazy study hall, I not only see rambunctious students, but I notice the beautiful mess on my marker board—the one that was so boring just minutes ago.

This is the day the Lord has made; let us rejoice and be glad in it.
PSALM 118:24

Rooted in Him

I recently turned forty-two, and in the past few years I have seen some "changes" in my body. People warned me this would happen, but I had hoped I might have a super metabolism and be able to continue binge eating chocolate with minimal effects.

Well, I don't. And I can't. So I started a new workout program. Every day I make time to push myself toward better health. And I'm realizing I need a new routine for what will be a long-term lifestyle change.

It's the same with my faith life, as well. I haven't invested the time needed to develop a solid connection with my Father, so when trouble hits, I'm filled with doubts and fears. I know an established relationship takes time. Yet having an unwavering pursuit to know God keeps my faith strong. When challenges come, I will be able to stand firm and confident in His plans for me.

Just as exercise energizes my physical body, time in His Word benefits my spiritual health. Making God a priority brings me joy. He is my strength, my shield. And I am grateful for the opportunity each day to know Him more.

Therefore, as you have received Christ Jesus the Lord,
walk in Him, rooted and built up in Him and established in
the faith, just as you were taught, overflowing with gratitude..
COLOSSIANS 2:6–7

Holding It Together

The sterile smell of antiseptic filled the early morning air. We had walked through the familiar routine of registering my husband for what would be his seventh procedure under anesthesia in less than a year. It was not clear whether this would be his last.

The prayers of this weary soul could be reduced to only one word to keep it together—Jesus. Whispering this one-word prayer can make the enemy tremble. Jesus—the name of the One who trumps death and is above all names.

I know that Christ could have previously healed my husband. But these various trials have shown me Christ's love in ways I could have not known otherwise.

Christ showed His love through the nurses who quietly joined us in prayer and hugged me when tears threatened to fall. I don't understand it, but I have to accept that there will be struggles in this life—Jesus said so. We live in a world that needs Him—the only One who can save us, heal us, and hold all things together.

My husband wakes in recovery asking for some ice to chew, and I am able to whisper three words of prayer this time. "Thank You, Jesus."

He is before all things,
and by Him all things hold together.
COLOSSIANS 1:17

Who You Really Are

Our five-year-old is going through an identity crisis. He feels the need to remind us who he is by telling us his name. A lot. As though we might forget. So I reassure him that I know who he is. Yes, he is Gabe, my son, and I haven't forgotten.

To be honest, I'm not so different than him. My wandering heart gets distracted by the things of this world. And before I know it, I forget who (and whose) I am. And instead of coming to God, I let the voice of condemnation whisper lies. Then I end up losing my temper and yelling at my kids over something trivial. Because when we forget who (and whose) we are, it doesn't just affect us. The insecurity and ugliness seeps into the relationships around us.

Thankfully, there's a remedy for an identity crisis: God's Word. It lives and breathes life into shame that tries to condemn. When I sit in a brief moment of quiet, His Spirit within me confirms I am His. He says I have nothing to fear because He has sealed me as His own. Just like my persistent reminders to Gabe, God tells me as many times as I need to hear it. I simply have to go to Him.

You did not receive a spirit of slavery to fall back into fear, but you received the Spirit of adoption, by whom we cry out, "Abba, Father!"
ROMANS 8:15

Singing the Words by Heart

My sweet eight-year-old popped into the car and announced, "Today I heard one of my favorite songs, but it was just the instruments playing. It didn't have the words, but I knew the words by heart so I sang them anyway."

Her words rang through my entire being. There are seasons in life when we don't hear the Words to our life's song—the words we're desperate to hear in our hours of deep need.

Some days I feel like the apostle Paul when he said he felt like "the least and unworthy" (1 Corinthians 15:9). But I know this: Life is hard, and every one of us is overcoming something.

God's Word dwelling richly in us will save our souls if we brand it over our lives. Knowing His Word by heart begs the song to sing itself out into our realities. We may have days when we don't know a lick about how to live through it, but if we can whisper out those memorized words and sentences strung together that tell the story of redemption, we are going to make it through.

So if you don't hear the words today and all you can hear are the faint recollections of an instrumental background? Sing the words of the Word by heart.

Let the message about the Messiah dwell richly among you,
teaching and admonishing one another in all wisdom, and singing psalms,
hymns, and spiritual songs, with gratitude in your hearts to God.
COLOSSIANS 3:16

God Uses You Every Day

At lunch, my new friend opened up and shared some struggles going on in her life, and I was able to speak truth into her. When I got home, I shared about our time with my husband. "It was the first time in a very long time I felt like God had used me," I told him.

He looked at me and solemnly said, "God uses you in this family every day, baby." His words meant the world to me. Chances are, you need to hear the same thing.

God uses you every day. When you cook dinner for a group of friends, He uses you. When you are sitting in a cubicle, answering emails, He uses you. When you get up in the middle of the night to rock your crying daughter, He uses you.

Sometimes in life's mundane moments, it can be difficult to see that He's using you, can't it? But it's true. So today, right where you are, I pray and ask God to show you how He is using you. Because if you are like me, you don't think of God using you in the ordinary. But He is. He uses you every day.

The Son of Man did not come to be served, but to serve,
and to give His life—a ransom for many.
MATTHEW 20:28

JUNE 21
The Gifts to Be Discovered

Some things in life are never-ending. Take dirty laundry. I'm beyond thankful I don't have to scrub clothes in a bucket and hang them to dry on a line, but still somehow I find myself entangled in this battle of never being finished. Some days feel like I'm rolling the same boulder up the same unending hill. And it can make me feel so tired . . . so defeated.

The daily things are so cyclical—cooking, cleaning, laundry, bedtimes, and then again with the cooking, cleaning, laundry, bedtimes. Sometimes we feel as though there are always more tasks to complete, whether it's laundry at home or a pile of paperwork at the office. Our work is never done, and in that never-done place, it can be easy to grow weary. It's easy to lose the joy and desire to do all things to the glory of God.

In a recent season of extreme busyness, I felt the Lord remind me that in these spaces there can be joy hidden in the mundane. In all of the things we do, there are hidden gifts to be discovered. And in places where we might be tempted to grumble or complain, His glory still shines and invites us into praise and thanksgiving.

Therefore, whether you eat or drink, or whatever
you do, do everything for God's glory.
I CORINTHIANS 10:31

Cultivating the Good

If you've ever driven through the Midwest in springtime, you've probably seen farmers in gigantic tractors, tilling their land in preparation for planting. They know a crop doesn't begin with planting seeds. It begins long before that—with soil management months in advance. And once the crop is underway, there's a whole science of tending, watering, fertilizing, and harvesting at precise moments for the best yield.

The same is true for our lives. It's our job to cultivate with intentionality the groundwork for the kind of crop we'll harvest someday. Preparation and cultivation help create an atmosphere for growth and health.

For example, for a healthier lifestyle, create a meal that features an array of vegetables. For spiritual growth, memorize Scripture or join a Bible study. For a deeper relationship with a friend, ask her how she's really doing and be prepared to love her even if her answer shocks you.

Today, let's think about the kind of life we want to live and the kinds of relationships we want to have, and then let's take the necessary steps to cultivate that life. A crop will never grow out of rocky, untended soil. But with the hard work of preparation and cultivation we'll reap the benefits many times over.

Remember this: The person who sows sparingly will also reap sparingly, and the person who sows generously will also reap generously.
II CORINTHIANS 9:6

A Good Fix

As the oldest child, I slipped right into the role of dutiful daughter and older sister who fixed things. When my mom and dad argued, I'd strategize how I could fix it. When my little sister got hit by a bully, I took action with fire and vengeance. In school, I loved the tests that gave partial credit if you fixed the problems marked wrong.

My fixing ways deepened as I grew. But before long I was headed for a life of overwhelmed delusion or the white flag of surrender. Thankfully I chose surrender, and I began to learn the value of broken things . . . and broken people.

Now when I'm faced with broken things, I see that a premature fix can sometimes be more damaging than a break. And that the God who was willing to be broken Himself can do amazing things with our surrender in broken places.

Watching a loved one struggle is painful. But how often is our desire to "fix" their problem really a desire to protect our own heart from their pain? Might real love be willing to simply *be* with a friend in the breaking? In the broken places of life, encouraging words and the reassurance of constant love may just be the best fix we can offer.

"Am I a God who is only near"—this is the Lord's declaration—
"and not a God who is far away?"
JEREMIAH 23:23

The Legacy We Leave

I attended a funeral recently and was surprised by the tears that would not stop. Why should tears surprise me at a funeral? At age ninety-three, Mr. Wallace went home to be with the Lord, and I was overjoyed for him. No reason to weep over that good news!

Instead I wept in confession. Behind all the outward appearances, Mr. Wallace was a man who lived and loved sacrificially. He was all about service to his country, his family, and his Lord. He loved his wife of sixty-seven years.

I am inspired by his life and overjoyed that he is home, free from the pain of this world. But I also realized why his remembrance brought tears: I get in the way. I get in the way when it comes to living and loving sacrificially. My insecurities and worldly desires. My self-protection and self-exaltation. It all gets in the way of living the exemplary life he lived.

Mr. Wallace wasn't published, well-known, wealthy, elected, sought after, or followed on social media. He wasn't famous, except with the Famous One—who I am certain welcomed him with, "Well done, good and faithful slave."

His master said to him, "Well done, good and faithful slave!"
MATTHEW 25:21

The One Short Prayer That
Will Change Your Life

We were on the way to church; I was so angry I couldn't speak. The outfits had been cried over and breakfast was a train wreck. We were so late it almost wasn't worth going. Plus my post-baby body couldn't squeeze into anything without looking like a slouchy mess.

But I knew I couldn't stay angry because it was our first day back at church since I'd had the baby, and I knew people would gather around and ask how I was doing. I prayed silently: *Lord, please fill me with Your Spirit of power, Your Spirit of love, Your Spirit of self-control, and of a completely sound mind.*

A shift began in my emotions, and I prayed further, deeper: *Lord, please fill me so full of Your Spirit that my cup overflows, that Your Spirit overflows onto everyone I interact with at church. On my children. On my husband.*

As we stopped at the intersection just before church, I knew God had just parted a Red Sea in me and led me into a powerful truth. Instead of all that anger, I had joy and peace. I was able to walk into church and worship. I was free to focus on others and not myself. I was *free*.

If you then, who are evil, know how to give good gifts to your children,
how much more will the heavenly Father give
the Holy Spirit to those who ask Him?
LUKE 11:13

Finding the Missing Peace

My big sister was the first-chair clarinet in junior high band and a cheerleader in high school. She was a straight-A student in honors classes, with a part-time job.

I was a daydreamer. I ran late for everything. I hid notes from the teacher in my desk and spent time figuring out how to skimp on my homework.

I couldn't measure up to my big sister no matter how hard I tried. I always focused on the places where I fell short. My identity became a long list of needed improvements.

I brought my brokenness into my life of faith and awoke every day feeling like a failure. No one told me that I wasn't "holy" enough, but that's what I believed.

Then God showed me in His Word that holiness isn't about me. It's about Him. Paul says we've been declared righteous by faith and we are at peace with God. Jesus made peace between God and us and this harmony is constant, not something we undo with each mistake we make.

We aren't made righteous by what we have done, but by our faith. Faith is recognizing what Jesus has done and knowing that He will continue to keep the peace between God and us, even when we can't.

_____

_____

_____

_____

_____

_____

_____

Therefore, since we have been declared righteous by faith, we have peace with God through our Lord Jesus Christ.
ROMANS 5:1

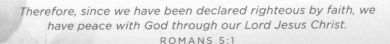

Other Women

Other women seemed to do it better. They managed to keep their houses clean and artfully decorated like a Pottery Barn catalog. Other women ran marathons and started nonprofits and had careers. Other women matched ankle booties to skinny jeans and layered infinity scarves without strangulation of any kind. Other women mastered the messy bun without looking as if a small woodland creature were nesting in their hair.

Other women rose at 5:00 a.m. to have quiet times next to their vases of fresh-cut poppies grown in their gardens, which they'd Instagram next to their journaling Bibles with handwriting that looked like a custom font. Other women did all this, while starting a clothing company from fair-trade-organically-sourced ministries in their spare time.

Other women do it better, I thought . . . and believed for far too long. But today I sow grace for myself. To be where I am, to be who I am. Other women are running their own races. No one can outpace me when my route is different.

I breathe deep and bare my heart before God and feel the width of my soul stretching out like limbs hungry for a race. I look to what is set before me, and I take my place in the lineup.

I have fought the good fight, I have finished the race, I have kept the faith.
II TIMOTHY 4:7

Wherever I Am, God Is Enough

I had just graduated college and thought, *Surely I will get hired quickly. I will figure out what to do with my life.* But God doesn't work in my timing. So there I was stuck between jobs. Doors to potential jobs closed in every direction.

To make some money I began working at a thrift store. As I cleaned a dusty area filled with trinkets, I cried out to God, "Surely I am called for more than this?" Every time I cleaned the bathrooms and sorted through used clothes, I would ask Him again.

As time went on, God began a refining work in me. He whispered into my heart: *"Lovelle, I am enough."* Regardless of my current job—a cashier, a CEO, or a stay-at-home momma—He is enough. I can do everything my heart desires, but if God isn't my contentment, then nothing I do will ever be enough.

As time went on I did get a job offer. It's not my ending point but it's going to give me the tools I need for the future. And where God has placed me for now is enough. Friends, He has you right where He wants you too. So when discouragement tries to seep in, hold on to these words: God is always enough.

And whatever you do, in word or in deed, do everything in the name of the Lord Jesus, giving thanks to God the Father through Him.
COLOSSIANS 3:17

Cast All on Him

The noisy engines drowned out the hammering in my chest. I yanked on the straps to double-check—secured. The hatch opened. "Are you ready?" I knew what he said only by reading his lips. Here I was, only a few steps away from casting my body out of a plane to plummet 12,000 feet through the air. For fun. Who does this?

But cast myself I must. Time to trust the process and proceed. Likewise, it can feel scary to cast our burdens to God. Will He come through for me? Can I trust Him to catch me when I fall?

Wind smacked my body at surprising speed. But even more surprising was the exhilarating feeling of weightlessness. Even though I was rushing at 120 miles per hour to the ground below, it felt like I was floating. A laugh escaped me as I felt incredibly free!

There was a tap on my shoulder from my instructor—my guide and protector—signaling to pull the cord. *Shwooosh!* The parachute exploded open above us and we floated gently toward solid ground.

Let's not be afraid to cast every single weight onto Jesus. Let's experience the exhilaration of burdens lifted. Nothing is too heavy for Him to hold. He will secure your fall.

Cast your burden on the Lord, and He will sustain you;
He will never allow the righteous to be shaken.
PSALM 55:22

The Joy of Pressing Through

I love the summer Olympics. I'm mostly a fan of track-and-field, but I still really enjoy watching the other sports.

For two weeks the world watches and cheers on the best of the best. We sit in awe of the magnificence that is possible with passion, focus, and persistence. Seriously, how is it possible for someone to run a mile in less time than it takes me to walk out my front door to my mailbox? How do you fall down during your race, get up, and finish as the winner?

The sacrifices these athletes make and the lessons they've learned about themselves is something no one can take from them.

For Christ-followers, this life of faith we live is the ultimate test of endurance, and our training never ends. On those days—when the hurdles of life have the potential not just to slow us down, but to knock us off our feet—the book of James encourages us to hold on to joy, even amid the trials of life.

Consider it a great joy whenever we experience various trials? Really?!

We hold on to joy in times of pressure, because when we do, the end result is a deeper faith and a greater joy that can't be taken from us.

Consider it a great joy, my brothers, whenever you experience various trials,
knowing that the testing of your faith produces endurance. But endurance must
do its complete work, so that you may be mature and complete, lacking nothing.
JAMES 1:2–4

JULY 1
The Truth About the Dark Days

I turned around from my kitchen windowsill, slid down to the floor on my knees, and cried. I thought: *I think I'm in a bit of a depression.* Depression is this weird thing that you can't really explain or give reason for. It just is. It's a darkness that seems to be a rhythm of my life, so I know it will lift.

When it hits, I can be mostly okay, but in my home, going about the hours, everything is a mountain. I had a professor once say that when you find yourself in a depressed place, when everything feels hard, just do something small. Maybe you can make the bed. Do that. My small thing, right now, is writing this down, because there is something in the writing that helps.

So while I am sharing that I'm depressed, I'm also hopeful because God is with me. He knows my heart and soul, and He will be kind and tender with me through this. I've been here before. You may have been here before too.

Let's agree to be gentle with ourselves and keep knowing we aren't alone. Because of Jesus, we are free, and we trust the healing in the heaviness.

Why am I so depressed? Why this turmoil within me?
Put your hope in God, for I will still praise Him, my Savior and my God.
PSALM 42:5

JULY 2
Peace in My Place

Isigh over the scattered toys that make up my daily life. While the kids nap, I read an article about a woman in leadership at a well-known organization whose work I admire. Looking around again at the clutter, I slump back into the couch. Anytime someone else seems to be living the dream I dreamed for myself, I quickly forget the joy of living in God's presence right where I am.

While coming to terms with my place in this season, God whispered, *"Hold the door."* Then He gave me a vision of an open door, of a greeter, of someone who makes room for others. In that moment of conviction, I realized that my perspective of my life was terribly skewed.

I had viewed door-holding as underappreciated, overlooked, insignificant. I'd lost sight of my calling. Convicted, I had to confess that what I craved was recognition and admiration.

But God sees me already. How much joy had I forsaken by longing for a different life? I actually don't want to be anywhere else. I know the best place to be is where God calls me—in His presence.

Our best work is done in the kingdom for His glory alone. Making peace with our place is where we find the better life.

Better a day in Your courts than a thousand anywhere else.
I would rather be at the door of the house of my
God than to live in the tents of wicked people.
PSALM 84:10

Hospitality Redefined

With gloved hands, I pull the chicken casserole from the oven. To my own amazement, I didn't burn it. Relief fills me. I have only fifteen minutes before our guests arrive, so I take a special packet of seasoning and carefully sprinkle a fine layer over the casserole. Then I step back to admire my handiwork. For the first time in my life, I've actually cooked something edible.

My husband rounds the corner and gasps, "Why did you cover it with that seasoning? Denise, they had one request: *No MSG.* And that seasoning is full of MSG."

Apparently the family I'm cooking for is allergic to it. And I've dusted the entire casserole with it. So we order pasta to-go from Olive Garden and welcome our guests with my cooking failure.

When it comes to hospitality, I used to think I didn't have much to offer, because cooking just isn't my thing. But over time I learned that real hospitality is about making others feel welcome, not impressing them with my culinary prowess. While some folks have a knack for cooking, hospitality is something we can all do. Hospitality can include a spread of food, but even more, it's about making others feel welcomed and wanted. And that's what I love doing most.

He brought them into his house, set a meal before them,
and rejoiced because he had believed God with his entire household.
ACTS 16:34

When You Wish That Hard
Thing Would Just Go Away

As I chatted on the phone with a friend, we swapped snapshots of what's going on in our lives. Then she asked me those four plain but powerful words: "How are you doing?" And because she isn't interested in the over-sifted "I'm fine!" answers, I knew she wouldn't settle for less than total honesty.

So I told her the truth: "I feel endlessly tired, ridiculously so. And really, I've been saying this for a long time." She asked me to tell her more, so I did.

She warmly listened and agreed with me that I had good reason to be tired. That's when I noticed my tears slipping south. What a relief it is to find an advocate who listens and validates what you're feeling.

I don't know what difficulties you face today, but if they're wearing you out, let me say, "You have good reason to feel the way you do." There will be seasons when hard things hang on even after you try to shove them out the door. Just don't shove out hope instead. Because while the wind howls and the lion roars, the Lamb reigns. Jesus is our advocate. He is interceding on our behalf this very moment and every moment we need Him.

Therefore, He is always able to save those who come to God through Him,
since He always lives to intercede for them.
HEBREWS 7:25

The Ministry of Tears

I have cried more in the past three weeks than I have since my mother's death, and that was a long time ago. The "why" of it is ultimately good: we sold our house. But packing up and purging the house undid me.

My husband and I have been married for thirty years now, and downsizing to a much smaller house forced decisions I didn't want to make. To toss any "thing" felt personal, as if I were saying that memory didn't matter. Suddenly everything mattered and I was paralyzed by emotion and indecision, and just about anything could trigger my tears.

I was grieving a certain kind of loss, but I quickly realized that crying wasn't weakness, it was simply cathartic. Tears are a way for the body to express itself when words aren't enough. They're a gift from God. They aren't arbitrary. Some *thing* in our home would trigger a memory that made me cry and then laugh almost simultaneously. Though I felt crazy at times, I paid attention and began to understand what all those tears were telling me.

Selling our home represented a final letting go of one thing to be free to grasp another. These tears are evidence of a great love and for a life that has meant something special, even important.

You Yourself have recorded my wanderings.
Put my tears in Your bottle. Are they not in Your records?
PSALM 56:8

In Every Day and Every Season

Wisdom is sensing what you need—or don't need—and knowing how or what you need to fulfill it. *Sometimes I need a sermon*: a preacher to preach strong and tell it to me plain. My life is out of alignment. It's for my spiritual survival to hear the preacher preach.

Other times I need a book. I need the beauty of truth in raw words.

And sometimes I just need to make everyone's opinions go away for a while. The older I get, the more I can't stand noise, and not just the loud radio kind. Sometimes I need to quiet my spirit, go solo, and rest.

The trouble is, most of us don't stop to ask: *what do I need right now* for joy, peace, and contentment? Too often we just keep doing the same thing we've always done. We continue to do the same things in every season, under every circumstance, and plug them in methodically, as if they will bring the same results as they did before. But life isn't a neat-and-tidy formula.

Bottom line: it's important to take time to evaluate, and reevaluate, what we need and be open to what God reveals in order to be at rest in our souls.

But seek first the kingdom of God and His righteousness, and all these things will be provided for you.
MATTHEW 6:33

Hurry, Climb Down

In college, I had a list of theological books I thought would give me the best glimpse of Jesus. I rehearsed theories about the atonement as I studied while overlooking the front lawn of the chapel. This was my sycamore tree—if I climbed up the best theories and thinkers, I would be able to see Jesus passing by.

What I longed for was the ability to see Jesus without the openness of heart it demands. But when Jesus sees Zacchaeus, He doesn't just say, "Come down." Jesus calls him by name: "Zacchaeus, hurry and come down because today I must stay at your house." Jesus approaches Zacchaeus. He offers Zacchaeus the chance to welcome Him into his heart with joy.

This is how Jesus comes into our hearts—not by us staying in the safety of the tree, but by hurrying down to the One who came to seek us out.

After that semester of memorizing, I had climbed far up into the tree. And Jesus, in His grace, came to me in the warm joy of summer, catching me off guard with a simple request: "Hilary, hurry and climb down, for I must stay at your house today." Jesus calls us out of our trees, to abide with us, to bring us salvation.

When Jesus came to the place, He looked up and said to him,
"Zacchaeus, hurry and come down because today I must stay at your house."
So he quickly came down and welcomed Him joyfully.
LUKE 19:5–6

In Defense of an Ordinary Day

Five weeks and four days ago—not that I'm counting—my brand-new dishwasher decided to quit on me. So I'm looking at a sink full of soaking dishes as I type. Until an installer comes with a replacement unit, I'm up to my elbows in suds.

Recently I've suffered from an assortment of skin allergies on my neck, chest, and face. Some I've identified and some leave me baffled. There's no peace, waking or sleeping, when you are—quite literally—uncomfortable in your own skin.

I'm the mother of a large brood, and my family gets separated. Last night the seven members who still live at home spent the night in four different places spread over two different states. It always feels like someone is missing (because they are).

I will fall on my knees in gratitude when I've got a dishwasher that needs to be unloaded, skin that doesn't demand calamine lotion, and my children snug in their beds at home. In other words, my heart will sing with thankfulness for what I take for granted on an ordinary day. And on my better days, I'll praise Him when those ordinary gifts are absent. Now if you'll excuse me, I've got some dishes to wash.

Be satisfied with what you have, for He Himself has said,
I will never leave you or forsake you.

HEBREWS 13:5

When It's All Said and Done

Stop by the pharmacy. Pay the utility bill. Pick up the dry cleaning. When I looked at my to-do list for the day, I realized just how mundane my life can be. A sharp contrast from Solomon's life. A world leader, Solomon reached the end of life and summated: wisdom is about fearing and obeying God.

Sounds a lot like another Man near the end of His life—"Love the Lord your God with all your heart, with all your soul, with all your mind, and with all your strength . . . Love your neighbor as yourself" (Mark 12:30–32). From the Old Testament to the New, our priority for life is revealed: love God and love others. This is our purpose. This is why we're here, to love the Lord with abandon and to love others the same way.

So, what if we shift our focus? What if, instead of seeing all the places, we choose to see the people? What if we stop focusing on the lists and start focusing on love? Then our mundane tasks on our to-do lists turn into missional opportunities to share the love of Christ with others. At the end of even the most uneventful days, we can rest in the assurance that we've honored Him through our love of others.

When all has been heard, the conclusion of the matter is:
fear God and keep His commands, because this is for all humanity.
ECCLESIASTES 12:13

On Pouring Out and Filling Up

I open my laptop and stare at the screen, blank and bright. The cursor blinks as if it's expecting a next move. Except I have no next move. I'm empty, spent. With not a word to be found in my brain or my heart.

This heart that has always penned its feelings is dry. There's been no great catastrophe, nothing life-altering, I'm simply weary with the daily stuff of life—meetings, deadlines, and full squares on the calendar.

There's no room just to *be*, and I am dried up.

This feeling scares me. And refueling my heart seems impossible because there's no time to escape to a quiet sanctuary. An idyllic setting is fleeting.

My life is loud, and I'm afraid that if I am still, underneath the chatter, there won't be anything worth saying. But God calls us to stillness, to a deep sense of calm. He speaks most clearly when I am most quiet. It's in the quiet He shines clear. When we are most dried up, He will do some of His finest work. We may not see the new works, the new pathways. But He is at work—in us and for us. And in spite the blinking cursor and dried-up heart, we can be still and know that to be truth.

Look, I am about to do something new; even now it is coming.
Do you not see it? Indeed, I will make a way in the wilderness, rivers in the desert.
ISAIAH 43:19

JULY 11

The Woman in the Navy Suit

I was a fifth-grader, laying down, chin propped up with fists, when a commercial came on TV. I turned to my mom and said, "That's what I want to do. I want to be her," pointing to the TV. The commercial had shown a woman dressed in a dark, skirted suit, briefcase in hand, boarding a flight. I'm sure my mom was wondering, *Where did she get such a notion?* I had no idea, but for the first time, I could see and respond to part of the vision God had planted in my heart.

I didn't realize what was happening, but my mom knew in that instant that something was taking place. She saw a vision being birthed: His vision in me. One she didn't quite understand but wanted to encourage.

My mom recently reminded me of this pivotal story. Sometimes we forget how God has prepared us and need others to remind us.

How does this story end? Well, I don't know. It's still unfolding. But I do know that God is faithful to plant seeds of a dream, sometimes years before they come to fruition. He has gifted each and every one of us, and His purpose for each of us is steadfast and sure.

Take delight in the Lord, and He will give you your heart's desires.
PSALM 37:4

By God's Design

Iam not a crafty person. Knitting needles seem scarily pointy and dangerous. And back in my high school home-economics class, while learning to operate a sewing machine, I accidentally sewed my shirt to my project. I rest my case.

But some of my best friends have great prowess with craft projects. They are Pinterest ninjas, gourmet chefs, and painters. One friend recently enrolled in a ceramics class.

There are two things I really love about my friends' creativity. I love tasting their edible creations and receiving their art as gifts to display in my home. But what I love most is seeing God at work in their creativity.

Truth be told, my friends don't always see the great value they bring to the world. The church tends to elevate people with gifts in teaching, preaching, and administration. But God gave the artists their gifts too. When I see my friends making art, I imagine them cocreating with our Creator God.

Maybe that's you. Maybe you're a baker, a poet, a scrapbooker, or a quilter. Don't underestimate the usefulness of your gifts in making this world a more beautiful place. With every stroke of the brush and every turn of a phrase, the Holy Spirit is bringing a fabulous dimension to your work.

I have filled him with God's Spirit, with wisdom, understanding, and ability in every craft to design artistic works in gold, silver, and bronze, to cut gemstones for mounting, and to carve wood for work in every craft.

EXODUS 31:3–5

It's Okay to Not Be Okay

I sat on the edge of her bed, and she didn't look up. I was visiting a friend who was not okay. It was more than a bad day; it was a sad season for her.

I thought back to days when I haven't been okay and remembered what I needed the most in those moments: I hugged her and whispered in her ear, "It's okay not to be okay." She sighed in relief. Permission not to be okay is sometimes exactly what we need.

Today, you might not be okay. You might be facing a mountain of sadness or impossibility. You might be walking through a valley of despair. You might not even know why you aren't okay. And you've probably exhausted every possible solution to stop the struggle in your soul.

But only one thing can refresh and renew and save our soul. And that's God's Word. It is alive, and it cuts to the broken places and heals what we cannot. There's only one place to restore our soul and find comfort and that's in His arms, where it's okay not to be okay. Because one day He will make everything okay.

The Lord is my shepherd; there is nothing I lack. He lets me lie down in green pastures; He leads me beside quiet waters . . . Even when I go through the darkest valley, I fear no danger, for You are with me.
PSALM 23:1–4

The Color of Courage

I'm six and courage is school-bus yellow. It's my first day of kindergarten, and my sweet mom says she'll drive me, but I stubbornly take steps to independence. I ride the bus.

I'm twenty-one and courage is wedding-dress white. I wait at the end of an aisle to become a wife. I make vows about for better or worse and wonder what the future may hold. I risk for love.

I'm twenty-six and courage is pregnancy-test pink. I discover once again I'm ready to start our family but God has other plans. I learn to live in the waiting and discover that sometimes bravery means remaining in the unknown. I'm still there now.

I'm thirty and courage is shiny-laptop silver. I sit in coffee shops, the library, or on our porch—writing. I'm putting my heart on display, like giving birth, like nothing and everything I'd hoped. And it scares me silly.

I once thought of courage as a single color—fire-engine red. But I am finding it is more like a kaleidoscope. It changes with the seasons of our lives, with who we are becoming, with what God is asking our hearts to do. And through all the shifting, this remains . . . in every color, every life . . . courage is breathtaking.

Wait for the Lord; be strong and courageous. Wait for the Lord.
PSALM 27:14

I've Never Been Told That Before

Clutching the note, I held my breath as I reread the words by my university's Admissions Director: "Jennifer, thank you for your servant leadership this year on our Admissions staff. Your hospitality welcomes each visitor, and your quiet and gentle spirit blesses each one." I wept. I'd never been told that before. Since childhood, my outgoing personality made that godly disposition seem elusive.

It started in kindergarten when my first progress report indicated "lack of self-control" and said, "Jenny needs to stop chatting." By the time I could pen New Year's resolutions, I'd write, "You'll be more popular if you'd be like the quiet girls." As my identity took shape, I failed to embrace the positive remarks like, "Jenny is a friend to everyone. She always has a smile." Those words didn't matter. I wanted to be a sweet, quiet girl. I wanted to stifle how the Lord had wired me.

I've learned, however, that this verse is referencing a heart issue. It's the "why" behind the "who." My desire is to love the Lord my God with all my heart, soul, mind, and strength. That sometimes manifests itself through an outgoing personality, while at the same time demonstrating a meek and gentle spirit.

God desires for us to cast aside the labels we've carried far too long, and embrace who we were created to be.

Your beauty should not consist of outward things like elaborate hairstyles and the wearing of gold ornaments or fine clothes. Instead, it should consist of what is inside the heart with the imperishable quality of a gentle and quiet spirit, which is very valuable in God's eyes.

I PETER 3:3–4

When You Feel Like Damaged Goods

Carol walked down the aisle of the discount grocery and noticed a bin labeled "Damaged Goods." Filled with dented cans and unlabeled boxes, the collection of random items caught her attention. Although they weren't considered shelf-worthy, an aching sense of empathy washed over her. She was keenly aware of how it felt to be unwanted.

An unexpected divorce left her with that unwanted label. She felt like damaged goods, no longer worthy of a place on the "Christian" shelf at church, in marriage, or in ministry.

Perhaps you have experienced the deep pain of a broken relationship. It can cause us to doubt our value and question whether anyone would want us.

But the truth is: Jesus paid the same price for all of us.

That day in the grocery store, my friend was determined to find something of value hidden in the rubble of rejects. She leaned over and picked up a dented can without a label. When she got home, she slid the mystery can under her can opener and removed the metal lid. Much to her delight, she discovered peaches! Not only was she thrilled to find her favorite fruit preserved inside, but it served as a "sweet" reminder that good things can still come from something that's been broken and damaged.

You will be a glorious crown in the LORD's hand,
and a royal diadem in the palm of your God.

ISAIAH 62:3

Walking Arm in Arm

I sat in the church pew with my friends—Michelle and Lyla—to sing songs, pray prayers, and listen to the message. I wanted to reach out and grab their hands, but I didn't. Fear of freaking them out meant keeping my hands in my lap. Later, I told them, "I almost grabbed your hands, but I didn't want to freak you out."

"You should have," they both told me. "It would have been fine."

Friendship is a gift. Finding someone who will talk you back from the edge of emotion, encourage you to follow your dream, stay up until 3:00 a.m. to hear your darkest confessions without flinching, and keep showing up anyway? That's a gift. No, a treasure.

If you've got one good friend, you've got a treasure, that's for sure. If you've got more than one good friend, you have what I've heard called an embarrassment of riches. I want my friends to know that sometimes my heart overflows with gratitude and love for them. So I'm turning a deaf ear to the voice that tells me I might just freak out my friends if I let them know how much they mean to me.

A friend loves at all times. It's as simple as that.

The one who walks with the wise will become wise . . .
PROVERBS 13:20

Peace and Thankfulness

When we pulled out of the driveway, heading toward seminary, part of me wondered if we were crazy. But we had prayed about this change for months and invited our family, friends, and church leaders into the discernment process. We felt sure of our trajectory, sure of where we were headed. The thing we were most unsure about? Money. My husband quit his job to become a seminary student; I quit mine to move. We knew we wouldn't have much money coming in for a while. But what we *did* have in front of us was a choice. Would we worry? Or would we choose thankfulness?

We had experienced lean times before and I had spent years worrying about paying the bills. This time, however, I made the intentional decision to say no to worry and yes to peace. To say no to fear and yes to thankfulness. It wasn't easy. I tend to be fearful rather than fearless. So I chose gratitude for what we had—health, time together, food on the table, and the opportunity to trust God afresh. And I found that choosing gratitude sustained my spirit over months of uncertainty. Focusing on God's provision for us, even in the smallest things, turned my mind to thankfulness and praise.

Let the peace of the Messiah, to which you were also called in one body, control your hearts. And be thankful.
COLOSSIANS 3:15

God-Sent Safety Measures

I push down and turn it to the right. The lid still won't open. So I try again. Push down. Harder. I scrunch up my face, somehow thinking the added effect will mysteriously help. I turn the cap right and . . . nothing.

Childproof locks take practice, but I've learned how to open the Tylenol bottle and Ragu jar. As I tried and tried again to open the mouthwash bottle, I began to realize that there's a lesson to be gleaned: Children aren't supposed to open certain things. Protective devices are one way of saying "Keep Out!" But as children we go meddling in with our little fingers, twisting and turning until, suddenly, the cap lifts off. It's fascinating. But it's also dangerous.

We do this as adults too. We meddle with our words, our actions, our mouths. We stick our heads into business that isn't ours. We whine and meddle to get our way.

This behavior might seem harmless on the surface, but it could be dangerous not only to us, but to those around us.

The next time we're facing an obstacle or a closed door, maybe we should just back away from the situation. Maybe it's like a childproof lock from our Father, and maybe we should just let it be.

"For My thoughts are not your thoughts, and your ways are not My ways."
This is the LORD's declaration. "For as heaven is higher than earth,
so My ways are higher than your ways, and My thoughts than your thoughts."
ISAIAH 55:8–9

Your Life Is Never Too Small to Qualify for Big Ministry

I've heard the whispers. The rumblings. Women with shy, embarrassed eyes pull me aside to share this worry that what they do doesn't count because what they do doesn't require a passport. Or because they think you need a pulpit for your voice to matter or to make a difference.

Sister, don't tell me you don't make a difference, that your life is small. Don't tell me that pulpits are only found in churches and speeches only come from stages. Don't tell me that microphones are necessary to be heard. Don't tell me that Cheerios, diapers, laundry, and dishes somehow don't count as serious service.

Don't tell me we're playing make-believe when we dress up our daughters in all the courage and conviction to last a lifetime of love stories found in the pages of God's Word.

Don't tell me that all the hours sown into sons between soccer practice and football matches, between pouters and bullies, isn't wild obedience. Don't tell me that holy dirt beneath the fingernails doesn't look like blog posts, carpool, science projects, and teaching Sunday school.

Don't tell me we can't leave the back door open for that misunderstood word, "ministry," to come quietly in. Along with the neighbor's kids. All the dirt in the backyard. And Jesus.

_____

_____

_____

_____

_____

_____

Abram believed the Lord, and He credited it to him as righteousness.
GENESIS 15:6

It's Not Too Late for You

Recently, I went camping for the first time with friends. We packed ourselves into the car and headed for the beach—driving with the windows down and the music blasting. We toasted s'mores by the fire and told stories of the people we loved when we were four years old. Later that night, there was a single layer of fabric between the stars and me.

I laid there thinking of the series of firsts for me lately. Small things, like camping or standing in the Pacific Ocean, and larger things like buying my first car, and deciding, after waiting for four years, to attend college. God keeps whispering to me: *Aliza, it's not too late.*

Then I thought that one of the things I love most about the night sky is that neither a camera nor words can capture its glory. It's a secret love letter between you and God—you can't fully explain it to anyone. I laid my head against the ground and watched three stars shoot across the sky.

In the midst of my feelings of wonder and gratitude, I whispered back to Him, "Thank You for fresh starts and first times. Thank You that it's never too late for me."

Friend, the same is true for you. It's never too late. Never.

"For I know the plans I have for you"—this is the Lord's declaration—
"plans for your welfare, not for disaster, to give you a future and a hope."
JEREMIAH 29:11

Above the Noise

Our house is situated slightly higher than the surrounding homes in our cul-de-sac. Because of its elevation, the view offers me ease in keeping a pulse on the comings and goings of my youngest son. When I need him, I just step outside and call his name.

My son is not always playing in our cul-de-sac, so using a loud voice ensures he hears my call. And it won't surprise you that sometimes my call is met with silence. As his mama, I know I'm calling for his benefit. Good things await his response, so I call again. He may not always see how responding to my call is to his benefit, but he has learned to trust the heart of the one who calls.

I love that Jesus used a loud voice to issue an invitation, in the middle of the commotion of a great festival, by speaking over the noise. He clearly desired to be heard. He is still calling us today—to eat, drink, rest, and be filled up. His invitation awaits our response. His offer is far better than the "noise" that fights for our attention and offers temporary satisfaction.

May we listen for the invitation of Jesus, come believing, trust the goodness of His provision, and find complete satisfaction in Him.

On the last and most important day of the festival, Jesus stood up and cried out, "If anyone is thirsty, he should come to Me and drink! The one who believes in Me, as the Scripture has said, will have streams of living water flow from deep within him."
JOHN 7:37–38

On the Comforts of Home and Finding My Fit

I was born into a homesickness for Tennessee bottomland where my daddy grew up. We live in Arkansas now, and I do love it here, but it doesn't make up for the weekends of lap-sitting, morning biscuits, and percolated coffee back home. Sometimes I'll wake up suddenly overwhelmed to go back, so I'll sling what I can into bags, load up the boys, and drive with abandon.

Once there, I rush to my daddy's chest and melt at the sound of his heartbeat—the little girl in me recognized, pampered, and invited. And though it is very good, it's not long until I realize that no state here on earth befits me. I'm learning that I was really born into homesickness for the heart of God.

So I go there, to the God whose throne sits on my own heart, and I ask what keeps me from craving the comfort He offers. And I know the answer immediately—I don't believe I can be "grieving yet always rejoicing." What the Spirit calls comfort is not what I call it: giving Him my all, my whole complete self. It is there I find the tastes and sounds of home. And there, at His heart, is my only fit.

Grieving yet always rejoicing . . .
II CORINTHIANS 6:10

The One Place That Has Taken Me
the Longest to Call Home

If you asked me "Where are you from?" my answer would include a pause, followed by: "Well, it's a long story, but I live in Illinois now." After eight years you'd think I would call this home, right?

My entire life has been in a place of transition. Since birth, I have moved twenty-three times. Half of those moves happened before I got married, and the rest have been with my adventurous husband. Looking back, it's no wonder it has taken me awhile to call this home, even though I've lived here the longest.

But here's the truth: This place really isn't home. Home isn't about the name of a town or a mailing address. Home is about the people. With every move, my husband and I have said, "It's not about the place, it's about the people." Everywhere we've lived, we've met some incredible people we now call family.

Your roots grow where you plant your heart. Some places require a little more work—to prepare the ground for the seeds that will be sowed. Thankfully, God brings new people into our lives who give us a renewed sense to embrace our new surroundings. And here's the biggest truth of all: Whether this place is our final destination or not, it's just a tiny glimpse of the place we will gladly call home forever—heaven.

Our citizenship is in heaven, from which we also eagerly
wait for a Savior, the Lord Jesus Christ.
PHILIPPIANS 3:20

When You Need a Hug from God

I woke up in a funk. Maybe it was the gloomy weather or the fitful night's sleep. When I get in a funk, I am unproductive. My brain feels thick. I wander aimlessly from task to task, never quite landing on what to do. I'm emotionally vague and directionless.

I did a few chores, and finally . . . I paused. I knew something had to change and it needed to be me. So I pulled out my Bible, asked God to talk to me, read one verse, and wrote it down, word for word. As I continued this routine repeated countless times in the past, I felt my heart shift. I felt my burden lighten, my perspective change.

Hearing God speak to me through His words in the Bible feels like a giant hug from Him. And all it took was ten minutes—tops. God's Word does that. This isn't just true for me; it's true for all of us. God promises that we'll find Him when we seek Him with all of our heart.

Reading the Bible—and allowing it to transform your life—is this simple. And here's the best part—you don't have to wait until you're in a funk to do it.

This book of instruction must not depart from your mouth;
you are to recite it day and night so that you may carefully observe everything
written in it. For then you will prosper and succeed in whatever you do.
JOSHUA 1:8

More Than What We See

It's the creases around my mouth I used to hate the most. I'd pull back my skin to make the lines on the sides of my mouth disappear. That is the real me, right? A face young and vibrant—because that's how I feel inside. How could this aging body of mine represent the beauty—the youthful energy—that God produces in my heart?

It doesn't. And I am learning that it's okay. Because at this time in my life, it's freedom I want—freedom from self-contempt, from comparison.

I ask to see how God sees. Varicose veins the reminder of carrying my sweet son in my womb. Sun freckles on my hands reminiscent of my beautiful grandmother's. Lines on my face testify to years of laughing and working, trusting and falling.

My Father tells me, day by day—I am only just beginning to shine. And we shine when we grow more in our fullness in Christ. With trust and surrender, we become more of whom we are created to be. Our physical selves might not show it, but our hearts do. And that is what I choose to have faith to see.

Therefore we do not give up. Even though our outer person is being destroyed, our inner person is being renewed day by day.
II CORINTHIANS 4:16

When You Need a Bigger Towel

We'd been at a charity event downtown and had to park a block away. It didn't seem like a bad idea . . . when skies were clear. But as a huge storm blew in, we began to regret our walk back. The rain was insane! Finally, soaked and shivering, my brother and I jumped into my car. He reached for the napkins I keep in my glove compartment, and he handed me a single napkin. I was completely soaked, head to toe, down to my underwear, if you must know. And he handed me one napkin! I needed a towel, like the kind the store actually calls a "bath sheet." I needed a big, fluffy, extra-large bath sheet to soak up all that rain.

It's kind of like life, isn't it? Some problems can be fixed easily. But other challenges—other storms of life—require a lot more than the equivalent of a leftover napkin from last week's McDonald's run.

It's okay to say, "I need a bigger towel!" It's okay to ask for help, to seek wise counsel. Jesus assured us that this world would bring us trouble. He knew we'd face hard times, but He also knew He'd be right here beside us. He gave us this promise: "Take heart! I have overcome the world."

He said to them, "Why are you afraid, you of little faith?"
Then He got up and rebuked the winds and the sea. And there was a great calm.
MATTHEW 8:26

JULY 28
The Worst Breakup

As a single girl, I've had a few breakups. But of all the romantic breakups in my life, none have hurt more than with who used to be a best friend. Years of deep friendship ended and the ripping apart felt the way a sheet looks when it is torn in two. Shredded. Loud. Sudden.

Isn't your best friend the one you talk to when things are broken? What do you do when things are broken with your best friend? How do you tell the other friends that a central friendship in your life is over without being gossipy?

It's all very messy. I bet Paul and Barnabas would agree. But while I hate how things ended, I don't regret what came of it—Jesus revealed a very unhealthy relationship. And He wanted to heal me—to make beauty from those ashes.

The more I say, "The hardest breakup of my life was with a friend," the more nods and tears I see from other women. You are not alone if your heart is broken over a friendship. And you should talk about it. Let Jesus into the ripped places. He will show you a tapestry you could not see before. And somehow, in ways we don't get, it will be beautiful.

There was such a sharp disagreement that they parted company,
and Barnabas took Mark with him and sailed off to Cyprus.
ACTS 15:39

The Gaze of His Eye

I stood in the center of a kitchen that hadn't seen the likes of a mop for weeks. Crumbs scattered on the floor, goo stuck to the table, and something mysterious clung to the countertops. I felt as if I might explode. *I can't do it all!* I thought.

The reality of my life—the countless needs and the never-ending feeling that life won't stop—made me wonder: *God, do You have more for me than nights of kitchen cleaning and mornings of kid-caretaking?*

I needed God to answer. I prayed my heart out, as if my all-good effort would bring good results. I waited. Nothing. *Where are You, God?*

I then found myself gazing out the window into the density of night. There, a blur in the distance took shape.

The moon—I could see it. It was imperfectly formed—shaped like an eye. All I could think was, *God, You see me. You know where I am going. You have a plan for me in my darkness. You have a way for me in my wilderness, even when I can't see.* And in this, I can rest.

I will instruct you and show you the way to go;
with My eye on you, I will give counsel.
PSALM 32:8

Let Me Hide Myself in Thee

I love to make memories of hiking wild trails of flowers growing along the river and jumping with arms flinging wildly while running into the coldest of lakes. They are times when God's goodness pours down sunshine and the sugary scent of peaches lingers in the air. Those are the days when hope rises up and I find solace from the weary days of winter. But there are times when depression sets in and tears me and my sunny world apart. All I know to do is pray, "God, please, not now."

I'll feel close to despair but know without doubt that God is with me, in the dark and the long loneliness when I have no answers for the sadness.

I feel like Moses in this verse, glimpsing the back of God's glory as He passes me by, tucked in the rock under the hand of the Almighty.

Should the battle come again, I need only to be still because I know my God will fight for me. I accept that this is my cup to bear, my thorn piercing deep. His strength made perfect because I am weak.

So I say, "Yes, Lord, I am here. Your joy is my strength."

The Lord said, "Here is a place near Me. You are to stand on the rock, and when My glory passes by, I will put you in the crevice of the rock and cover you with My hand until I have passed by. Then I will take My hand away, and You will see my back, but My face will not be seen."

EXODUS 33:21–23

When You Think You're Not Doing Enough

Recently I have been struggling with the thought that I'm not doing a good job discipling my kids. Other moms I know do nightly devotions. They have prayer cards on their dining room table, and they have prayer time every night. One writes beautiful letters to her kids, and another teaches large portions of Scripture to memorize. Compared to them, I feel as though I'm not doing enough.

So I emailed a former mentor and asked how she discipled her children. She wrote back: "I usually read the Bible to them before going to bed. And sometimes we'd have a special quiet time with them."

Hold up. *That's it?* She just read the Bible and sometimes had special quiet times? This godly woman who has discipled hundreds of women and co led a ministry with her husband just "read the Bible" to them when they were young?

Sometimes we get so wrapped up in what we think is right or wrong and forget to simply set our minds on things above—which are the simplest: Jesus, *the* Word, and reading His Word. Yes. That's what I will do. I will turn my focus from my earthly fears and failures onto the things above—on Jesus and His Word.

So if you have been raised with the Messiah, seek what is above,
where the Messiah is, seated at the right hand of God.
Set your minds on what is above, not on what is on the earth.
COLOSSIANS 3:1–2

When You Feel Like You Missed the Giving of Gifts

I used to struggle with knowing my God-given gifts. I knew that Ephesians 2:10 proclaimed that I was His workmanship, created in Jesus specifically for these good works that God had prepared in advance for me to do. But as I noticed other people using their gifts, I grew discouraged and kind of jealous too.

One day at Bible study, a woman asked, "How do you really know what God wants you to do?" My heart skipped a beat because that was exactly what I wanted to know but didn't have the courage to ask—I thought everyone (except me) already knew the answer!

The teacher said, "God has already told you what He wants you to do. His Word gives very specific instructions to love and serve, to be a light, to refrain from ungodly behavior. If we focus on what He's already told us to do, we'll be better positioned to hear what else He wants us to do."

So I changed my focus from worrying about the gifts of others and started working on how well I did what I knew to do. Opportunities soon came that allowed me to serve in such particular ways, I realized I wasn't waiting anymore.

And He personally gave some to be apostles, some prophets, some evangelists, some pastors and teachers, for the training of the saints in the work of ministry, to build up the body of Christ, until we all reach unity in the faith and in the knowledge of God's Son, growing into a mature man with a stature measured by Christ's fullness.

AUGUST 2
The Value of Rest

As a young bride, desperate for approval, I worried there was something wrong with the way I did life. I simply couldn't sit still if I knew there was a chore to accomplish. Of course, there was always another chore to do.

In the midst of so much doing, two important parts of life can be eroded—rest and relationships. If I don't slow down, I won't be able to connect with the people God has placed in my life, nor will I find the refreshment needed to keep doing the mundane.

There is a type of "doing" that's an overflow of our passion, but even that "doing" can lead to burnout without rest. So we need to be intentional about finding rest, no matter our personality type or our wiring.

By God's grace, He has guided me in this process of putting off the tyranny of the urgent. Sometimes it looks like leaving the laptop while I snuggle with my girls and listen to them pour out their hearts. Other times, it looks like playing a round of Uno with the twins (and I'm not a game person). Yes, I'm active, but it is rest for my soul.

Embracing rest means walking away from unfinished tasks while choosing to enjoy the present moments.

For the Lord God, the Holy One of Israel, has said: "You will be delivered by returning and resting; your strength will lie in quiet confidence."
ISAIAH 30:15

AUGUST 3
The Prayers We Neglect

I looked around the room and asked the women present, "How many of you gather in a small group setting like a life group or Bible study?" Most nodded. Then I asked, "How often do your prayer requests include a relative three times removed in another part of the country? Most of the hands went up with a few knowing smiles and slight chuckles.

Then I asked the question I really wanted to ask, "How many of you pray for what's going on in your own heart?" Not one single hand.

We are so quick to ask for prayer for someone else's obvious need, which is easy to talk about. Yet, how often do we request prayer for the needs of our hearts to help us walk through life and grow in our faith? What steps could we take today to cultivate this kind of prayer among us?

The women, right then and there, clustered in groups of three to take turns sharing, listening, and praying. God will meet us in our darkest places when we cry out to Him in prayer. And He often chooses to do this through the gift of fellowship in community. May we pray for each other in the same way.

You will call to Me and come and pray to Me, and I will listen to you.
JEREMIAH 29:12

A Friend Like Esther

When I approached Esther, I didn't know exactly what it meant to be "discipled." But I had a longing to grow and hoped she would guide the way. So we started meeting in my dorm room my sophomore year of college. I guess I expected to learn about God's Word and how to walk with Jesus. But what Esther really taught was how to care for someone's heart.

At one of our meetings she pulled out a little keyboard and started typing. She said "I usually take notes about our time together later, but what you're sharing is important. I don't want to forget it." I must have had a strange look on my face because Esther quickly added, "I want to remember how to pray for you and what to follow up on. Does that make you feel uncomfortable?"

"No. Not uncomfortable," I said while wiping tears. "It makes me feel seen. Loved. Invested in . . . like no one ever has."

Sixteen years later, she is a soul sister and lifelong friend. May I be someone who influences many the way she did me, one woman on my block, a mom in my playgroup, or the college student at my church. May I share the love of Christ by caring for someone's heart.

The Spirit of the Lord God is on Me, because the LORD has anointed Me to bring good news to the poor. He has sent Me to heal the brokenhearted, to proclaim liberty to the captives and freedom to the prisoners.

ISAIAH 61:1

Everyday Grace through Faith

I became a Christian as a middle schooler. In my teenage bedroom, I placed my faith in Christ as my only hope for salvation. Vividly aware of my sin and separation from God, I eagerly accepted the glorious grace so clearly pursuing me. That first moment of faith was so easy and clear and powerful. God loves me. Christ died for me. Me!

Moving forward, things were not so simple. I attempted to live out my new life of faith, but I was often confused as to what it should look like. I wanted to live big for God and I thought drastic "faith-filled" decisions would prove my validity as a Christian. Slowly but surely, I felt I had to keep proving myself worthy of Christ's sacrifice.

Unfortunately, this led me to believing that God's acceptance was tied up in my performance. My relationship with God began by faith, but I moved forward by works. In doing so, I missed the point of grace.

It's been a journey, but I have learned that the work of everyday faith means drawing near to the presence of God, with complete certainty that He will accept me. Not because I have ever been good enough. Not because I ever will be. But because of Jesus on my behalf.

For you are saved by grace through faith, and this is not from yourselves; it is God's gift—not from works, so that no one can boast.
EPHESIANS 2:8–9

AUGUST 6
When You Thought No One Was Watching

I came around the corner to see my six-year-old daughter doing the exact thing I had told her not to do earlier. "Would you explain why you were doing that after I told you not to?" I asked her. She sweetly replied, "Sure. The reason is because I didn't know you were watching me."

I took in her innocent expression and kneeled down to look in her eyes and said, "It's important to do the right thing even when no one is watching."

Fast-forward and I was hosting a live seminar online when the video disappeared from the screen. I couldn't figure out what went wrong, so I fretted about the room and mumbled heatedly about technology. I growled at my computer. And used a few choice words that I wouldn't utter in the presence of my grandmother.

Then my phone dinged. I read the text message from my friend in horror. "I know you think your camera is off but it definitely is not. It is still broadcasting you live on the Internet."

Bless my heart. I was mortified and a bit shamefaced given my recent lesson to my kindergartener. What we do in the quiet, unseen moments comprise our character. It's by our actions that we make known the truth.

Little children, we must not love with word or speech, but with truth and action.
I JOHN 3:18

AUGUST 7
The View from My Window

I work in the inner city, and the reflective windows on the wall are what people use as mirrors. There's a tent outside my window, too, made of yellow and blue tarps thrown together for someone to sleep on the street. My heart becomes uncomfortably knotted every day—the world's pain seems too overwhelming for me to make a difference.

I feel led to wonder how we are to serve, how do we move both individually and collectively, so our acts of service make the most difference for those deemed the least among us, those whom Christ has also created in His image?

We tune in so we see rather than avoid what makes us uncomfortable. We pray for our neighbors in Christ and also for our hearts to be moved to service. We listen to the needs of those in our community who are crying for justice. And we begin today, standing up for what is true and right, demonstrating Christ's love in action.

Provide justice for the needy and the fatherless;
uphold the rights of the oppressed and the destitute.
Rescue the poor and needy; save them from the power of the wicked.
PSALM 82:3–4

When You Aren't Like Her but Wish You Were

As I read her words, the enemy hissed lies and I lapped them up like a ravenous kitten: *You aren't as good as her. You can't write as well as she can. Why do you even bother?* Waves of inferiority crashed over me. And it's 100 percent true: I will never write like her. That's how the enemy of our soul works; he mingles truth with lies because there's just enough truth to lend credibility to the lie.

You might not be a writer, but I bet there are ways your spirit receives a similar assault: I'll never cook like her . . . or excel at work like her . . .

We torture ourselves with unfair comparisons, but when we do, we're only comparing one aspect of another's life to the whole of ours. It's illogical. I am the only me who has ever existed, who will ever exist. When God made me, He broke the mold. Same is true for you.

You and what you have to offer have immense and intrinsic beauty, value, and worth, because you are created in the image of God. If you withhold what only you have to offer, you're withholding it from the body of Christ. Nobody can do something quite the way you can.

Now as we have many parts in one body, and all the parts do not have the same function, in the same way we who are many are one body in Christ and individually members of one another. According to the grace given to us, we have different gifts: If prophecy, use it according to the standard of one's faith.

ROMANS 12:4–6

I Number the Minutes

I number minutes like stars. The minutes Jack is in my arms. The minutes he sleeps while I monitor his oxygen levels. And the minutes of prayer.

I look lovingly at him—he has a mark from his IV in his hand, and I am reminded of the scars on Jesus's hands—the hands that, even in these long minutes, I believe are holding my son. I cannot number all the stars or all the minutes. But the Lord can. He can count the stars and name them all.

Who am I, then, to think that Jesus has not been mindful of these minutes? Who am I, then, to think that Jesus has not counted each one with me, His knowledge of them far more perfect than anything I could fathom? Jesus has seen each minute of prayer, of worry, and of desperate joy when my son is in my arms and I feel the weight of him, his hand grabbing my shirt, and Jesus is numbering the minutes with us.

Jesus knows each star, each minute—and He knows my son. Jesus holds us all, counting each breath.

He counts the number of the stars;
He gives names to all of them.
PSALM 147:4

When God Anoints You but Doesn't Appoint You

"He's calling me," she tells me on a drive in her car, and I can see how it pains her, how she feels called to things that her life, right now, won't allow. God's pull is strong inside, but she doesn't know how to walk in a call she cannot, at this moment, fulfill.

Living in the space of "not now" is perhaps the hardest and holiest space of wrestling. It almost feels cruel for God to give us a sense of destiny and then not release us to walk in it right away. But the waiting is part of the plan too. The spiritual disciplines of surrender, trust, and faithfulness make us more prepared for the appointing. The truth is, the anointing often comes before the appointing. Our job is to believe God and pursue holiness in the space in between. I think of David in the Bible. God knew what would happen if David became king before he was ready. God knew what he needed to learn and how he needed to grow.

So if you find yourself in that place now, in the holy hard space of waiting—for the anointed but not yet appointed—remember this: God knows what He's doing. And He is faithful. Every time.

Then the LORD said, "Anoint him, for he is the one."
So Samuel took the horn of oil, anointed him in the presence of his brothers,
and the Spirit of the LORD took control of David from that day forward.
I SAMUEL 16:12–13

Show and Tell

Do you remember "Show and Tell" in your elementary classrooms? I do. I remember distinctly how we couldn't wait until it was our turn to bring something special to school. Once, I brought a ceramic cat I had painted, and I still remember the quiet murmurs from my classmates when I held up my beautiful treasure.

After a few years, "Show and Tell" began to disappear because it seemed boastful. We think it's the opposite of humble—and good Christians should be humble. Consider your life for a moment. What are you making, doing, creating, or planning today that you love? I'll bet you'd be uncomfortable sharing your answers in front of a group of peers. But do you know that your gifts are the kingdom shining in you? Some of us want to put our kingdom shine under the bed, thinking that's what humility means. But that's not humility; that's hiding.

Your light shows other people who Jesus is, and it shows people how to find their way to Him.

Your light comes in many different forms: in your attitude, your kindness, your humility, and your generous heart. You are free to let your light shine for Jesus. Because of Jesus. Don't be afraid to let people see God's work in you.

He also said to them, "Is a lamp brought in to be put under a basket or under a bed? Isn't it to be put on a lampstand? For nothing is concealed except to be revealed, and nothing hidden except to come to light."
MARK 4:21–22

AUGUST 12
Work That Matters

From the time I was eight years old to just this week, I've spent too much time seeking the approval of people. And not just in my appearance. My insecurities come out in parenting, marriage, work, and even hobbies. But something changes when I'm confident about whose I am and what I'm called to do. I live differently.

When God called Moses, a feeling of inadequacy flooded over him. Three times Moses questioned God. Who am I? Will they believe what I say? Why not someone else more qualified?

Instead of trusting the sufficiency of God, Moses obsessed over his own inadequacy. He questioned, he compared, and he hesitated.

But when Moses stopped focusing on himself and started trusting God, God used Moses in history-changing ways. When we're focused on God—not our deficiencies—we can confidently live and do work that matters according to His purposes.

Let the favor of the Lord our God be on us; establish for us the work of our hands—establish the work of our hands!
PSALM 90:17

AUGUST 13
Use What You Have

Years ago I was certain God was calling me to an adventure. But I spent an entire year in confusion, praying and wondering what would come or where I was supposed to go. God seemed quiet. So I continued to pray and knew increasingly that I wanted to encourage women, but I felt ill-equipped and still lacked a sense of direction. There were no flashing directional arrows, no answers.

Finally, after a long year of praying and waiting, the clouds finally parted and I could see more clearly. My passion, purpose, and direction had been right in front of me all along! I turned a "use what you have" style of decorating into a business, because that's where my passion had been all along. I found it fascinating, even amusing, that God would finally encourage me with the obvious answer: *use what you have.*

Sometimes I think we forget that God already gave us our unique gifts, so we look high and low for the bigger passion and purpose in flashing lights somewhere, only to discover that all God wants is what we already have.

Based on the gift each one has received,
use it to serve others, as good managers of the varied grace of God.
I PETER 4:10

AUGUST 14
Freedom

I was tired of fighting within. I wanted to be free; my soul ached for it. But I didn't feel free—I had chosen darkness. But not anymore. I was ready to bring my sin to the light.

My friend encouraged me to call it out for what it was and what it is . . . sin. And as I confessed my sin, I felt the forces of shame, guilt, hopelessness, and grief begin to flow right out of me. I tangibly felt the freedom I longed for and recognized the change.

I let the words out and felt the light slicing the darkness. I let the tears flow and felt the comfort of a gracious Father's forgiveness. It was just the beginning of a new journey as I worked to get to the root of my issues, so I wouldn't return to old habits when life got hard. I learned my triggers and found the accountability I needed. And I was no longer feeling controlled by my own desires.

What a gift to be able to confess our sins one to another. What a gift to have Christ-centered friends to walk with us and point us to the light. What a gift we have in Jesus!

"Everything is permissible for me," but not everything is helpful.
"Everything is permissible for me,"
but I will not be brought under the control of anything.
I CORINTHIANS 6:12

When You're Trying to Remember Who God Is

"Remind me who God is." These words a mandate from a grieving friend as we stood near the casket of her twenty-six-year-old son. She grabbed my shoulders and repeated her edict: "Remind me who God is."

Who is God when real life comes knocking with a blow so forceful you can't stand against it? Who is God when everything you've planned for and dreamed of is altered forever?

Death. Divorce. Illness. Life has changed, and it will never look, feel, or taste the same as it did before. Who is God through it all?

I'm reminded of Shadrach, Meshach, and Abednego who refused to bow and worship King Nebuchadnezzar's golden statue. The king gave them one more chance to "do the right thing," but still they refused. Their rationale? "But even if He does not rescue us, we want you as king to know that we will not serve your gods or worship the gold statue you set up" (Daniel 3:18).

But even if He doesn't . . . these words, strangely, have given me hope. They have strengthened my faith as I process the death of a too-young man.

God has not left our side. He is there, walking right beside us, weeping with us. He grieves with us. Because He loves us.

"If the God we serve exists, then He can rescue us from the furnace of blazing fire, and He can rescue us from the power of you, the king."
DANIEL 3:17

Renewed from the Inside Out

As I walk down the grocery store aisle, the labels on various products call out: *Renew your youth! Reduce those lines and wrinkles! Look like a new you in three easy steps!* One tiny jar says I could look ten years younger in just ten days.

Imagine that.

I pass by the little jar of promise and looked for the milk aisle instead. The truth is, I'm okay with my age, and I'm okay with the lines around my eyes. I've earned every crease at my brow with every story I've lived. My stories make up who I am—wrinkles and all.

I wouldn't trade my stories—my years—for anything. Through them, God has shown Himself greater. And my trust in Him has grown, even as the lines on my face have lengthened.

My journey with God is not the kind of renewal that's promised in a store-bought product. Our journey of authentic renewal begins with soul surrender, yielding to the majesty of the Almighty. And with each day, our hearts are renewed as we spend time in the Word with the Ancient of Days, who is both matchless and ageless.

The instruction of the LORD is perfect, renewing one's life.
PSALM 19:7

Heads Up

My days are filled with puppy dogs and baby chicks, cuddling with a miracle daughter and planting seeds in our garden. We sit on the porch and pretend to play the harmonica. We go on tractor rides and take pictures of the pear trees we just planted. Sometimes I look at God's plans and marvel at how they're so different from the ones I had for myself. I never would have imagined the life I now lead.

The college-me wanted to climb the corporate ladder overseas. The single-me wanted to get married someday but couldn't fathom having kids. The married-me would never have thought about having a garden, much less a farm. The mommy-me thought I could juggle and do it all as a mom and the creative balance would easily transition.

I'm so thankful I was open to God's ideas, His desires, and dreams for my life. He has transformed me as He's guided me. I came to know intimately the Holy Spirit that dwelt within me, and my life became worship instead of plans.

Since we live by the Spirit, we must also follow the Spirit.
GALATIANS 5:25

AUGUST 18
Burden or Blessing

Every Sunday night, I packed my children's backpacks, tucked them in, prayed with them, then proceeded to complain to my husband. "I wish I didn't have to work tomorrow. I wish I could just stay home and be only a mom!"

I said this every Sunday night. And other nights of the week. When I had papers to grade, I'd complain. When I didn't have time to go to the grocery store, I'd complain. It didn't matter that my job was teaching at the same place my children went to school, I still complained.

Then, one night when my youngest said his prayers, his tiny voice said, "And thank you, God, for Mommy being a teacher at school so I can hug her." My heart dropped. My tired eyes flew open and suddenly the thought of my work became a blessing—seeing my kids in the hall for a quick smile; attending class parties because I was already there; teaching about Jesus's love to kindergarteners. My job was a beautiful blessing that not only helped me pay for their tuition, but also allowed me a chance to interact with my children during the day! What I saw as a hindrance, God used to bless not only my kids, but me as well.

Indeed, we have all received grace after grace from His fullness.
JOHN 1:16

Filled with Wonder

Iinhaled. The air was crisp, yet before long, my quick running pace warmed me. I ran believing I was moving away from the battle and into something better, something powerful. I needed "something better," because I was tired of my monotonous life and other women's sparkling success stories wrapped neatly in social-media status updates.

I wondered what would happen if I disappeared. Would anyone notice?

Would anyone miss my love? The darkness above hung heavy, like a dome I couldn't escape. It symbolized my feelings: I'm not valuable. Not worthy. I wanted to run and escape these feelings. But, as always, there was no escape, nowhere to go, it seemed. The only thing left to do: look up and seek God.

I saw the clouds parted slightly and small rays of light cast down upon the earth, near the horizon. The beauty of God's glory displayed beckoned me. It's as if He was saying, "My daughter, move where I am, into the light of My love. For under My light, you cannot be consumed by darkness."

Today, let's choose to dwell with God. Let's notice how God's presence reminds us of His providence, His power, and His good plan to help us, and be with us, wherever we go.

Then He replied, "My presence will go with you, and I will give you rest."
EXODUS 33:14

Test for the True

When my cousin and I were kids, we swam at a large public pool on hot summer days. It was a simpler time when people weren't afraid to drop off their elementary-age children for an afternoon of fun in the sun.

One day we discovered that some change we brought for snacks, which we hid under our pile of clothes, was gone. Another child pointed to the thief.

With righteous indignation, we reported the criminal to the pool authorities.

Only we were wrong.

We publicly accused someone of something they didn't do, and it felt awful. I don't know if the child we blamed remembers this incident, but I have never forgotten it. All my children know the story, because I remind them of it whenever they point fingers without the facts about what someone else has done, said, or intended.

It's easy to make assumptions about people based on their differences. But stereotypes rarely reflect people accurately. That painful childhood lesson taught me to trust what I see and hear firsthand more than what is related to me secondhand and not to assume what I don't know to be true.

Test all things. Hold on to what is good.
I THESSALONIANS 5:21

This Is Your Life

When I was a little girl, I always asked, "What's it like to be you?" Somewhere early in my journey I realized that my life was unlike any other. Somehow I understood that each life is a note in the music of God's creation.

One day, worn out by my tireless inquisition, my mom said, "You should ask your teacher that question."

The next day I stood at my teacher's desk and asked her, "What's it like to be you?"

I can't tell you what she said, as she struggled to answer a question for which there really is no answer, but I realized no one can fully articulate their existence. It's too magnificent.

Your life is spectacular. Don't miss it by continually wishing you had someone else's. Don't miss the beauty of playing your one note in the symphony of God's creation. You are a treasure—the only you there will ever be. Be you. Tell your story. Paint your canvas. Get dinner on the table. Create beautiful code. Because the way you do it is magnificent.

Yet Lord, You are our Father; we are the clay,
and You are our potter; we all are the work of Your hands.
ISAIAH 64:8

An Easy Way to Bless Teachers

Teachers play a powerful role in our lives. I can tell you the name of every teacher I ever had growing up, as well as something about them.

Now as a parent I have an even deeper appreciation for teachers and the way they love the children they teach—including my own. They love on my children while my husband and I work. In some ways, they are an extension of us—loving, teaching, and shepherding our kids in our physical absence.

So I think a lot about how to bless the teachers at my children's preschool. Last year, my son colored cards to deliver to his teachers, and his thoughtfulness was appreciated. This year, we decided to give each teacher a journal, wrapped with a tag of thanks.

As I wrapped the rope around the journals, I prayed that each teacher would feel loved. That they would know they are valued. That this small gift would minister to them. Honoring teachers doesn't require that we spend a lot (or any!) money. Something as simple as fresh baked bread or a gift card for a cup of coffee is a thoughtful way to show you care.

The one who is taught the message
must share all his good things with the teacher.
GALATIANS 6:6

Take the Training Wheels Off

Our two older kids were in preschool when we taught them to ride their bike—the kind without training wheels. After several weeks of scraped knees and a few tears, we wondered if they would reach puberty before they got the hang of it.

Their upcoming preschool bike rodeo was our motivation for doing this. The school encouraged the parents to get the kids to the place where they didn't need training wheels.

When the day of the rodeo came, our kids realized there were very few kids still riding with training wheels. Discouragement quickly set in. But then it set a fire under them. Later that day they asked us to take off the training wheels, so we did. We did all the things we had done with them before. They still fell. They were still afraid. But they had a steady resolve and, by the end of the day, they were both riding their bikes without training wheels.

Watching their determination that day taught me a valuable lesson. After watching their friends succeed, their faith grew enough to believe they could do it too. (Their little competitive spirits probably contributed as well.) God isn't holding out on us by playing favorites. Sometimes our faith is activated by witnessing success in someone else's life.

Then Peter began to speak: "Now I really understand that God doesn't show favoritism."
ACTS 10:34

AUGUST 24
Enough Light

I don't always wake up before the sun, but when I do, I anticipate its rising. I want to see the hot-orange promise of a fresh new day, warming me to all the inevitable challenges that will rise with the sun. Yet this morning there are thick, gray clouds covering the sky. And I ask myself if I can be content with just light.

My Bible sits open on my lap beside my current study and pencil, and I have hopes of seeing the sunrise here too. And many days I do. It crests between the words and begins to glow. My heart feels the warmth and my mind wakes up with the illumination. When I'm done, it's a bright new day, and I'm feeling fulfilled.

But some mornings, it's just light—enough to chase away the dark, but the sky is still gray. And I ask myself: *Can I be content with just light?* No warm fuzzies. The chill of life's trials right there beside me on the couch. Light undeniably right there in my lap. Truth illuminating the gray just enough for me to take the next step.

It's 7:20 now. I take one more hopeful look out my window to the east. And my day begins.

From the rising of the sun to its setting, let the name of Yahweh be praised.
PSALM 113:3

The Table

The table . . . it's basically four legs with a slab of glass or wood on top. But buying one requires thought. Square, rectangle, or round—there's not much creativity in geometry there. Chairs with arms or no arms? Chairs with cloth or wood? In our house with little ones, it's always safest to go with wood, without decorative scrolls for the back. Mac and cheese will surely find its way to those crevices.

The most herculean task is when we have to convince the family to leave the screens and sit at said table for a meal. Sometimes I'm tempted to forget it and just turn the dining room into an office.

But after more than three decades of marriage and almost as many years raising a family, I can tell you one thing I have learned: the table is the most precious piece of furniture you will ever own.

The table hears it all. The heated arguments and celebrated announcements. The table remains steadfast and silent at the telling of the most heart-wrenching story, and she releases no squeal of delight at the most exciting news shared. The table simply stands, waiting for you to gather around and share life. For the sweetest moments in life happen there.

When the hour came, He reclined at the table, and the apostles with Him.
LUKE 22:14

AUGUST 26
Reaching across the Divide

I stepped through the doors of The Pantry and entered a hive of activity, alive and buzzing with purpose. An elderly black woman manned the front desk, a middle-aged white man stocked shelves in the pantry, and a young Hispanic woman walked the halls with a determined step and a stack of official papers. All around me, men and women of all ages and races came together with a singular goal: to feed local families in need.

The Pantry opened after local houses of worship combined their separate food-assistance programs into one. They recognized that the need was too great and their individual resources too small to make an impact if they remained divided.

"Neighbors helping neighbors" are the words that guide their mission.

As believers, those words should guide our own lives too. But often we stare across great divides—of age and race and economic status—and feel unable to cross them.

If we are to bring the kingdom of God here on earth, then we must reach across with eager hands to bridge the gap. When we join hands, we become braided together with a common purpose gathered from the strands of neighborly love. We become a cord that cannot be broken.

_____

_____

_____

_____

_____

_____

_____

If a kingdom is divided against itself,
that kingdom cannot stand.
MARK 3:24–25

Friends Don't Let Friends Tell Themselves Lies

It's been a rough season for me in the friendship arena. I've felt rejected, disappointed, deserted, and excluded. I don't know about you, but when I struggle with friendship and community, it's way too easy for me to move from thinking sad thoughts about the situation to thinking sad thoughts about myself.

If I were cooler . . . If I were thinner . . . If I didn't make so many stupid jokes . . . If I had more time or more money . . . If I weren't so me . . .

When I start thinking that my lack of friends is a result of my inability to measure up, I open God's Word for a dose of reality and a reminder of who—and whose—I am. In Christ, I am enough. In Christ, I am loved.

The God of this universe would do anything for us—and *He has.* And when we forget that, let's point each other straight back to the truth. We can't let each other sit in doubt and insecurity and petty lies. We must be a community that points, pushes, drags each other to truth. Let's not dwell in the lies any longer, friends. Let's run, not walk, "do not pass go" back to the Truth. *I'll meet you there.*

_____

_____

_____

_____

_____

_____

For I am Yahweh, the Holy One of Israel, and your Savior,
give Egypt as a ransom for you, Cush and Seba in your place.
Because you are precious in My sight and honored, and I love you,
I will give people in exchange for you and nations instead of your life.

ISAIAH 43:3–4

AUGUST 28

The One Sure Way They'll See Jesus

There's something disconcerting about waiting for someone to stick a huge needle into your back. I was about to have my third C-section, and fear hit me all at once. My husband, who was my rock, was not yet allowed in the operating room.

I sat trying to be patient when the nurse noticed tears welling in my eyes.

"It won't be much longer. Waiting is the hard part," she said.

I agreed with a nod. She and the doctor left the room, promising to return a few minutes later. What I didn't know was that while I was waiting, the nurse and the doctor were with my husband. He was giving them advice to help calm my nerves.

When the doctor returned, he held my arm where I still had some feeling. The firmness of his grasp reassured me. He talked to me about my boys, bringing a smile to my face. So even though my husband wasn't in the room, his presence was there. And when we love others in a way they can see and grasp, Christ is there too.

We have the opportunity to show the lost God's presence here on earth. We don't have to complicate it or water it down. We can simply love. It's the one true and perfect way.

No one has ever seen God. If we love one another,
God remains in us and His love is perfected in us.
1 JOHN 4:12

The Difference That Makes All the Difference

The house was quiet, and I was feeling productive. I had planned a fun family dinner and game night. Life was peachy. And I felt like such a good mom. Then my kids came home from Grandma's house, and one of them did something not-so-peachy. Then my other child did *not* do something I asked him to do. Suddenly I lost my peace and patience and our family night didn't go so well.

Later, harsh words replayed in my head. Guilt convinced me I was a terrible parent. Shame pointed its finger and told me I was the worst mom on earth. But I knew the difference between conviction and condemnation. Condemnation comes with cruel general statements: *You're so hypocritical, Renee. You are never going to change.* God's conviction is specific and points toward love and repair: *Your words were harsh, Renee. All you need to do is apologize and ask for forgiveness.*

Condemnation says we'll never change. But godly conviction shows us how we can. The next morning, I apologized to my kids and asked for forgiveness. And we did a makeup date for our family night. I'm so grateful for grace that convicts me and helps me put back the pieces of my broken attempts to be humble, gentle, patient, and kind.

Therefore I, the prisoner for the Lord, urge you to walk worthy of the calling you have received, with all humility and gentleness, with patience, accepting one another in love, diligently keeping the unity of the Spirit with the peace that binds us.
EPHESIANS 4:1–3

Meeting God in the Silence

Sometimes it feels like God isn't anywhere near. The truth is, His Spirit is within us at all times—we just don't stop often enough to recognize Him.

And the only way to be faithful to His call for our lives is to make time each day to sit in the profound silence of heaven intersecting earth and listen to His Holy Spirit speak.

Jesus called His disciples away to a quiet place to rest because ministry without pause can bring both weariness and waywardness. Jesus's example of coming away to rest can be difficult for those of us who pride ourselves on productivity. I'm like a young child who's been told it's nap time. I throw my head back and protest, "But I'm not tired!"

Do you have trouble with taking time to rest? I do. So to help me with my need to achieve, I bring God's Word and a journal to my time of rest. Then it's not long before I sense the Lord's presence speaking to my soul. Rest time isn't a place to achieve; it's a place to receive.

He said to them, "Come away by yourselves to a remote place and rest for a while."
For many people were coming and going, and they did not even have time to eat.
MARK 6:31

Chasing Space

When it comes to eating a meal around a table packed full of people, I can squeeze into any chair just fine and be comfortable. But when it comes to my schedule, I need space in my days and weeks and months to think and mull and ponder. Because when I don't get that, I want to escape—I start to wish for a faraway land to live in. I want to walk barefoot in the grass and read stories. I long for money and chocolate to grow on trees. I consider buying a new toilet instead of cleaning my old one. I dream about having lots of space. And in all that dreaming, I find myself beginning to worship space and chasing after it—and all the while it seems to become more and more elusive.

In my quest to experience space for my soul, to pin it down and plan for it, a voice reminds me that it isn't simply space I want. It's Jesus. I need Him in my space. I want the calm and strength and understanding only He provides. I want to be known fully, loved wholly, accepted unconditionally. That is really what I want.

You are my hiding place; You protect me from trouble.
You surround me with joyful shouts of deliverance.
PSALM 32:7

Releasing Expectations and Finding True Friendship

I hadn't heard from her in over a month. And I didn't feel a release to send another message until she responded. Sometimes in friendship, we need space. We need to process all that's happening inside and respond when our heart is ready—when we have something meaningful to say. So I waited. And I prayed.

It was hard to wait because I wanted the friendship on my terms. I wanted interaction and connection now. I longed to hear her heart and deeply desired her to hear mine.

Because to me, that's what friendship does. But until someone decides to reply, there's not much one can do but wait. A relationship can only be vibrant, close, and growing when both people mutually give. And sometimes that dance takes a long time to learn. It's not until we lead and follow, and then follow and lead, that the dance becomes graceful, elegant, and smooth.

In our friendships, may we live with purpose and focus. Only purposeful lives of focus—refusing to let others set our agenda, yet still loving them deeply in the moments we're able. And sometimes the space and in-between moments make our renewed connection all the sweeter when it finally comes around again.

Dear friends, let us love one another, because love is from God, and everyone who loves has been born of God and knows God.
I JOHN 4:7

The Mentors We Need

When I think of those I most want to model in my life, Kelli comes to mind. She has taught me, by example, what it looks like for one generation to pour into the next. These are a few of the things I (and you) can begin to emulate as we grow and mentor younger women:

1. Invite her out for coffee. Conversations over coffee cultivate relationships.
2. Ask her how you can pray for her. Then follow up to see how she's doing.
3. Don't settle for her "I'm fine" response. Ask again.
4. Share your story and what you're learning in your own life.
5. Send a card with a verse of encouragement.
6. Invite her the next time you go to the park. Everyone needs a short break and some sunshine.
7. Keep communication lines open. Text or call regularly. Something as simple as, "I knew you could do it! I'm proud of you!" speaks volumes.

Most of all, know you don't have to have everything together before inviting someone into your life. Trust that she wants the friendship just as much as you do.

In the same way, older women are to be reverent in behavior, not slanderers, not addicted to much wine. They are to teach what is good...
TITUS 2:3

This One Is for All Us Expert Worriers

Most mornings when I wake up, I stumble from bathroom to kitchen thinking about my to-do list. I'm thinking how my hair has more gray than last month. I'm googling videos that show how to fix the leak underneath our kitchen sink.

My mornings don't involve a list of God's mercies; they involve a list of my own worries. I can rattle off all my very specific fears and worries without even having to think very hard. I can sit in the house of my dreams and miss it all because I'm so busy counting worries. And then an old hymn rolls around in my head—the one about His great faithfulness. And the new mercies I see. But that "all I have needed" part is what makes me stop. Do I really believe that?

Of course, there are the big things like a home and clothes and warm food. But I'm waking up more to the little things—the ordinary glory of fresh chocolate chip cookies. Bike rides. Clothes warm out of the dryer. His faithfulness is new every morning in a hundred different ways. On the stormy days as well as the mild ones. It's the one thing that doesn't change. And I so desperately want to become an expert at believing *that*.

_____

_____

_____

_____

_____

_____

_____

Because of the Lord's faithful love we do not perish, for His mercies never end.
They are new every morning; great is Your faithfulness!
LAMENTATIONS 3:22–23

When Grace Chases

I am stuck. I twist left only to see dark, and I scurry right to seek help, yet I am alone. It's not a moment of anxiety. It's my identity—I feel like it's been lost.

The search is visceral and daily. I look and I look, and I begin to feel small for my wandering. My mind is confused by the juxtaposition of feeling stuck while actually moving away from my Keeper, my God.

But grace chases. It finds the orphaned in me and whispers worth. My eyes take in a beautiful me surrounded by His majesty.

Not all of me is restored, but for that which reflects the Creator, a song plays. It beckons me to the truth of being known and feeling held, instead of alone and stuck. Although I don't always understand my purpose or potential, I trust that He does.

The search for me is exhausting and at times thwarted by depression or triggers from the past. Yet the search ends when my Comforter draws near. His care is evident as the Spirit intercedes.

He draws me close and into sacred space where all my canyons of hurt are held by His holiness. I rest in being His. There, on His holy mountain, I find identity and true peace.

Send Your light and Your truth; let them lead me.
Let them bring me to Your holy mountain, to Your dwelling place.
PSALM 43:3

SEPTEMBER 5
It's All about Perspective

A few years ago, I was absolutely enchanted with the aspen forests in Colorado, displaying their fiery fall foliage on the mountainsides. I couldn't wait to experience the blazing colors from underneath the incredible leaves.

From the road the forest looked massive and formidable. I couldn't see the individual trees, just a bright wash of color. But up close, I could see each aspen had its own space. And high above, branches touched and interlocked to create a shimmering cathedral ceiling.

While standing there, I was reminded how, in life, a vantage point makes all the difference. I thought of the times I've been so focused on the obstacles I faced that I missed the grace God was providing to get through them. I'm forever thinking tasks are so big, so intimidating, that I don't see the small, simple things I can do to accomplish them.

Perhaps you're facing something too big to handle. You can see the forest in front of you, but not the trees it will take to clear your way through. Let's step back and ask God to help us see beyond it in order to focus on the work He is doing. Changing our vantage point will give us new perspective and lighten the burden we're carrying.

You will indeed go out with joy and be peacefully guided; the mountains and the hills will break into singing before you, and all the trees of the field will clap their hands.
ISAIAH 55:12

Stop Waiting to Be Ready

When it comes to projects, my train of thought goes like this: "I want to paint my desk, but I can't until I clean the deck so the desk can sit on it. And we can't clean the deck until the kids are in bed because they love playing on it." Can you guess what piece of furniture still isn't painted?

I've heard the "wait till you're ready" argument used for getting married, buying a home, or changing careers. These are huge decisions, and there are steps to take before diving into some things. But there are other things we simply can't be ready for, and if we wait until everything is in place, we might miss it.

In Scripture David chose to fight a giant. David wasn't trained or ready, but he was victorious—because of God. And then there's Rahab, a prostitute who risked her life to help some Israelite spies further God's kingdom. But she didn't wait to clean up her life first. She accepted the opportunity when it came to her.

We too can choose to follow God's call in our everyday-yet-extraordinary ways—despite our lives being messy. We may not be ready, but He is. So let's take the risk. Give a *yes*. And paint that desk.

For you are a holy people belonging to the Lord your God.
The Lord your God has chosen you to be His own possession
out of all the peoples on the face of the earth.
DEUTERONOMY 7:6

The Gift of Presence

My dad's high school yearbook told the story of a popular teen with the world at his fingertips—track star, editor of the school paper, class council president. He was so full of promise and potential. He went on to work his way into a high-paying management position.

He got married and had three beautiful daughters. But the majority of his adulthood was marked by pain and broken dreams. He distanced himself from almost everyone. So when we gathered at his memorial to mourn his passing, I could count on one hand the number of people who were there for him.

But the sanctuary was far from empty. Rows and rows were filled with friends and loved ones—of mine. Of my sisters. They gave the gift of their presence.

When I stood behind the wooden podium I looked out and saw not only my husband and sisters, I saw my community. There was nothing left for them to say or do. They were just there. That is one of the greatest gifts we can give anyone on their journey of grief. We can give the gift of our presence.

Now when Job's three friends—Eliphaz the Temanite, Bildad the Shuhite, and Zophar the Naamathite—heard about all this adversity that had happened to him, each of them came from his home. They met together to go and sympathize with him and comfort him.

JOB 2:11

When He Calls You Beautiful

You don't forget the first time a boy calls you beautiful. That word, directed at you, has the power to make you blush and turn shy in an instant.

"You are beautiful."

But you don't truly perceive the power that handful of syllables has . . . until you hear them from Jesus. Jesus, in His utmost love for us, calls us beautiful. His fingertips formed ours, His very breath seeps from our lungs. And it's His love that whispers . . . "I think you're beautiful. I do. I think you're beautiful."

He's not a boy who makes you blush or turns you shy—He's the Poet who created the universe. The Artist who made you worthy. The Writer who authored the story you're living. And He calls you beautiful.

As He also says in Hosea: I will call Not My People,
My People, and she who is Unloved, Beloved.
ROMANS 9:25

Daughters of the King

Everything was unfamiliar to me. The sounds. The smells. I didn't know a single person in this new city with fast-moving cars and people rushing around. Now, staring at all the empty moving boxes that I had unpacked in my apartment, I felt a little empty myself.

I needed a friend, at least one person to connect with. So I prayed: *God, please, I need a friend.* I visited a new church that following Sunday, and there were thousands of people there. You'd think I'd find one friend in such a large crowd, but instead, I felt overwhelmed with despair.

Then across the sanctuary I recognized someone and wondered, *Can it be?* She looked toward me and our eyes connected. A spark of remembrance flashed behind her eyes! A long-lost girlfriend from four years earlier when we both worked on staff at a Christian summer camp. A friendship I thought lost was now rekindled, and she continues to be one of my truest, most trusted friends today.

In that moment, when I first saw her at church, God reminded me how much He sees us and answers our prayers. I had regained a friendship, but more importantly, I remembered the everlasting friendship I already have in Christ Jesus.

*No one has greater love than this,
that someone would lay down his life for his friends.*
JOHN 15:13

God Isn't Afraid of Our Big Feelings

I've struggled with mental illness for most of my adult life. First, postpartum depression ripped the joy from the births of my children—I carried feelings of hopelessness, fear, and isolation, even as I rocked them in my arms.

Later, all I felt was the cold insides of a dark and unrelenting shadow life.

But the Psalms were a balm to my battered and weary soul. The Psalms reveal just how empty and scared and tired we can become. The Psalms aren't afraid of our humanity, and neither is Jesus. My faith in Christ helps me to know I'm not alone in my pain.

Scripture reminds us we are never alone.

Not in our frustrations. Not in our loneliness. Not in our fear, or anxiety, or sadness. When I feel depressed, I'm reminded that God is with me in the shadows, and His mercy never comes to an end. Even when I don't feel it, He holds me to Himself like a mother rocking her babies through the night.

God hears our cries and is attentive to our prayers. When we are overwhelmed and feeling as though our hearts might falter, remember, He is there. He shelters our hearts, and He isn't afraid of our feelings. Take refuge, friend, for you will find rest for your soul.

God, hear my cry; pay attention to my prayer. I call to You from the ends of the earth when my heart is without strength. Lead me to a rock that is high above me, for You have been a refuge for me, a strong tower in the face of the enemy. I will live in Your tent forever and take refuge under the shelter of Your wings.

PSALM 61:1–4

God Is in Control

Our five-day-old son snoozed soundly in his crib at Children's Hospital. Diagnosed with the congenital birth disease Hirschsprung's, he needed to have a colostomy the next morning.

My emotions whirled from the diagnosis. "Lord, I beg You. Calm my wavering heart." I exhaled my short, choppy prayer. My husband said he'd stay through the night so I could go home and rest. Exhausted, I gathered my belongings to leave while all the "what-ifs" danced through my mind.

Pulling onto the highway, the radio played a song by Twila Paris, "God Is in Control." And the tears flowed. As I wept, the spirit of the Lord whispered, "Remember, your son is Mine." The one true living God spoke truth straight to this momma's heart. My Savior loves my tiny babe more than I ever could. He always has and always will.

God's vessel for reaching me that day? A song. The outcome? A life change. As I pulled into the driveway, His peace enveloped me. It was one of the scariest evenings of my life, and I slept soundly. So often it's through ordinary things of life that God reaches out and ministers to us. I love that about Him. We just have to quiet our hearts and listen expectantly in order to hear Him.

Jesus Christ is the same yesterday, today, and forever.
HEBREWS 13:8

From the Old to the New

Irecently moved to a new city. Before the move, I had a career that brought a tremendous sense of importance and influence, as well as a strong reputation. I had deep roots. I was known. And the familiarity was a comfortable and constant companion.

In a new city, I felt strangely emptied. I had no career, no reputation, and no history. And as I met people, I struggled with insecurity. I missed being respected, admired, and accepted. Mentally and emotionally, I longed for those things that once gave me significance.

But I soon came to realize that my flesh took pride in my accomplishments and caused them, over time, to swell my vanity. My pride became a stumbling block—and I became complacent.

But God is good. He disrupted my complacency to move me forward and remind me that as long as we feel adequate in ourselves, we won't reach for Him to make us complete.

The grace of Christ now seems infinitely sufficient for me. Don't get me wrong. I'm not completely free of the struggle. But I'm thankful for the pruning. It's the way we're transformed as we grow into the likeness of Christ.

Then He said to them all, "If anyone wants to come with Me,
he must deny himself, take up his cross daily, and follow Me."
LUKE 9:23

SEPTEMBER 13
Remain in Me

In desperate defiance I declared a monthlong fast to finally be loosed from the burden of fear and anxiety that had plagued me for years. One month later, on the first leg of a flight to Chicago, I had my first panic attack. I cried in the airport bathroom—I simply could not make the connecting flight for fear that I would die en route. I was heartbroken that God had not delivered me.

At my next doctor's visit, words like *anxiety*, *grief*, and *rest* swirled around me. Then I heard in my spirit the gentle whisper, "Rest, abide, and remain." I did everything but obey the whisper in my soul. And the panic attacks continued, joined by insomnia, neck spasms, and headaches. I begged the doctor to do something, anything. But then I heard, "Abide. Remain in Me." And this time I listened.

More peace is found when remaining in Christ, choosing to spend time in constant prayer and reading His Word. Asking Him before committing to (or rejecting) something. Staying connected to Him—and true to Him, and focused on Him. In Christ alone, this is where freedom and fruitfulness reside.

Remain in Me, and I in you. Just as a branch is unable to produce fruit by itself unless it remains on the vine, so neither can you unless you remain in Me. I am the vine; you are the branches. The one who remains in Me and I in him produces much fruit, because you can do nothing without Me.

JOHN 15:4–5

What Jesus Prayed for You and Me

I signed up for a mission project the summer after my sophomore year in college. My youth director at church sensed my excitement mingled with fear and invited me to the Sunday night service for prayer. I accepted considering my wave of emotions.

At the service, I went to the front of the church and quietly sat down on the front platform. Filled with fatherlike compassion, my worship pastor put his hand on my shoulder and began to pray for me and over me. The tenderness and power of his words broke my heart. I could not stop the flow of tears.

I imagine a similar tender scene in John 17 when Jesus prayed on the night of His betrayal. He did something that also breaks my heart wide open: He asked His Father to set us apart (or sanctify) us with truth. And He made a provision as well.

We read in His Word, "I am the way, the truth, and the life. No one comes to the Father except through Me" (John 14:6). His Word was the truth tool always pointing to Him. He is that truth. What He prayed for us that night changed our lives forever. It's meant to. Let's sit at His feet and let it do just that.

Sanctify them by the truth;
Your word is truth.
JOHN 17:17

No Longer Afraid

We were in a frozen yogurt shop when my son had an allergic reaction. Two bites into his dairy-free frozen treat and some trace contamination caused his throat to swell shut. A stranger pulled an Epi-pen from her purse and handed it to me. I struggled to uncap the pen because my hands would not stop shaking.

My son quickly recovered, but me? It took a long time for my hands to stop shaking and an even longer time to realize all the fear I had carried for him. I realized that I could never keep my son perfectly safe. I understood that life and death are so much more than the love a mother has for her child—that both life and death are held in Someone else's hands.

It is written, "Perfect love drives out fear." But fear is powerful. Enormous. It takes a very big love to drive it out. I am thankful our God's perfect love for us is even bigger and able to do just that.

There is no fear in love; instead, perfect love drives out fear, because fear involves punishment. So the one who fears has not reached perfection in love.
1 JOHN 4:18

The Courage of No

With one foot, I was bouncing a fussy baby in her bouncy seat when the phone rang. I recognized the name on the caller ID as a well-known woman from our community who ran a sizable nonprofit. And she was calling *me*!

Mrs. Very Important called to see if I might be interested in serving on the nonprofit's board of directors and asked if I would let her know within the week. A huge part of me wanted to say no. I was a busy mom with freelance projects on the side. But two days later, I called her with my yes.

I served out my board term, but in hindsight, I should have said no.

I learned that God never intended us to say yes to every good thing that comes our way. I also learned that it takes courage to say no to an enticing offer.

I am older these days and have learned that courage looks different depending on the circumstance. Sometimes it sounds like a yes while other times it sounds like a no. I encourage you toward a courageous yes if you are called outside your comfort zone. But if you need to say no, I cheer you toward that response because there's another kind of courage—the courage of no.

For every one of God's promises is "Yes" in Him.
Therefore, the "Amen" is also spoken through Him by us for God's glory.
II CORINTHIANS 1:20

SEPTEMBER 17
Fixin' My Stinkin' Thinkin'

I smelled something wrong. An odor that came from my daughter's room. A quick look inside, though, indicated that everything was fine.

So I opened the closet doors. I peered under the bed. I opened each drawer. And nothing. Until I saw, sticking up from underneath a sock, a half-eaten piece of pizza and a Styrofoam cup with a moldy strawberry smoothie. Ewww! And right there next to her dresser was a trash can! What was she thinking?

This story reminds me of how often we tidy up the outside while holding on to emotional or relational garbage. I call this "stinkin' thinkin'." We hold on to thoughts that stink up our hearts, our relationships, and our peace of mind. But we can, and should, do something about it. What controls our thoughts controls our feelings. And what controls our feelings controls our joy.

The easiest way to know whether a thought should be tossed or kept is how you answer this question: Does this thought bring life and peace or does it bring death? Death of peace. Death of hope. Death of confidence. Death of faith. Death of unity.

When we realize we're holding on to stinkin' thinkin', let's do the one thing that makes sense: let's throw it in the trash.

For the mind-set of the flesh is death,
but the mind-set of the Spirit is life and peace.
ROMANS 8:6

Focus and a Yellow Rolling Pin

I'd given my ten-month-old son a yellow rolling pin as something to play with, a new shape to occupy his ever-curious little mind. And as soon as I handed it to him, my two-year-old came running in from the other room and wailed as tears streamed down her cheeks.

"But I want the rolling pin, Mama!"

Let's be honest. A yellow rolling pin is a little cool, but not really.

Yet she was wailing for it like a possessed hyena.

How often do I focus on, and therefore magnify, what I don't have? And then grumble about it. What if, instead, I magnify the things I'm glad I have, and not always even things, but the small joys that come my way each day.

What if I move my gaze from the mess on the carpet to the built-in bookshelf that I love? What if I let my eyes draw up to notice the little spiral light fixture in our high-up hallway ceiling. It is beautiful, quirky, and unique. Why hadn't I seen it before? How is it that even the tiniest things can start to shimmer when we stop and say thanks?

Rejoice always! Pray constantly. Give thanks in everything,
for this is God's will for you in Christ Jesus.
I THESSALONIANS 5:16–18

Keeping Guard

In my growing-up years, there's one thing the teenage Kristen did all too often—argue. Especially with my parents. My dad would shake his head while reiterating one classic response, "Kristen, never become a lawyer, because every judge you encounter will hold you in contempt of court for disrespect."

Yes, I liked to argue my position ad nauseam for one chief reason: I wanted to be right.

As an adult, I still see within my heart the desire to be right. Where the heart leads, the mouth follows, and before long I'm explaining away my position when I really should keep quiet.

Psalm 141:3 offers a literal picture of a guard placed in front of my mouth. A guard is used not only to prevent harm from coming in, but also to prevent anything harmful from coming out. So if I sense the Holy Spirit telling me not to justify myself, I imagine that guard preventing the escape of retaliatory words.

When frustration causes regretful words to spill over, let's speak them vertically rather than horizontally. Let's share them with our Father who isn't put off by our honesty, nor unfamiliar with our struggles. Let's rest knowing our defense and reputation are right where they belong: right in the hands of Christ.

Lord, set up a guard for my mouth;
keep watch at the door of my lips.
PSALM 141:3

A Solid Foundation

When storms hit, the incessant raindrops are powerful enough to create landslides and floods, crush roads, and break up foundations. The same can happen in life. Financial troubles, relational tensions, illness—all shake the faith we thought was solid.

In the midst of those stormy seasons, I often wonder if my faith will endure. Will the things I profess to be true in my faith *prove* to be true when the rubber meets the road?

The longer I journey with God, the more I learn that faith is not only given to us by grace but is also built through obedience. Each act of trust, each act of obedience is a brick laid. It's a slow process of knowing God's character, becoming familiar with His ways, listening to His voice, and then actually doing the things He tells us to do. And like the muscles that grow in our bodies, faith becomes strengthened with practice.

Whenever I tell the Lord I love Him, I now hear Him say with tenderness, "If you love Me, you will keep My commands" (John 14:15). Friends, if we love Him, we'll obey Him. The little yeses we say now in the mundane rhythms of our lives will eventually help us to stand firm when we face the raging storms.

Therefore, everyone who hears these words of Mine and acts on them
will be like a sensible man who built his house on the rock.
MATTHEW 7:24

SEPTEMBER 21
Why We Don't Have to Feel Ready

I often work in coffee shops where conversations swirl around me as thick as the scent of espresso. I've heard everything from scandalous confessions to details of doctor's appointments. One morning I found myself the recipient of some unsolicited wisdom . . . .

A young man and his mentor were talking about faith. The young man asked, "When am I going to be ready to help someone else?" The mentor paused and said, "I think you're asking the wrong question. As long as you ask 'Am I ready?' you'll always reason you're not. A flaw. A struggle. Something you think you need to learn more about. The better question to ask is, 'Have I received something?' If so, then you have something to share. And when is the best time to start passing it on? *Yesterday*."

I looked over for a second just to be sure he wasn't talking to me. Hearing those words made me realize that we never feel completely qualified. We rarely feel like we've got ourselves "together." But God isn't looking for perfect. He is looking for ordinary people willing to simply love one another. He's calling the messy, the broken, and the incomplete. That means our role isn't to show off; it's just to show up.

For the eyes of Yahweh roam throughout the earth to show Himself strong for those whose hearts are completely His. You have been foolish in this matter. Therefore, you will have wars from now on.
II CHRONICLES 16:9

When Her Life Is Better Than Mine

I have a friend. She lives in an amazing house and has more than enough money for every need and want. Oh, and she's beautiful. And if that isn't enough, she's a wonderful person who has a servant's heart. I used to think her life was better than mine. You don't have to be a genius to realize that some people have it better than you. You only have to be *human*.

It's in our nature to compare our lives to others. *And we grieve God when we do.* When I compared myself to my friend, it only magnified my own insecurities. It only left me feeling discouraged. It created a desire in me to be something other than I am.

As believers, we're all in a race. But not against one another. We're all running toward the prize of Jesus. And we're all first-place winners by finishing the race.

My friend's life isn't better than mine. It's just *hers*. A year ago, she started a blog but didn't write on it once. After a few months, she e-mailed and said, "I wanted to have a blog like yours. But I just can't do it. It's not me." She has her job and I have mine. I wouldn't trade our lives for anything.

For we don't dare classify or compare ourselves with some who commend themselves. But in measuring themselves by themselves and comparing themselves to themselves, they lack understanding.
II CORINTHIANS 10:12

Abundantly and Lavishly

Not long ago my anxiety revealed a pent-up sin—envy. In my affliction, I blurted out to God: "I wish I had her life. I've loved You and obeyed You all these years, and this is all I get? Nothing? It seems like You love her more than me!"

I was feeling sorry for myself and anxious. I knew better than to pine away for another person's life, but I did. Elizabeth and her husband Zechariah were righteous people, yet Elizabeth couldn't conceive—a source of tremendous suffering for her. Eventually, God blessed them—with John the Baptist. Elizabeth could then have been the object of envy by others.

Christianity is not formulaic; obedience to God seldom entails worldly success. Throughout Scripture we see those closest to God suffering greatly. Yet when we don't get what we think we deserve, we become jealous of His generosity to others.

Scrolling through Facebook, we tend to see only people's good experiences. Very few advertise their anguish. With our eyes on others, we fail to see God's lavish generosity on our behalf.

Once I put my eyes back on Jesus, instead of my perceptions of my Christian sister's life, I was able to accept God's Word to me: "Everything I have is yours" (Luke 15:31).

Both were righteous in God's sight, living without blame according to all the commands and requirements of the Lord. But they had no children because Elizabeth could not conceive, and both of them were well along in years.

LUKE 1:6–7

When Jesus Wore Camouflage

We stood in line waiting to pay for our meal. My husband, Darren, had just returned from a long business trip. The weariness still weighed heavy on his shoulders. In front of us, I noticed a couple with three young children.

"I left my wallet in the van," said the mother as she shifted the baby in her arms while herding the other two little ones. The man gave his wife a glare and headed out the door. As Darren approached to pay our bill, he said to me, "I think I'm going to pick up theirs."

"Sure, but hurry up before he comes back," I said. After Darren paid, we hastily made our getaway. Suddenly, we heard the man's voice. "Sir, sir . . ." Darren turned around. He had caught up to us.

"Did you pay for our meal?" said the big, burly man. Dressed in hunter camouflage, the husky man towered over my husband. Darren extended his hand. The man, however, wouldn't shake hands. There, under the glow of a business sign, I watched as two brawny guys embraced. With genuine authenticity, the men acknowledged their mutual brokenness and each became wrapped in the arms of Grace.

In our stress, in our struggles, in our suffering, Jesus meets us . . . sometimes wearing camouflage.

Now the God of all grace, who called you to His eternal glory in Christ Jesus, will personally restore, establish, strengthen, and support you after you have suffered a little.

I PETER 5:10

Trusting God in the Terrible Seasons

"Why is this happening?" my friend choked through her tears. Over the previous two years, it seemed every dream and plan she had for her family had slipped away or fallen apart. After months of putting on a brave face, her faith wavered.

As we sat together in the silence, I, too, wondered why. Before leaving, I prayed for my friend to know the nearness of God and to know His peace in the middle of her circumstances.

David's words in the first verse of Psalm 60, "God, You have rejected us; You have broken out against us," resonated with me in light of my friend's circumstances and our conversation. Maybe they resonate with you too?

At some point, we all experience seasons when it's difficult to remember that it's God who will tread down the foes (verse 12). But, friend, He will! He is our Deliverer. And His timing is perfect. When I get lost in the situations around me, I need to be reminded of His sovereignty. He will deliver us fully from the heartache and sorrow of this broken, sinful world.

We cannot put our hope in anyone or anything other than Jesus. Whatever your situation, Christ is the hope and assurance of God's presence and power.

Give us aid against the foe, for human help is worthless.
With God we will perform valiantly; He will trample our foes.
PSALM 60:11–12

SEPTEMBER 26
Kicking Guilt to the Curb

I used to feel guilty all the time. Mainly, mother guilt. But I've had wife guilt, housecleaning guilt, homeschooling guilt, eating guilt, and a slew of other guilt, if you will. In fact, I would say that for most of my adult years I've lived in a perpetual state of guilt. I'm talking about the guilt of always feeling like a mess.

It's a plague—a plague I've not only allowed, but invited. I've let the guilt in to do its dirty work, to keep me looking down instead of up. It wants me bound up, not free and wide open, head back, gazing up.

It's our humanity of quirks and bents and weaknesses wrapped up in a flesh that will struggle until that glorious day when Christ returns. We're never going to "get it right" on this earth, but we have a God who is willing to live inside us, to guide us and comfort us until that glorious day. We're not meant to wear those guilt shackles. We're meant to live free. Jesus gives freedom, the real kind. Be free.

Therefore, no condemnation now exists for those in Christ Jesus.
ROMANS 8:1

Looking for God in a Billboard Sign

I saw a movie once about a guy who had a "talking billboard" that helped him find love. I can relate with the desire to have a message spelled out for me, in big letters—an unmistakable message from God. How easy would that make life?

Driving down the road in prayer, asking God for direction, and then passing an electronic billboard and—*voilà!*—your answer appears! How could I argue God's direction if it were plastered on a billboard?

That scenario might seem perfect, but what would happen to our faith and trust if it were? The times I've faced the unknown—when I trusted God's love and provision although I couldn't see or feel it—those are the times I have been closest to God. It's in those desperate moments that I go to the feet of my Savior. If He flashed an answer saying that everything will be okay, would I miss the beauty in my journey with Him?

While an electronic billboard sign might be the easy way out, ultimately the journey to the discovery of all that God has planned for us would be so much less sweet. When we look for who God is in His Word, we find all the answers we need.

Then he said to Him, "If I have found favor in Your sight, give me a sign that You are speaking with me."
JUDGES 6:17

SEPTEMBER 28
The Best Way to Know What to Say

It's a hot Texas day, and I've just returned to my apartment when suddenly someone bangs on my door and yells, "Fire!" I don't think. I just grab the two things I value most and run out the door.

"Grilling accident," I overhear someone say, and I glance over just in time to see a guy with scared eyes holding a spatula. The flames from his apartment are spreading, inching closer to mine, and I am grateful my wedding dress and my Bible are safe with me. Thankfully, the firemen put out the fire right before it reaches my apartment, and the scary event ends.

Looking back, that moment of crisis revealed what I most valued and also shaped the message I'm now committed to live and share. Because the truth is, our message is discovered by determining what life lesson we most value. It's the one question we must ask ourselves: *What would I grab in a fire?*

In the same way, we can also ask ourselves: *If I could only say one thing to someone, what would it be?* If the stopwatch said you only had time for one sentence, *what would you preach?* Your core message. Your most treasured thing. It's the best way to know what to say on any given day.

_____

_____

_____

_____

_____

_____

_____

But collect for yourselves treasures in heaven, where neither moth
nor rust destroys, and where thieves don't break in and steal.
For where your treasure is, there your heart will be also.
MATTHEW 6:20–21

Because of Jesus in You

Are you too tired or overwhelmed to know how to serve those in need? Do you wonder what ability you really have to make a difference in someone's life?

Because Jesus knew who He was—secure in God the Father's love—He could love the utmost and serve the lowest. Because Jesus knew whose He was, Jesus could listen to the whisper of God's voice and obey, serving those who loved and hated Him.

As the Holy Spirit lives and dwells in us, we can rely on Jesus to empower us to do the good works He has prepared in advance for us to do.

I can't count on myself, but I can rely on Jesus to empower me to take the hard steps the Holy Spirit is calling me to. Then I will grow closer to Jesus and become more like Him—and have life to the full. Because we can be secure in the Father's love, we can be led by the Spirit, hear clearly His moment-to-moment instructions, and glorify God by our service.

[Jesus] got up from supper, laid aside His robe, took a towel, and tied it around Himself. Next, He poured water into a basin and began to wash His disciples' feet and to dry them with the towel tied around Him.

JOHN 13:4–5

Sometimes Friendship Is a Piece of Cake

I've spent most of my life being the pursuer in female friendships. From junior high through college, I was the one who invited other girls over to my house or out for coffee dates. Even now, I'm the one who plans the get-togethers.

The other day, when I mentioned scheduling another dinner, one of my friends laughingly responded, "I was just thinking to myself, Ann needs to organize another girl's night!" And I don't mind it, really. I like bringing women together. But sometimes I forget how special it feels to be pursued by other women in friendship.

Last week, I was reminded. While planning a weekend retreat for students at our church, a friend knocked on my door holding a piece of cake. But not just any cake . . . my favorite flavor from my favorite bakery in town.

I enveloped her in a hug and laughed. She had me pegged; chocolate is one of my love languages. More than that, though, I felt loved and known by her. She took time to drive across town, pick up a piece of cake, and bring it to my home. And it meant a lot. It meant that she valued our friendship and she was, in a real and tangible way, pursuing me.

Now, may the Lord show kindness and faithfulness to you, and I will also show the same goodness to you because you have done this deed.
II SAMUEL 2:6

OCTOBER 1
When God Writes Your Story

I'm not a great scrapbooker. Crafting isn't really my thing. But a friend of mine has inspired me to think about ways I might become a curator of my story.

The Lord is the Author of all of Life. He knows us so well and plans our special moments before we are born. He sees all the messes we are going to make, and He loves us anyway. In fact, God sent His Son to make sure that all of our stories, even the hard ones, are used for His glory.

Do you ever think about how God wrote your story? Next time you share pictures on social media—of your family vacation or dinner with friends—remember that every bit of your story was written before you were born. God has left nothing to chance. God is always at work to fulfill His plans for us. He makes it so we can grow in wisdom and love and peace. He invites us to walk with Him closely, each and every day. And He will stop at nothing to meet you, right where you are.

Your eyes saw me when I was formless; all my days were written in Your book and planned before a single one of them began.
PSALM 139:16

Getting Nudged Out of Our Comfort Zones

I have this cat, Peanut. And she's really sweet, but what drives me nuts about Peanut is that she's stubborn. Or lazy. Or both. When I try to make her move—off my spot on the couch, off the dining room chairs at dinnertime, off my leg when I'm trying to sleep at night—she refuses.

And, well, I suppose it's a lot like how I behave when God asks me to move. Get up early to read my Bible? Reach out to that person who makes me feel uncomfortable? Apply for that job? Move to that city? Stay here? Talk to a new person?

It doesn't really matter what God asks of me. From small changes to big risks, my first instinct is to dig my claws into the couch and stay put. So when He asks me to follow, my immediate response isn't always one of obedience. But no matter what feels safest to me, my calling—to love Him, to follow Him, to trust Him, to obey Him—is more important than my comfort. It's not easy, and sometimes I still act like my grumpy, stubborn cat. But I want to move *with* God, instead of making Him resort to pushing me off my proverbial couch.

_____

_____

_____

_____

_____

_____

_____

This is love: that we walk according to His commands. This is the command as you have heard it from the beginning: you must walk in love.

II JOHN 1:6

When There Are Eggshells in Your Washing Machine

My mother would dutifully empty the pockets of every pair of pants in a basket before putting them in the washer. She kept the money she found in a green glass jar and called it a laundry tax. Now I am responsible for sorting and folding, and I think a laundry tax should be mandatory, if only I could remember to check pockets!

My lack of attention to housekeeping is why I just spent twenty minutes vacuuming broken eggshells out of my washing machine. It was not my idea of a fun afternoon, not to mention that you can't buy a latte with eggshells. I had imagined my gospel-sharing self as a jet-setter—and I imagined myself with really great hair and a delightful accent. (I've had very grounded daydreams.)

But I have learned that we can't "serve one another through love" and assume it looks the same for everyone. Today I'm sorting laundry and spreading peanut butter on bread for our lunch, and my daughter is beside me doing the same. She slips sandwich after sandwich into a brown paper sack and then we deliver them for the local food pantry. Today love looked a lot like eggshells, broken up bits of ourselves wrung out in the rinse cycle and strewn throughout the world.

For you were called to be free, brothers; only don't use this freedom as an opportunity for the flesh, but serve one another through love.
GALATIANS 5:13

Drawing Near

A dear friend was facing something scary, and I felt helpless. I tried to pray, but it had been a long time. Too long. Without meaning to, I'd let the busyness of life take over.

So that night I poured out my heart to God. Over and over, I begged Him to make everything okay for my friend. I told Him how sorry I was that He'd come last. I tried to thank Him for His blessings. And then I begged some more.

That text from her began several weeks of waiting and praying . . . and it also began a journey that would change my heart. I started talking to God more all throughout the day. While I was driving, while I was cleaning, even while I was feeding my baby. And in that difficult season of leaning into my Father, I began to crave even more time with Him.

My friend ended up getting good news, and believe me, I celebrated with her and thanked Him over and over. I still do. But whenever I think about that hard time, I'm humbled . . . because it was in that painful, uncertain season that my Father became my refuge and showed me just how good it is to be near Him.

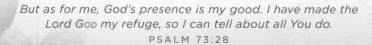

But as for me, God's presence is my good. I have made the Lord God my refuge, so I can tell about all You do.
PSALM 73:28

OCTOBER 5
Just Me and Him

My husband is an active-duty sailor in the US Navy. So I am regularly raising our kids solo while he's on a ship on the other side of the world. When he's away, I'm exhausted more often than I admit. I find myself lonely in an overstimulated world. And sometimes I'm fearful of the future. But what I've found to be absolutely crucial for making it through each day is carving out precious time with God.

Jesus's ministry must have been draining—sharing the Good News, healing the sick, combating opposition on every side. So He separated Himself to be alone with the Father. Four of those times were:

- fasting in the desert before His temptation from Satan;
- after the death of His cousin, John the Baptist;
- after speaking to the masses during the height of His ministry; and
- in the Garden of Gethsemane before He faced Pilot.

My day-to-day can in no way compare to Jesus's burdens. But I know I need to seek out time to be alone with the Father. It's my time to sit at His feet and feel His love and care for me. To be enveloped in peace and quiet. Moments when my empty cup is refilled so I can complete the work He has given me to do.

After dismissing the crowds, He went up on the mountain by Himself to pray. When evening came, He was there alone
MATTHEW 14:23

OCTOBER 6
Tangled and Tied

One time my kids were having a blast on a yellow Slip 'n Slide in the backyard when some visitors showed up, and suddenly there I was, tangled and tied up. My house was a mess and my stretch marks were glaring for the entire world to see.

But if I could go back, I'd tell myself that one day the kids will be grown. And all they'll remember is the joy of sliding down a sudsy Slip 'n Slide while their mama threw her head back laughing.

You know that old lady in the store who gives advice when you don't ask for it? I don't want to be her, but I am reaching out to every woman now to say: don't spend one more minute tying yourself in knots over things that don't matter.

Messing up the kitchen making cookies with your kids is far greater than the dishes in the sink afterward. In the long run, you realize that perfection was never a worthwhile goal.

Let's provide room for mistakes and growing through them. Let's choose which things that matter and not worry about what others may think. Let's give each other a little grace, and while we're at it, let's pour some over our own heart too.

Woe to those who drag wickedness with cords of deceit and pull sin along with cart ropes.
ISAIAH 5:18

OCTOBER 7
Our Response Matters

I was driving home after dinner on the interstate when another car sideswiped mine—all because he was about to miss his exit! Instead of slowing down to go behind me, he sped up to go in front of me and hit my car. While going 65 mph! He didn't slow down or pull over. He just hurried away, barely making his exit. This could have been a horrible accident, but thankfully Benny (my truck) only suffered a few scratches.

Many things that happen to us are beyond our control. What matters is how we respond. My initial response of yelling and honking my horn was understandable. And if I'm honest, I wanted to chase him down, but I probably would have caused another accident.

I didn't pull over to see if Benny was okay because she was driving fine and she wasn't making any crazy noises. So I just drove home.

I pulled into my driveway and the anger I felt the previous ten minutes was quickly washed away with gratitude. I was so happy to be home and not stuck on the interstate. Overwhelmed with gratefulness and relief, I walked into my house, hugged my husband, and kissed my kids good night. Home is where everything comes back into focus.

Enter His gates with thanksgiving and His courts with praise.
Give thanks to Him and bless His name.
PSALM 100:4

The Secret of the Secret Place

Have you ever wondered how to multiply your peace? Peter shared where to find more peace when he wrote: "May grace and peace be multiplied to you through the knowledge of God and of Jesus our Lord" (2 Peter 1:2). Our peace is multiplied in the knowledge of Him.

Not a "heady" or academic knowing, but a Spirit knowing. A closeness. A confidence. God is the One who made us, knows us, and loves us. It only makes sense that in knowing Him, we find the peace we were meant to have. It's the (not so) secret of the secret place.

In high school, I wrote Scripture cards to tape on every surface I could. As I read the verses, I wanted to write them down not just on the cards, but on the tablet of my heart. And God wooed me to Himself through His Word. He showed me His love, His nature, and His heart as I spent time with Him.

I didn't understand everything in the Bible, but He met me and spoke to me as I sought Him. This is the secret of the secret place, of finding peace—that we know Him, and, as a result, grace and peace are multiplied in our lives.

Tie them to your fingers;
write them on the tablet of your heart.
PROVERBS 7:3

When You Don't Feel the Love

You've probably heard the saying "Familiarity breeds contempt." But recently I wondered if familiarity can breed contempt specifically when reading Scripture. I don't mean a matter of disdain or unbelief, but more of having read or heard certain passages so many times that it's easy to gloss over them.

That's what I was thinking about 1 Corinthians 13. But there are important things to know about love, so it's good to reread that passage with my full attention.

Love is something we do, not just feel. Paul provides a beautiful way for us to love others when we've been wronged. Love—when companioned by emotional attachment, affectionate connection, and deep feeling—is a precious thing.

But we're called to love not just others, but our enemies too! How loving do you feel when your teenager disobeys you? When a friend betrays your confidence? When a coworker undermines your decisions? How can you love then?

Reread 1 Corinthians 13:4–5 and consider the ways you can show love to the hurtful people in your life. Thanks be to our Lord who loves us enough, not just to command us to love others, but to make a way for us to love people, and, in doing so, live out the gospel.

Love is patient, love is kind. Love does not envy, is not boastful,
is not conceited, does not act improperly, is not selfish,
is not provoked, and does not keep a record of wrongs
I CORINTHIANS 13:4–5

Because You Just Never Know

Every Sunday morning I walked down the aisle at church to smile, shake hands, and say hi. Everyone responded with cheerful greetings and hugs. All except one. This one lady never reciprocated any warmth toward me. She'd only mumble a weak "Hi" in return. And sometimes she'd just give me this blank expression and walk away. I kept thinking: *What's wrong with her? She's not friendly at all. In fact, she can be quite rude!*

One Sunday I sat next to a new friend and whispered, "Gee, she's not very friendly, huh?" I nodded in the direction of the lady.

"Oh, that poor woman," she replied, "She lost a young daughter a few months back, just before you arrived. It was so tragic." I felt convicted. There she was, grieving—struggling to breathe. And I judged her. It must have taken every ounce of her energy just to get out of bed, get dressed, and show up at church. I asked God to forgive me and to bring her face to mind whenever I meet someone I'm tempted to judge. You never know what heartache another person might be going through. One day maybe the woman in desperate need of an added measure of grace . . . is me.

_____

_____

_____

_____

_____

_____

_____

For with the judgment you use, you will be judged,
and with the measure you use, it will be measured to you.
MATTHEW 7:2

OCTOBER 11
Storing Up Grace

I was in seventh grade when she approached me with a smirk. "What brand are your jeans?" she asked. Those jeans were my best-kept secret, my "please-make-me-cool" prayer. But with one glance she knew, and she carved me with her smug question. I stammered out an answer, and she grinned and went on her way. That morning has never left my heart.

Now the midthirties me wonders why it's so much easier to store up words and experiences that hurt rather than save and treasure the ones that reward eternally. I recall with clarity receiving cruel, sarcastic, and hurtful comments, but I have to dig deep to dredge up the kindnesses.

When I was a college-age camp counselor, we began each day with declarations. We'd gather around the flagpole, plant our feet, and loudly declare, "I am a child of God! I am more than a conqueror! I am beautifully and wonderfully made!" It was the best way to start a day—with truth stored up and spoken aloud.

Today, let's choose to fill our hearts with truth and grace, to forget the old and ugly, and to treasure and ponder that which He says we are: Blessed. Loved. His.

But Mary was treasuring up all these things in her heart and meditating on them.
LUKE 2:19

How to Recognize the

Glorious Ordinary in Your Life

It's ridiculous how much of our lives we consider ordinary. Yet Wednesdays are holy nights in our family because we offer an open call for our kids to come into our bed—mostly to try and keep them out of it the other nights.

Of course, they never go straight to sleep. It's from under the blankets their questions will flow. And, if you pay attention, you'll find that you're living the *extra* part of your ordinary. You watch as his hair falls just so across his eyebrows—it needs to be cut again. And you can't even believe these tall, gangly limbs were once folded in prayer inside your belly. He's a living answer to prayer lying in the rumpled bed, and you dared to think your life ordinary?

No, these are the moments for kneeling in delight as you absorb every nuance on the face that can split your gut in ridiculous jokes one minute and crunch your heart the next. This is living. It's *the people* that make us extraordinary.

Don't believe ordinary for a minute. Life is so full of glory it will weigh you down if you just stop to let it sink deep into your here and now.

Don't neglect to show hospitality, for by doing this some have welcomed angels as guests without knowing it.
HEBREWS 13:2

Set Apart

Every year my mom would plot ways to improve her secret recipe for our traditional pancake breakfast. She treated each concoction like a secret formula, examining the batter, adding a bit of water or a handful of flour, and heating the griddles just so.

Unlike her top-secret recipe for pancakes, God's recipe for incense was not to be altered. This anointing oil was to cover everything in the Holy of Holies to set it apart for the Lord, including the ark of the covenant. Anyone using it for personal consumption would be cut off from the community.

The ark of the covenant was the place God said, "I will meet with you there." Once a year, a priest representing the people would enter the Most Holy Place where the ark resided. Everyone else stood outside and waited.

Jesus changed all this with His own blood of the new covenant.

It was no longer necessary for the incense recipe to be guarded. The Most Holy Place is now open to everyone who calls on His Name—we are the dwelling place of the Most High God. And He still meets us at the mercy seat because He is holy, just as you and I are holy.

Tell the Israelites: This will be My holy anointing oil throughout your generations. It must not be used for ordinary anointing on a person's body, and you must not make anything like it using its formula. It is holy, and it must be holy to you.
EXODUS 30:31–32

OCTOBER 14
Why It's Okay Not to Be Enough

One of the things I've been asking of God is that He would make me a servant. Then He puts me in a position where others are serving me. My one-year-old son is the size of a four-month-old—my milk has not been sufficient—and keeping the feeding tube away from his feisty arms is demanding. So God surrounds me with dear friends and family, some of whom have the very least of resources to give. They stop and sit with me and my children in their own not enough-ness.

Sometimes I think about Paul's thorn, how he must have thought, *If only it were gone, I would finally be enough.* If only my milk were better. If only I read more. But God's response? "My grace is sufficient for you." When He says this, it's the same as saying, "Don't give Me your excuses—you're not the one doing it anyway."

I suddenly feel free to shirk the pretense that I could possibly have anything together, and I'm learning that boasting in this weakness—it's the gospel. My temptation is to say that if I nurse him more or read the Bible more or pray harder, I'll be enough—that my works are sufficient. But God's grace is sufficient.

Concerning this, I pleaded with the Lord three times to take it away from me.
But He said to me, "My grace is sufficient for you,
for power is perfected in weakness."
II CORINTHIANS 12:8–9

When Prayer Goes Unanswered

I was furious with God. He failed me. For the past six months I had pleaded with God and believed He was going to come through for me. But He not only *didn't* come through, He hurt me.

Have you ever felt abandoned by God? Maybe someone is still sick. The spouse is still mean. A child won't return. Your finances are in the dumps. A friend has hurt you. Whatever is going wrong, it's because God has gone rogue, right? Looking back, years later, I see things through a different prism, a different angle.

Sometimes we don't receive the lesser prayer because God is answering a bigger prayer. And the waiting produces patience. It is in the wait we learn faith.

What looks like rejection is often protection. We see life horizontally, but God sees life horizontally, vertically, cross-diagonally and inside out. He also sees how closing a door may prevent our foot from getting jammed in it.

God hasn't given up on you. Just as He hasn't given up on me. He doesn't discount our prayers as frivolous or worthless. God loves us and He has a plan. Just wait and see.

The LORD of Hosts has sworn: As I have purposed,
so it will be; as I have planned it, so it will happen.
ISAIAH 14:24

Sinners in the Hands of a Loving God

When I was a girl, I would go forward for every altar call. With each opportunity, I would raise my tiny hand as if I were a student waiting to be picked for my right answers. I would repeat the sinner's prayer with my eyes squeezed shut and hope that this time it took.

I was afraid I didn't do it right, because later I'd fight with my brother, think mean or envious thoughts, or I'd disobey my mom. I thought this disqualified me from God's love, and I vowed to try harder next time.

In my teen years, I'd imagine God a distant and angry taskmaster for all the wrong I was. I realize now how distorted my view of grace was, yet sometimes I find myself slipping back—I still think I need to earn grace and that it's possible to lose it. Sometimes I am still that little girl with her arm raised, hoping to be seen and loved by God.

But while we were sinners, with tempers that flare and petty thoughts, with insecurities and selfish intentions, with bad mom days and flesh that wills against God, Christ died for me.

I can put my hand down and rest in the arms of my Savior.

But God proves His own love for us in that while we were still sinners, Christ died for us.
ROMANS 5:8

OCTOBER 17
Saying Yes to Courage

I was petrified. I hadn't been to college before, and it was my first day. I was going to college four years later than my friends, and I was certain the other students would know I was different.

I arrived an hour early and sat in my car, gathering the courage to go find my classroom. Fear was trying to tangle its way inside me and snatch away the joy of my new experience as it had so many times before.

When I went to Africa, I was scared of missing out on what was happening back home, scared of falling too deeply in love with a continent, and I was petrified of snakes. But in almost every case, I said no to the fear and yes to the experience. I said yes to going to college four years later. I said yes to Africa, and yes to choosing bravery.

I want to keep saying yes. Yes to Jesus, yes to courage, and yes to letting go of fear. I'm still in college, but I'm not scared anymore. I go out and face it. I keep saying yes to courage and no to fear.

This is what the Lord says: "Do not be afraid or discouraged because of this vast number, for the battle is not yours, but God's."
II CHRONICLES 20:15

OCTOBER 18
Slowing to Listen

As I'm watching my boy run to the playground, the lovely mom I'm chatting with mentions the daughter she lost the previous Christmas. I look at her beautifully pregnant belly, her toddler playing in the stroller, and her kindergartner with the pink bow skipping toward the playground. Never would I have guessed the grief and sorrow she has lived. Never would I have known her full story.

She smiles as she talks about the light and joy her little girl brought for nearly three years. "It's hard," she says, "but we are blessed by the time we had with her and now have with these little ones."

I want to weep and hug this woman. I want to hold my son and not let him go. "We still miss her beyond words," my new friend says, "but we know we'll be with her again one day, and there is so much hope in that."

I say goodbye and travel the sidewalk toward home. I thank God for the gift of this glimpse into another woman's story. A glimpse of His grace. I walk to my front door—filled with sorrow, filled with hope.

And thankful for home.

For as the sufferings of Christ overflow to us,
so through Christ our comfort also overflows.
II CORINTHIANS 1:5

What Jesus Means by Salt

I told my kids I'd make brownies for them this week. So last night after supper, our home filled with the lovely smell of butter and chocolate and the sound of children counting down with the oven timer. After a long fifteen minutes of cooling, plates were passed, bites were taken, and confused and disappointed faces appeared.

I immediately knew the problem and said, "Oh, I left out the salt."

Voices exclaimed, "That's the problem!" and "That's what's wrong!" Plates were pushed to the side and no one took another bite. Because three sticks of butter, three cups of sugar, and seven squares of baking chocolate cannot make up for the absence of that teaspoon and a half of salt.

When Jesus tells us to be the salt of the earth, He's not talking about a little seasoning sprinkled on the side. He's talking about a living, breathing faith that permeates everything we say and do—a light that cannot be hidden, a tangible hope.

I was determined not to let three sticks of butter and seven squares of baking chocolate go to waste in my kitchen, so I continued to nibble on those brownies and grimace. And I felt glad that Jesus can use even my failings in the kitchen to help me see Him more.

You are the salt of the earth. But if the salt should lose its taste, how can it be made salty? . . . In the same way, let your light shine before men, so that they may see your good works and give glory to your Father in heaven.
MATTHEW 5:13, 16

No Regrets

"What should I do?" My plea sounded more like a whine when I asked my dad this question back in college. But he wouldn't tell me what to do. It was time to make my own decisions. Even the tough ones. I felt frustrated. And confused. Looking back, I realize I wanted to shift the burden of decision-making off my shoulders and onto his. I thought I was seeking wisdom, but I was avoiding responsibility.

Have you ever been in the midst of a decision-making process and prayed something like, "God, just tell me what to do! Show me in neon lights!" Then . . . crickets.

It may be because God knows the Bible studies you've attended, the sermons you've heard, the deep conversations with Christian friends you've had, and the Scripture you can recall. If God seems radio silent, it may be because it's time to apply what you already know.

God rarely reveals His plan to us in neon lights. Instead, He asks us to seek Him through His Word. The question, "What should I do?" has one primary filter: Does this express my love for God and does it express my love for others? If I'm seeking to please God and extend love to others, then I do right.

When I was a child, I spoke like a child, I thought like a child, I reasoned
like a child. When I became a man, I put aside childish things.
I CORINTHIANS 13:11

There Is No Safe Gospel

I'm in a circle of thoughtful and kind people, and I've been asked to read the gospel lesson. God's Word is living and active, but this is an uncomfortable parable for me. *Why did I have to read it? Why couldn't I have read the one about the pearl of great price or the mustard seed or the treasure in the field?*

My struggle is, I don't really want to proclaim the teachings I don't like or understand. I don't want to be that close to some of the teachings, because speaking them out loud makes *me* uncomfortable.

There is no encounter with the Word that will leave us comfortable. Comforted, perhaps, but only first through the upheaval of our worlds, the collapse of our presuppositions, the relinquishing of our desire to have the easiest story to tell. We cannot claim "Behold, the Lamb of God who takes away the sin of world" without the uncomfortable parables or the uncertainties or the radical promises or the hardest questions.

I'm still wrestling with the parable of the nets. But it's in the midst of my wrestling that I'll learn what it means to preach this life-changing gospel in my life, in my heart, in the world.

Again, the kingdom of heaven is like a large net thrown into the sea. It collected every kind of fish, and when it was full, they dragged it ashore, sat down, and gathered the good fish into containers, but threw out the worthless ones. So it will be at the end of the age. The angels will go out, separate the evil people from the righteous, and throw them into the blazing furnace. In that place there will be weeping and gnashing of teeth.
MATTHEW 13:47–50

Tied to the Dock

As a kid, I loved the water and riding in boats. And I learned early on that if you aren't tied to the dock, the boat will float away—even in the smoothest of waters.

We can learn much from the person in Psalm 1. Scripture speaks of him as blessed because he walked with intention and treasured God's Word. He lived his life like a tree planted by water. He paid attention to where he was walking, standing, sitting. He didn't allow his life to drift like an unfettered boat.

The written Word of God brought this man delight. When I think of the things that bring me delight, I think of getting to sleep in, treating myself to a pedicure, and indulging in my favorite raw-sugar-no-foam-with-whip latte drink. A facial? Yes, please! These are all things that bring me pleasure. Though I must ask myself: Do I delight in God as much as these? Do I delight in His Word as much as these?

We're blessed when we're in His Word every day. Because God's Word is the truest anchor, preventing us from drifting with the currents of cultural trends. Blessed is the woman who is tied to His dock.

He is like a tree planted beside streams of water that bears its fruit in its season and whose leaf does not wither. Whatever he does prospers.

PSALM 1:3

Catching the Next Wave

We had just arrived in Florida for a family getaway and some boogie-boarding. With a board strapped to my wrist, I'd position myself to literally "catch a wave."

Each ride would end the same way . . . I'd land facedown with a mouthful of sand. But that moment with a mouthful of sand was not the place I intended to stay. I'd go back out for another chance at victory.

Boogie-boarding soon shed light on my parenting, with moments of defeat and victory alike. Wading into the adventure of potty training when she finally got it. Victory! Then, a note from school for biting. A mouthful of sand. Wading into elementary school as an advanced reader. Victory! Next, he was suspended for bullying. A mouthful of sand. Wading into the teen years, I had an employed teen, with a bank account and debit card. Victory! Next, overdraft notices pouring in. A mouthful of sand.

Parenting has moments of victory and defeat. But I did figure out one thing. The mouthful-of-sand moments would not be the place I'd choose to live. Instead I'd address the failure (spit out the sand) and then move on (wade back out to catch the next wave of victory). We would live in the victory!

Brothers, I do not consider myself to have taken hold of it. But one thing I do:
Forgetting what is behind and reaching forward to what is ahead, I pursue
as my goal the prize promised by God's heavenly call in Christ Jesus.
PHILIPPIANS 3:13–14

Why God Allows Change

"Hey, Mom, I'm leaving," he said. Looking up from a book, I see my twenty-one-year-old son with a backpack and pillow under his arm. His wedding day was approaching and suddenly I realized he'd spent his last night sleeping under my roof. The weeks and months that followed brought more change—the unexpected loss of my father, and the company I worked for shut its doors. I wanted my old life back.

Perhaps you're wrestling with some big changes right now. I've learned that with every change that brings pain, God allows something new to be born. It's okay to grieve or regroup, but let's not linger too long there.

The same is true in our spiritual life, trusting Jesus to transform the shades of our faith, making them more brilliant, no matter what season we are in—be it the hurts or the joys. In time, my empty nest became a place of beauty. I found new purpose and went back to school. My husband and I found a new depth of love and joy in our relationship. And God has taken away the fear of change. I've finally realized that every season the Lord brings into my life is lovingly filtered through His precious fingertips.

There is an occasion for everything, and a time for every activity under heaven.
ECCLESIASTES 3:1

OCTOBER 25
Friendship Heals Our Broken Hearts

One year when we attended a new church, I began each Sunday morning with a panic attack. Sitting on the bed I tried to fill my lungs with air. Sometimes I'd turn on the box fan in the window to drown out the sound of my heart pounding in my ears.

I'd been down this road before—I'd had my heart broken by women who shared my faith in Jesus. And each time, it caught me off guard and sucked out the air, leaving me empty and sore. I don't know why we break each other the way we do.

We carry the glory of God in our earthen pots with dirt caked on, yet He has a way of bringing glory out of ashes, grace transforming disgrace, and healing banishing disease.

Eventually, I opened up my heart to new women over coffee or tea or a good book. I kicked off my shoes, tucked my feet up on the sofa and listened to stories other women shared. This heart, all tender and broken, has been filled with breath and life and hope—hoisted on the shoulders of women who love well with bruised hearts of their own. The good with the bad, and God right there in it, working it all for His good.

Your heart must not be troubled. Believe in God; believe also in Me.
JOHN 14:1

301

Holding on to Hope

I can tell my son is nervous as he steps onto the diving platform. I can see his muscles tense, but then . . . he leaps. We clap for him as he emerges from the pool with a grin, his chest swelling with the triumph of having overcome.

Watching my boy step up to jump again, I remember my own moments of stepping up, taking that leap. And I wonder if I will ever stop being afraid.

God constantly presents opportunities to choose fear or faith. I'd like to say the choice is simple. Sometimes it is. But I'm still learning that faith cancels fear. In fear, I lose hope. Hope overcame death so that I could live constantly under hope's wings.

I am learning, like my boy, to step up, to believe that when I leap, God will catch me. I am learning to hold fast to that hope because it does not disappoint. I know I cannot leap by myself, and yet this human heart tries. I'm learning to trust and believe that with hope in the cross, in the saving grace of Christ, I can overcome, not by my own strength, but by His.

Now in this hope we were saved, yet hope that is seen is not hope, because who hopes for what he sees? But if we hope for what we do not see, we eagerly wait for it with patience.

ROMANS 8:24–25

To Believe the Best

I have a friend who did something some people didn't like. And no matter how much he now shows a pure heart, they judge him.

Another friend is sure that God won't use her like He does others. That she won't be what she's always dreamed of being. It's a reality that all of us at some point struggle with—to believe the best, in others and even ourselves.

But when we don't believe the best, we're really saying to God, *I don't believe people can change or be considered as worthy unless I deem them to be.*

This mind-set is the stuff of humans. To believe the best is the stuff of God. He's the Maker of all things new, the knower of the heart, the turner of things around. God asks us to place our faith and trust in Him without trying to put that job in our own hands.

And if someone does disappoint, we will have honored God by believing the best. And if our life doesn't turn out to match our dreams, it will be beautiful anyway. We all have past moments we're not proud of. Everyone has been less than faithful, less than honest, less than good. And yet God doesn't give up on us. Shouldn't we, then, too?

Do not judge, so that you won't be judged.
MATTHEW 7:1

OCTOBER 28
Play Your Note

In elementary school I wanted to read, write, and draw like Grace Su. I partnered with her for a "Young Authors" contest, and it was the only year my entry received recognition.

Middle school and high school ushered in more inadequacies to discover. From best friends to book smarts, from the right clothing to a cool hairstyle... I was mostly a day late and a dollar—or $20—short.

Then, when I became a mother, a new layer of inadequacies developed. Comparing sleep habits, feeding schedules, and milestones was a real issue. I had to fight against comparison because it left me feeling disappointed and fearful. But after all those years, I decided to say, "Enough!"

I now have a friend who says, "Play your note." It's easy to get sideways about the notes that others get to play and forget that I have a note to play too. And so do you. The song is better when I add my note—and when you add yours—by exercising the unique gifts and talents given to each of us.

Together, let's say, "Enough!" Let's walk confidently in the "you-niqueness" we've been given by God. When we're each playing our note, we bring God the greatest glory.

For as the body is one and has many parts, and all the parts of that body, though many, are one body—so also is Christ.
I CORINTHIANS 12:12

OCTOBER 29
The Ball Field

It was the state playoffs and my daughter was running hard. As she slid onto home plate, the catcher lost her balance and fell on Megan's leg. We could tell she was injured, but she insisted on finishing the game.

When it came time for Megan to bat again, it was clear she would not be able to run. So another girl from the team would be a pinch-runner in her place. The girl they chose wasn't great at fielding or batting, but when Megan hit the pitch, the girl began to run. Around first base, then second, then third, then home! We all realized she had an amazing talent to run. Because of this opportunity, Megan and this girl bonded as friends, which opened the door to us inviting her to church.

It's hard to understand God's plans for achieving eternity. It can sometimes appear as if He's being unfair to us. But it could be that He is using our afflictions to work out eternity for us, or perhaps to work out eternity for others through our wounded places. So we trust that He sees more than we ever could, and we trust that His purposes are good. In this way, we choose to live by faith.

The righteous one will live by his faith.
HABAKKUK 2:4

Saying Yes to Hospitality

With my due date just two weeks away, I was overwhelmed by the thought of a family of five staying with us. But they came and our time together was wonderful. After they left, I was glad that we flung our door open wide and made everything work.

The following day I got a text from a friend who was in town with her family, asking if we could do lunch. I was still worn out from the previous week, but I knew that seeing her would be a gift.

But instead of going out to lunch, I invited them over to our house in spite of the state from our prior guests. Of course they didn't care—they didn't come over to see a dust-free mantel or a spotless living room. We spent more than two hours together and our time was rich with conversation.

Lunch was simple, the kids played, and everyone enjoyed each other's company. When they left, I was again reminded that hospitality is not about the condition of our homes, but the condition of our hearts. Hospitality is about saying yes. It's not about perfection. It's easy to get busy and miss out on opportunities to demonstrate hospitality. But let's not miss those chances. Let's be the friend who invites others in.

I opened my door to the traveler.
JOB 31:32

How to Pour Coffee Like a Believer

Reaching for the creamer, I realize there's only a small amount left in the container.

A voice in my mind shouts two words—*not enough!* Those words reveal a belief I've been holding on to for a while now: *there will never be enough.* Those words—*there will never be enough*—haunt.

The whispers grow and sound something like: "If you work faster, then you'll be more successful. If you had more time, then you'd be a better mom. If you were thinner, then you'd be enough."

I'm all too familiar with "if-then" theology. It started back in the garden, with a liar who said: "If you eat this fruit, then you will be like God." It's a lie that tells us we have to *do* something in order to *be* something. And we've been buying it ever since.

After pouring my coffee, I spend a little time in my chair by the window, allowing all the if-thens to float to the surface and letting Jesus still those voices on my behalf. He has redeemed those false statements and replaced them with new ones—ones that make me enough in God Himself. Because the one who lives under the protection of the Most High dwells in the shadow of the Almighty.

In fact, God knows that when you eat it your eyes will be opened and you will be like God, knowing good and evil.
GENESIS 3:5

Clothed in Strength and Dignity

Growing up, my favorite amusement park ride was a roller-coaster called Tornado. When I stood in line with my dad, I had the tension of wanting to get on but fearing I would plummet to my death.

When we reached the platform, there was a Chicken Exit for anyone who decided to back out. But with Dad at my side, I felt brave. We plunged straight to earth and rocketed up another hill together, and we laughed the whole ride. When it was all over, I'd beg Dad to get back in the line again.

Looking back, I see how life is a lot like waiting to ride the Tornado. We *want* to live life with adventure, but we're pulled to the nearest Chicken Exit. Yet God gives us strength for the adventures of life. He even gives us the ability to laugh in the face of our fears!

Sometimes I want to take the easy way out, but I realize that if I did, I would miss out on the adventure my Father intended for me. The same goes for you. He is inviting you to sit next to Him. And He'll guarantee you the ride of your life. You might even hear yourself say, "Let's do it again, Dad!"

Strength and honor are her clothing, and she can laugh at the time to come.
PROVERBS 31:25

When You Wonder if You'll Ever Measure Up

I don't remember the first time I felt it. It could have been in the third grade when I was the last one picked for the kickball team. Not being enough has been a faithful companion in my life . . .

I may not remember the first time I didn't measure up, but I do remember when I stopped measuring. I was a freshman in college, rooming with my twin sister. I called my mom on the phone and said, "Mom, did you know I'm petite?"

She laughed and said, "Of course, honey. You're 5'2". That's petite by most standards."

I replied, "But, Mom, I'm the big twin!"

I had spent my entire childhood being compared to my smaller twin sister. We were born five minutes apart and I towered over her 4'10" frame. But I had been measuring myself by the wrong perspective. And that's what comparison does: it skews our view of ourselves and we believe lies that say we aren't pretty enough or smart enough or whatever enough.

We can never be all those things, but that's okay. We don't have to be enough. Because Jesus is. All the time. He takes our inadequacies and exchanges them for His perfection. And that is enough for all of us.

It is not that we are competent in ourselves to claim anything as coming from ourselves, but our competence is from God.
II CORINTHIANS 3:5

NOVEMBER 3

From Heaven, with Love

When my mom lost her battle with breast cancer, my office gifted me a beautiful bright pink orchid. It was a busy season of life—changing jobs and a son going off to college—so I didn't have time to research how to care for an orchid.

To my surprise, the flowers lasted a long time. Then my husband accidentally bumped into the stem and cracked it off. We were convinced we killed it.

A couple of years later it was showing no signs of life. But I couldn't throw it away. Then one day I noticed a new shoot at the base. And soon it grew up with tiny buds at the tips.

Then one morning I was greeted by two full fuchsia blooms proudly standing at attention. I smiled and thanked God for the brightness it brought to me.

As I sat down to spend time with Him, He gently reminded me of my mom's homecoming to heaven. I blinked back tears as I reflected on His tenderness and goodness to reach down from heaven to remind me of my mom's new life in eternity.

Sometimes God smiles at us from heaven and reminds us that He never forgets and He is always bringing forth new life.

Look at how great a love the Father has given us that we should be called God's children. And we are!

I JOHN 3:1

NOVEMBER 4
Confidently Going in the Right Direction

When my son was born, my husband took our daughter, not yet two, to *The Lion King*. Eventually I'd get to see it too, and if you polled any member of our family today, it still ranks as one of our all-time Disney favorites.

When we first meet Timon and Pumbaa, a fun-loving duo in the form of a banded mongoose and warthog, Simba is depressed, wrongly believing he is responsible for the death of his father. Well-intentioned, Pumbaa advises for him to put his past behind him and then launches into a spirited performance of "Hakuna Matata."

The sweet characters of Timon and Pumbaa make an important point, a lesson that serves us well to learn early: we can't change our past. It's futile to dwell on it. I think it's even dangerous to be anchored to our past. It's a form of bondage that's holding your future hostage.

Regrets. Bruised feelings. Bitterness. Anger. Grudges. Even if you were wronged by no fault of your own, holding onto the past is limiting and unhealthy. If we're only looking in the rearview mirror, we won't be able to move on to all the Lord has for us ahead.

Do not remember the past events, pay no attention to things of old.
ISAIAH 43:18

Celebrating the Middle

She was sitting at her computer, muttering to herself and shaking her head. My sixth grader fumed, "Mom, I just want to hurry and get my work done, so I can have some fun." She had always loved school, so what happened? Instantly I knew, and it stopped me in my tracks. *It's me. I'm the one always rushing. I'm the one always hurrying.*

Let's get our reading done so we can relax! Let's finish our homework early so we can meet our friends at the park! Let's hurry up and do our chores so we can bake!

As I turned to walk back downstairs, I repented of my own haste. I don't want to model a life of hurry.

Do you ever find yourself rushing ahead? Wanting to get to the next place without enjoying the time in the middle? That day on the stairs got me thinking. We don't enjoy cleaning, but we love the shiny, sweet-smelling result. We don't love exercising, but we usually feel better after we do.

What if we accepted that most of life is lived in the middle. What if we started recognizing that God wants to meet us right in the middle of whatever we're doing, right now, wherever we are.

_____

_____

_____

_____

_____

_____

Whatever you do, do it enthusiastically, as something done for the Lord and not for men.
COLOSSIANS 3:23

Even When We Can't Be There, God Still Is

I answer the phone and hear the tears in her voice. I close my eyes and wish I had wings to fly the many miles to her side. I read the hurt in the e-mail that makes its way to my in-box. As I respond, I want to reach through the screen and put my arm on her slumped shoulders.

I want to be there for the people I love. I imagine you do too. I don't like the idea of missing even a moment when they might need me. Yet I know that God is an ever-present help in trouble. He is on the other side of the phone line after she hangs up. He is right beside her when she reads my e-mail reply.

There is never a time when God will not be with the people we love. They are not alone. And as much as the people in our lives care for us, they can't always be there for us either. But God is always available. He is with us even when the room is empty. He's not even a phone call, e-mail or hug away—He's with us right now, right here, every moment of every day.

God is our refuge and strength,
a helper who is always found in times of trouble.
PSALM 46:1

Let the Music Play

Music is moving. It connects us across the centuries and binds people together in profound ways. It is beat, melody, and harmony all in one. Art claims it, humanity is touched by it, and our souls are the holder of it.

When tragedy shatters the stained-glass window around you and the piercing sun blinds your eyes, keep breathing. Let the notes of courage and providence carry you to the next measure. Weep to the slow, riveting sound of the low tones and know this too is music. Heartbreak is still worship; in the wrestle and the raw, faith laid bare, do not mute the music now.

When joy paces your heart's arrhythmia and care from others brings your life's quality to notable goodness, keep living. Let the notes of confidence and community carry you to the next song of beauty. Sway to the rhythm, the momentous pulse of the strong tones, and know this too is music.

Hope is worship, for you and for those you can bless, so don't mute it. For tragedy and joy are some of the greatest complexities in life; we are intertwined with both daily. For both, I stay on my knees; join me. For all you enjoy and for that which calls you to endure, let the music play.

Sing to the LORD with the lyre, with the lyre and melodious song. With trumpets and the blast of the ram's horn shout triumphantly in the presence of the LORD, our King.
PSALM 98:5–6

The Importance of Sharing Our Stories

When my middle daughter was four years old, she was nearly killed by a falling tree in the middle of a tornado. When my youngest daughter was born, she had a collapsed lung and pneumonia, causing her to spend a week in the NICU. Several years ago I spent twelve days in the hospital, eventually undergoing a serious surgery that saved my life.

These stories are told at birthdays, and we share them with friends and family. We return to these stories again and again because they remind us of God's faithfulness.

God told His people, the Israelites, to share their stories, to write them down, to remember. These weren't just feel-good stories to bolster their faith in that day, but they're also for future generations, that they would praise the Lord.

I hope that one day, because of all our family stories, my grandchildren and great-grandchildren will know and follow Jesus with abandon.

All of us can share our stories so that future generations will praise the Lord. When we share God's goodness with those in our lives, we all are encouraged to give Him the praise.

This will be written for a later generation,
and a newly created people will praise the Lord.
PSALM 102:18

Less Words, More Presence

I used to work hard at encouraging my friends, especially in the difficult times. And when I sensed that my efforts weren't resonating, I felt helpless. I was trying to be a savior, in a sense, but now I know I couldn't soothe anyone's ache using my own logic. It wasn't until I came face-to-face with my own inadequacy that I was able to enter into someone else's pain. When our own transparency surfaces, we become two broken daughters on a journey together, to love God and each other, and know that neither of us has the strength to go it alone.

Because Christ is in us, we can be His arms to hold others close when the tears flow and the grief is thick. As we listen to Him we can His use discernment for knowing the right words, for giving sound counsel, and most importantly, for praying with more fullness of heart.

A text on my phone read, "Thank you for being present, for understanding and being helpful this morning . . ." A smile made its way across my face and gratitude filled my heart. This was the sweetest compliment to me—because it confirmed God's continued grace and growth in my own life.

If anyone thinks he knows anything, he does not yet know it as he ought to know it. But if anyone loves God, he is known by Him.
I CORINTHIANS 8:2–3

NOVEMBER 10
The Canopy

My dad grinned and motioned for the salesman's attention. In my small hands were new bills recently exchanged from quarters, birthday checks, and little tuck-ins from Meme. I unfolded the magazine ad and showed it to the man—a white four-poster bed with a beautifully adorned gauzy canopy had been my dream bed for over a year.

Fast-forward twenty-eight years and I still love that bed. It's traveled with me from my parents' house to my first home to the storage shed after I married. And now, it sits in our garage.

The other morning I glanced at the four posters sticking up over cardboard and realized that its purpose was being wasted. So I started to pray for God to show me what to do with this bed, plus the matching desk, chair, and side table. (My parents bought the rest of the set after I purchased the bed.)

It's funny how God prompts us to pray—and prepares our hearts. He orchestrates timing and reasons that are beyond our imagination. A day later, I read an announcement in our church bulletin about a Furniture Loan Program to international students at our local university. But it's a gift, not a loan. And God will answer my simple prayer through it.

Everyone must appear with a gift suited to his means, according to the blessing the LORD your God has given you.
DEUTERONOMY 16:17

NOVEMBER 11
How Great Thou Art

We gather every month in the yellow community room at the nursing home. They're a beautiful bunch, this gathered assembly. As we sing, some join in while others simply nod along as the familiar words touch a soft spot in tired hearts and worn bodies. Their mouths gently form the words of their beloved youth.

As we begin to sing "How Great Thou Art," a gentleman stands with a grin on his face as he pulls out his rusted tambourine and the tiny cymbals mix with the out-of-tune piano.

As the last note ends, the tambourine player bows his head low, and I steal a glance to see his face . . . and it's glowing. A man whose words are difficult to understand had used his shaking hands to worship.

As I look around the room of withering bodies and faltering minds, tears slip from my eyes as I whisper a word of thanks for being in such a holy place. We pray one more time and then stand, all who could, to sing one last hymn.

Afterward we shake hands and thank our friends for letting us share their morning, and I realize once again how much God sees each and every one of us and how He calls us to love.

Yahweh is great and is highly praised; His greatness is unsearchable.
One generation will declare Your works to the next
and will proclaim Your mighty acts.
PSALM 145:3–4

The One We Should Go to First

My husband and I were having dinner with another couple, and she told me she always asks her husband about everything from weekend plans to activities for the kids. That got us started on a whole conversation about who we ask for advice.

For advice I often go to my husband, my sister, my brother, my parents, and even my sixteen-year-old daughter. But going to God is often a last resort. If I'm confused about something, I'll go to my close friends or family. Most of the time I'm seeking affirmation of decisions I already made! If I'm worried, I'll talk over the best-case scenario with my mom and the worst-case scenario with my husband. Prayer often comes after I have talked to everyone else.

When Nehemiah needed to answer the king's question, Scripture tells us that he said a quick prayer to God. How many times would my decision-making seem clearer if I went to God before I asked other people? Or maybe just offering a quick thank-you could change my thinking? How easily I forget that I have a God who has everything in control and wants to hear me ask about decisions, share about my day, and come to Him with any worries or questions I have. He is in control over everything!

Then the king asked me, "What is your request?"
So I prayed to the God of heaven...
NEHEMIAH 2:4

When Healing Brings Hope

It was a new season for all of us, in a new home and a new town, with new rhythms and responsibilities, and I was feeling just a bit overwhelmed.

Adjusting to a new life is hard when you only remember the good of what you left behind. It's easier to remember the highlights of the past instead of clinging to hope in the present moment. There are moments in this new every day that feels like the wilderness, and I pine for the good of what was. Yet moving wasn't about leaving the bad and finding the better. It was about obedience. We asked and God answered. God led and we followed.

So while I cry out to the Lord for understanding, the response I get isn't about my circumstances. It's always about Him. My heavenly Father gently whispers to my soul . . . "I've got this. I've got you. I'm doing a new thing. Just abide in Me."

Maybe He's orchestrated all this so I'll lean more on Him and less on myself. Maybe it's about not clinging to anyone, anything, or any idea, but learning how to cling more to Him alone.

Be strong and courageous; don't be terrified or afraid of them.
For it is the LORD your God who goes with you;
He will not leave you or forsake you.
DEUTERONOMY 31:6

NOVEMBER 14
The Rules Are Tools

"Mikey, don't stand on Maddie's stroller. Mikey, step down!" He looks at me, steps up higher, and loses His balance. The stroller tips backward and through tears he asks, "Mommy, why did you let me fall?"

I want to grab him and say, "Why didn't you listen to me?"

How often are we like Mikey? How often do we push the boundaries just a little bit more and think, *I can get away with this; I'll be okay.* We want to do things our way. We think that grace will cover us. But even though His grace secures us in eternity with Him, our actions still have consequences.

God lovingly laid down instructions for our lives. He's given us a road map for knowing where we are headed and informs us of the places we shouldn't venture. Why? Because we may get hurt. His directions keep us from shame, guilt, and regret. Even more, they offer us joy, fulfillment, and purpose.

If only we'd see God's commands as tools instead of rules. Tools to keep us in places of contentment and peace. When we live within the boundaries He has set, we'll live lives that are focused and purposeful. Then we can walk with God in confidence toward the destination He has set before us.

*For I am commanding you today to love the Lord your God,
to walk in His ways, and to keep His commands, statutes, and
ordinances, so that you may live and multiply, and the Lord your
God may bless you in the land you are entering to possess.*

DEUTERONOMY 30:16

The White-Space Challenge

One not-so-fine day I woke up to catch my computer deleting all my photos. One by one, *gone*. My son's birthday party? Poof! My daughter's graduation? Goodbye!

My computer had been saying that my disk was full for *ages*, but I was "too busy" to deal with it. Hitting "OK" to get that pesky message to go away got me back to all the more pressing things on my to-do list.

In my panic to restore everything, I pushed all the buttons! I googled "SOS! White screen of death!" I was hoping that some really smart guy at Google would have the answers. Fortunately, this disaster ended well, offering me more than just a restored computer, but my photos miraculously returned safe and sound.

Just as I needed to heed the early warnings to free up disk space, I must also get better at building intentional white space into my day. I'm a *doer*. I thrive when I'm busy, checking things off my list and doing as much as possible. My soul craves slowing down to simply *be*. No amount of "doing" will ever satisfy. I need quiet moments with God—that free white space to refocus, reboot, recharge, and rejuvenate my life and my soul.

As a deer longs for streams of water, so I long for You, God.
PSALM 42:1

The Answer God Gives

"Mom, would you pray for me?" I looked up from the dish I was scrubbing. "Of course. What's going on?"

She hesitated. "Could you pray and ask God to give me the desire to do my schoolwork?"

I smiled and nodded. "I will, but you should pray too. God likes for you to talk to Him directly."

"I will, but I don't think He's going to do it."

I smiled again as I rinsed off the dishes I had no desire to clean from a meal I had no desire to make.

"No, He may not," I said, "but you know what? When you ask Him for something you know is right and He doesn't answer your prayer the way you hoped, He's giving you the opportunity to grow in maturity . . . to choose not to follow your feelings. Our feelings will take over our lives if we let them. But feelings are meant to be indicators, not dictators. A no to a good desire means a yes to the gift of perseverance."

Her eyes locked with mine and we shared a hopeful smile. Then she faced her books and turned the page as I scooped up the basket of overflowing laundry and went up the stairs, one step at a time.

Now these three remain: faith, hope, and love.
But the greatest of these is love.
I CORINTHIANS 13:13

Our Identity in Christ

My identity isn't what I thought it was. People often ask, "What do you do?" Before school, I felt as though I had nothing to say. But now I tell them, "I'm a journalism student. I am learning to be a truth-teller in all I do." I can easily wrap myself around the idea that being a journalism student is who I am because it's currently what I do.

But there's a problem with basing my identity on what I do. For example, the other day I received a mark on a writing assignment. It was a terrible grade. I saw the mark and instantly wilted. If I get a bad mark in a writing class, does that prove I'm a bad writer? Am I in the wrong program? Why am I taking journalism if I can't actually write?

It's astonishing what can happen when you make what you do into who you are. I'm a writer, even after that bad mark. But it's what I do, not who I am. I am a journalism student, but it's what I do, not who I am.

So who I am? I am one who is deeply, immeasurably loved by the God of the universe. This is who you are too.

I chose you before I formed you in the womb; I set you apart before you were born. I appointed you a prophet to the nations.
JEREMIAH 1:5

NOVEMBER 18
Louder Than Nutella

I tap my fingers on the table and check my phone again. Nope, I hadn't missed a text or a call. He said he would call. He hasn't. Another day is ending, and nothing. So I walk to the kitchen and pull a spoon out of the drawer. Just one scoop of Nutella will get my day back on track.

I pause at the cabinet. I stood there, spoon in the left hand and cabinet handle in the right hand. "I'm not hungry," I say, "I'm just sad, and I'm about to eat this Nutella because I think it will satisfy this hurt." My grip tightens on the spoon and I slowly close my eyes. "God, You're gonna have to be louder than this Nutella."

I keep talking about the deep hurts of my heart and all the ways I wish my life was different. When I finish, nothing happens. My phone doesn't ring. I don't feel some supernatural strengthening in my soul. I just put the spoon away and remember Psalm 73:25–26. My flesh and heart feel like they're failing, but He is the strength of my heart, my portion, forever. For today, my vice loses, my God wins, and somehow, my heart will survive it all.

Who do I have in heaven but You? And I desire nothing on earth but You. My flesh and my heart may fail, but God is the strength of my heart, my portion forever.
PSALM 73:25–26

To Know Him More

Iused to be afraid to trust God. And it bothered me. I wanted to slip my hand in His and let Him lead. I wanted to put my concerns in His capable arms and believe He could take better care of them than I could. I wanted to have more faith. But I didn't.

One day I realized it's hard to trust someone we don't really know. I knew a lot about God but I didn't really know Him. So I started spending time with Him like a friend. Having conversational prayers. Listening to Him through His Word. Relying on Him in faith as I struggled with different fears. I also began to learn about His character and faithfulness through the power of His names.

We can't know God as Jehovah Jireh, our Provider, if we aren't in need of His help. And when we are, we can trust Him and depend on Him to meet our needs. The more we do this, the more our trust will deepen and our relationship with Christ with be strengthened.

Those who know Your name trust in You because You have not abandoned those who seek You, Yahweh.
PSALM 9:10

NOVEMBER 20
Small Is the New Great

I'm a sucker for Christmas cards. I love creating one each year as well as receiving them from friends and family. I include a simple letter full of the good, the sad, and the joyful from the previous year.

The first Christmas I sent such a letter was the first year my husband and I were married. We'd read Psalm 126:3 during our wedding, so I included it as a send-off in our letter. It's been over ten years since that first letter went out, and Psalm 126:3 has been in the closing of each one. Not because every year has been sunshine and rainbows, but because there have always been great things—the births of our babies, financial blessings that came in the nick of time . . .

But even more precious were the small, everyday things that didn't make the annual letter but have brought great joy. Like sunshine in February. Hot morning coffee. Time with girlfriends. Wispy baby curls. Clean sheets. Small can be great—it may just be the new big. Joy can come from the smallest of places and be the theme of our years, no matter what.

The LORD had done great things for us; we were joyful.
PSALM 126:3

Put Me Back Together

I reach up into my mother's dish cupboard, past the plates and bowls. *Got it,* I think as I slide my fingers around the yellow ramekin. *This will be perfect for the olives.* But somewhere between the "perfect" in my head and the grip of my hand, I fumble. The dainty cup with ruffled edges smashes to the tile floor and spreads out in shards like a firework.

I clench my fists as my mom reassures me, "I got it on sale. It doesn't matter."

But the voice in my head says it does matter: *How could you do this? You are always screwing things up.*

They are thoughts from an old record that's played for years. But this time, I breathe in the fear and speak back in prayer, "My spirit is one of power, of love, of sound judgment." I start small and whisper, then speak out loud, and then know it is true. This power and love really is for me.

After my dad vacuums the floor, I reach up in the cupboard once more, praying I take the courage offered me . . . and lean on the far-reach of love that comes for me again and again, always ready to clean me up.

For God has not given us a spirit of fearfulness,
but one of power, love, and sound judgment.
II TIMOTHY 1:7

When It Doesn't Seem Fair

As the kids played soccer in the sunshine, I sat in my Suburban eager for some quiet time to read. Then another mom walked to my window and wasted no time.

"One of the moms in our group has a problem with you, and even though I defended you, I wanted to ask you something."

"Sure," I said.

"Why is it that you had an affair, yet you get a nice family and be happy, while I've stayed faithful to my cheating husband and my marriage is a mess? It's like you did wrong and got rewarded for it. It's just not fair."

In a split-second my heart flooded. Guilt. Shame. Regret. It had been over for fifteen years, but her words made the memory crisp. It's true I dove in; in time I did get out. But not by myself.

God heard my cry. He turned to me. I didn't deserve to be brought out.

I'd ruined everything. But He rescued me and gave me new life. God's mercy found me. The natural consequences of sin are real, but God's love is so great, He will lavish His mercy on those who don't deserve it. All we can do in response is thank Him.

I waited patiently for the LORD, and He turned to me and heard my cry for help. He brought me up from a desolate pit, out of the muddy clay, and set my feet on a rock, making my steps secure. He put a new song in my mouth, a hymn of praise to our God. Many will see and fear and put their trust in the LORD.
PSALM 40:1–3

My One-Word Vocabulary Shift

As the sun set on our back-patio conversation, my friend said, "Jen, my relationship with the Lord is stronger now than it was thirty-one days ago." I had no words. Just a month previously, her nineteen-year-old son went to be with the Lord. "God is still good," she reiterated.

On the morning of the funeral, it hit me. My son stumbled down the stairs airing his bad attitude. Eggs greeted him, but he didn't want eggs. He wanted pancakes. Yet I knew my precious friend would give anything for the same disrespectful morning greeting. For the rest of her life, she'll daydream about past breakfasts gathered at the table. Tragedy opens our eyes to perspective changes, and in that moment, the simplicity of a one-word vocabulary shift marked me.

This making of meals and tending to wounds and continuing on when I'm tired and worn out and really don't want to—it's a privilege. I don't *have* to, I *get* to. I don't have to go to work, I get to because it means we're employed and there's a paycheck coming.

This one-word gratitude challenge impacts how we do life. We can all press in and learn to love what must be done regardless of how we feel. It's the choice we get to make.

I say, The Lord is my portion, therefore I will put my hope in Him.
LAMENTATIONS 3:24

NOVEMBER 24
The Imago Dei

What would it look like if we lived as if we truly believed that every human being was created in the image of God? Including the boss intent on making your day miserable. The child breaking your heart. Your political opponents. Your ex. And his girlfriend. All of us knit together by the same Artist that spoke the universe and all its varied wonders into being.

Our hearts are intent on dividing humanity with hidden titles—love, like, tolerate, dislike, can't stand. Protecting ourselves behind a shield of indifference and even hate. Not my denomination. Not my political affiliation. Not my type.

But if we construct fences and build walls to "protect" our neat categories and hard hearts, we are stepping on our oxygen line. Because love is like air.

Inhale. Exhale. Both directions. And it better not stop, or you'll pass out. We're made for love. Sure, there's plenty of hard work involved. But when we choose to set aside our prejudices and silence the anxious judge and jury of our minds, we hold two things fundamentally in common with everyone: 1) the image of God and 2) our need for His grace. Suddenly, we are the acquitted and the only justice is to share the unmerited favor we've received. And love becomes simple.

So God created man in His own image;
He created him in the image of God;
He created them male and female.
GENESIS 1:27

The One Thing We Should Never Hoard

I'm jumping in the car to grab a spur-of-the-moment donut, and I get a text message from a new friend. She wants to know what I'm doing for lunch tomorrow. She suggests sushi. I do not like sushi. I don't like to feel like my food may be making eye contact with me.

She texts me again, *"All I want is your time. I want to talk about God and life and success and failure and moving on and being strong."* And there it is. It was never about the sushi. It was about the raw time—the biggest gift we can give each other. It was about taking the time to sit across the table from each other and dig into our lives and sift through the ordinary in order to really connect beyond the default *"I'm fine."*

How easily I forget that my relationships thrive on time. God spoke days and nights and seconds and hours into being and then He gifted them to us. I don't want to hoard my time. I want to be generous with spending time on the people in my life. Generously. The more the better. For both our sakes.

Then God said, "Let there be lights in the expanse of the sky to separate the day from the night. They will serve as signs for festivals and for days and years."
GENESIS 1:14

Hope Beyond the Pain

Earlier this week my daughters and I were watching a sitcom, and the mom on TV was having a baby. She was doing the stereotypical heavy breathing and moaning that is associated with dramatic (and comedic) television births, so my daughters began to question me about the validity of pain and childbirth.

They were horrified when I confirmed that, yes, women do typically have a great deal of pain with childbirth.

I also shared that a lot of women (myself included) report that they don't really remember the specifics of that pain. "Why else would people have subsequent children?" I joked.

I assured them that the pain of childbirth isn't comparable with the joy that comes with the birth of a child. It is, in fact, "worth it," which is a beautiful metaphor for the trials of life. Thankfully, even our omniscient God chooses to forget some things. Jeremiah 31:34 says he forgives our sin and remembers it no more. But God calls us to remember our trials and pain. And to remember how He brought us through. Because He will continue to do so until, finally, He brings us home. In Christ, there is always hope beyond the pain.

For I consider that the sufferings of this present time are not worth comparing with the glory that is going to be revealed to us.
ROMANS 8:18

The Soil of Friendship

One Monday morning I received a simple text from a friend: *"How was your weekend?"* I chose to be real and reveal that it didn't go well. *"My two-year-old woke up in the night with a sudden onset of croup. We spent an unpleasant four hours in the ER and didn't get home till after 3:00 a.m. But thankfully, he's doing much better and I'm hopeful for the chance to take an afternoon nap."*

Without skipping a beat, she replied, *"Oh no! Can I bring you dinner?"* In that moment, I faced a decision: decline help or accept dinner and be blessed while deepening our friendship. Yes, I would be fine without help. But what if being fine isn't the point? I accepted my gracious friend's offer.

A few hours later, I heard a soft knock and opened the door to arms full of delicious delights adorned with a "Get Well" balloon. As I thanked my friend, the light in her eyes beamed a genuine pleasure for the opportunity to help.

Over the past few years on my journey, I've learned that meaningful friendships are forged in the soil of service. We are meant to come alongside. To lean in and be held up. To do the holding. It's in needing one another that relationships bloom.

A friend loves at all times . . .
PROVERBS 17:17

The Name That Defines Me

The first time our eight-year-old realized I had a name other than "Mama," we were sitting at the dinner table and my parents were visiting. We could see the light bulb moment in his expression, but I made sure he knew that to him, my name would always be "Mama."

I wear the title proudly, and yet I don't let it define me. At times I have to remind myself that my identity exists outside the roles of wife, mother, and friend. These different roles shape me and mold me, but they don't determine who I am.

My search to discover who I was began after I became a mom. My former labels—student, worker, daughter—were eluding me. Now as a wife and new mother, I felt unstable, like I was failing at both.

Somewhere in my darkness I sent up a simple prayer, "Lord, help." And over time, God showed me I would never know who I am until I learn who He is.

The more I learned about Him, His love, and His unchanging character, the more I discovered my own identity. I learned that these different hats that I wore—mom, wife, friend, employee—were meant to enhance, but never define.

Look, I have inscribed you on the palms of My hands;
your walls are continually before Me.
ISAIAH 49:16

A Different Way of Looking at Success

Growing up, my family was fiercely competitive in board games. I'd stay up till 2:00 a.m. with my brothers to take over the world in the game of Risk. Our favorite games involved strategy like Chess, Stratego, and Empire Builder. In Chess, my big brother patiently taught me how to move each piece and checkmate the other person's king.

The queen might be the most powerful piece on a chessboard, but I liked the knight. I thought it clever how the knight could move in little L-shapes, so I played my knights exclusively until they died. Then I played my bishops, sliding across the board in grand diagonals. Meanwhile my brother methodically moved various pieces into position for checkmate. Game after game my brother won.

What I learned was that I can't become so fascinated with one piece and one move that I neglect the others. Each piece has a part to play, working together for a common goal. The church is like that too. We come together, with each person doing the thing we do best, being obedient to complete the work God has called us to do.

Tell Archippus, "Pay attention to the ministry you have received in the Lord, so that you can accomplish it."
COLOSSIANS 4:17

NOVEMBER 30
Home Is Where You Feel Wanted

While in college, I found it odd that a childhood friend visited my family before her own when she returned to town during university holidays. One day she confided, "When I walk into your home, everyone gets up, greets me with a warm 'Hey!' and wraps me up in a bear-sized hug. Your family makes me feel like a big deal."

My communications professor taught that the first three minutes of every human interaction—in the morning, at the office, when a family member comes home—sets the tone of your communication for the rest of the day.

No matter what time Dad came home, we'd hear his key jingling in the lock followed by a booming "Hello!" as he entered the doorway. Mom always answered with a cheerful "Hey!" Yes, they occasionally argued, but in the midst of it all, they never stopped making each other feel welcome and wanted. And they never stopped making others feel that way too. Because home is not merely where you're welcome; home is where you feel wanted.

Our Father in heaven opens His arms wide and lovingly invites us in. Best of all, His welcome lasts longer than the first three minutes. His welcome lasts forever.

How good and pleasant it is when brothers live together in harmony!
PSALM 133:1

The Strength of Our Lives

After a particularly challenging day, I abandoned the laundry, the dishes, and most of my responsibilities to retreat to a mindless binge of reruns on television. Avoidance comes naturally to many of us. Friends confess a dependence on food, alcohol, shopping, and even exercise to buoy them in tough times.

We constantly try to be strong. We muster courage, try harder, and grin and bear it. Rather than addressing our weakness, we avoid it or cover it up. But when we make the Lord our light and our salvation, we no longer have reason to avoid or be afraid, for the Lord becomes the strength of our lives! He is our stronghold—our refuge, our protection, our strength!

This strength comes not from Christ beside us, but from Christ in us. He is not merely the shield that encloses us; He is the internal foundation upon which everything else is built. He is not our exoskeleton, but the very bones inside of us, the endoskeleton upon which our whole lives hang!

When we can't, He can—in us and through us. In Christ we live and move and have our being. In Christ all things hold together. In Christ we can do all things because He is the strength of our lives!

The Lord is my light and my salvation—whom should I fear?
The Lord is the stronghold of my life—whom should I be afraid?
PSALM 27:1

DECEMBER 2
Jesus and Road Maps

Lately I've been asking for Jesus to show up with directions on Google Maps, because I'm really not sure where I'm going these days. I want something like a neon billboard, because I need a glaringly obvious sign.

I think that of all the characters in the Bible Jesus showed up for, He never showed up with a road map. Like Jonah . . . When he received his call—or his road map—to go to Ninevah, he ran in the opposite direction. (This is probably why Jesus isn't showing up with a road map for me.)

When Jonah eventually found himself treading water in a stormy sea, God showed up for him. God brought a whale—even though Jonah ran away.

Maybe I need to be swallowed up by a whale! I don't know. But what I do know is that Jesus always shows up when we ask Him to. He may not have a road map—He already knows where He's going. But He knows the number of stars He's placed in the sky. And today, that's enough for me.

Lord, lead me in Your righteousness because of my adversaries;
make Your way straight before me.
PSALM 5:8

How to Be Worry-Free

It was 11:58 p.m. on December 31, 1999, and I was on full alert, eyes glued to my computer screen. I sat in a newsroom full of other reporters, waiting to see whether our world would collapse under a predicted technological catastrophe called the "Y2K bug."

Many people believed that when the calendar switched from 1999 to 2000, computers all over the world would glitch out and end civilization as we knew it. You know, like grocery stores couldn't keep bottled water and canned goods in stock. So we reporters were called in to wait, watch, and then report. While I sat at my desk, the clock struck midnight. And? Nothing happened. All that worry . . . and it never came to pass.

This reminds me of the unproductive nature of worry. And I've been such a worrier lately. But the truth is, most of our worst fears will never come to pass—like the Y2K catastrophe that wasn't. Worrying about what might happen *tomorrow* does little more than distract us from what God is doing *today*. In the end, this truth remains: we can't fix outcomes, but we *can* fix our minds on Christ. Today, let's keep grounded. Let's listen to the Master of hope instead of focus on our worries.

Therefore don't worry about tomorrow, because tomorrow will worry about itself. Each day has enough trouble of its own.
MATTHEW 6:34

DECEMBER 4
When No Means Yes

To say my three-year-old is a picky eater is an understatement. She would be the happiest girl ever if only I'd stop pushing disgusting vegetables and chewy meat at every dinner.

And, well, to be honest, I'd probably be happier too, because then we could forgo the tears and forced gagging that occurs. But while her mood would be better, her body would suffer in the long run. And I'm more concerned with her health than her mood.

This is similar to how we are with God. We want "crackers" all day long. But perhaps He says no. Then He provides a plate of "vegetables" while making the "crackers" harder to reach. How many times do we ask for something in prayer, only to be given something else? How many times do we push Him for our will to be done, not His?

Sometimes I'm after that which is not the best for me. And God says no. He loves me by offering up something better—His best, for my best. That's when I recognize that His nos are a gift. God's no is really a yes to something better. So I am learning to give thanks for the nos, reminding myself that Abba knows best and He will provide everything I need to navigate this life.

And my God will supply all your needs according to His riches in glory in Christ Jesus.
PHILIPPIANS 4:19

DECEMBER 5
In Every Season God Is Enough

I've seen a lot in the few short years I've been on this earth. I've felt pain almost unbearable that was associated with choices others made that were not in my best interest. I've been homeless and hungry, scared and worried. Most of all, I've felt hopeless.

Trudging through life with no hope, God grabbed hold of my situation and my heart. He taught me that I am not defined by my baggage. When I seek Him for contentment no matter what life throws at me, I will come out as an overcomer.

Fast-forward a few years and here I am . . . stable, out of poverty, and prospering in ways I never thought possible. I was adopted at the age of twenty-one. I now have parents who love me so well—they are worth every bit of pain I endured prior to knowing them. I am married to an amazing man and have a baby on the way. God is using every bad experience I have ever walked through for His glory.

I've learned that I can't get through this life on my own. But in the end, I will walk with a better understanding of who He is and who I am in Him.

I know both how to have a little, and I know how to have a lot.
In any and all circumstances I have learned the secret of being content—
whether well fed or hungry, whether in abundance or in need.
I am able to do all things through Him who strengthens me.
PHILIPPIANS 4:12–13

DECEMBER 6
We All Break Differently

Our friends were taking some time off from going to church—time to process and to heal from some deep hurts they'd experienced, as did we and several others involved in our church plant. And who could blame them? What we went through was traumatic, exhausting, and life-changing. But my husband and I returned to our previous church the following Sunday and immediately got involved. So why weren't we doing the same thing? Why weren't we stepping away from "the" church to mend and heal? We all left with regrets and heartache, yet we all reacted to our exits differently.

To be clear, my way of coping wasn't better than anyone else's. I went back into church right away, but it was years before I felt safe enough to let a church family back into my heart. I've learned that we all break differently, though. We hurt differently. We react differently.

In crisis, every person will feel differently and respond differently. I think this is a lesson we all need to learn: we break differently and that's okay. God made each of us unique, so we need to give each other grace when we go through tragedy together.

Lord my God, I cried to You for help,
and You healed me.
PSALM 30:2

Consider It Joy

I had returned from a mission trip in Africa to my insular world called home. And I wondered if the North American church has missed out on a deeper relationship with God and each other because we're so surprised by injury and inconvenience, by suffering and difficult circumstances. We have learned to have a tidy life.

But the reality of following Christ is, there's nothing tidy about it. We are promised trials and hardships. Yet we distort the gospel when we say it will fix our problems. We become upset without ways to ease the wrinkles of our day, get shiny, full-bodied hair, and have perfectly behaved children. We want a warning sign or someone to blame when our lives get broken.

But if we fail to dig into a theology of suffering and the way we as Christ followers will hurt right alongside a broken world, we write off people's trials as an anomaly or a reaping they had coming instead of a place where God's solace is at hand. A place where peace and even a greater purpose is found while weeping with those who weep. For what does the gospel offer us in our pain if we cannot be people who grieve even while we believe?

The LORD is near the brokenhearted;
He saves those crushed in spirit.
PSALM 34:18

DECEMBER 8
For Unbelief, God, I Give You Thanks

I remember the day I stopped believing God. I see that day now as a doorway—one I walked through and was never the same. And I thank God every day for allowing me the grace to do what I had never yet done—doubt Him.

Growing up, my parents told me God is love and I believed them. But then I stood in church one Sunday and sang a song about God's love, yet I was in pain and saw no evidence that God had noticed. So I stopped singing. I no longer believed in a God who equaled love. I no longer believed His love saw me. Here is the thing about unbelief: it's like a fire. It burns away at the truth and the lies until all that is left is the perfect ground for new life.

Before I stepped through the door of that day, my view of divine love was a mixed-up mess of lessons I'd been taught, songs I had sung, parents who loved well, and my own lonely efforts to be a good person. Maybe that has been the greatest gift of unbelief. Embracing it, I let go of everything I thought made me lovable. And then love found me.

We love because He first loved us.
I JOHN 4:19

The Wide-Open Shore

We grasp hands and lean back, digging our toes as deep as we can into the wet sand. The waves crash against our legs and the seawater splashes into our open, smiling mouths. We stand side-by-side, heads back, delighted not to fall despite the surf's resolute heaving of itself onto the shore.

I don't want to miss a moment, so I put the camera and phone away.

I fight against every distraction, every obstacle threatening my awareness of love, joy, beauty. My heart needs to remember, needs to see, hear, be. No post on social media can adequately capture what God is doing in us, this moment: Me. My daughter. Standing barefoot in the crashing waves. I am practicing deeper awareness, for I'm hungry to experience true life.

There is something that is killed in us when we worship something other than Jesus. For me, it was other people's approval—my own approval too. Striving toward anything but Jesus is wasted time. Anything we do must have Him at the center.

So we run to the beach today with no plan, no agenda. We, His daughters, open our hands, our hearts, our lives to more freedom, more joy, more life. More of Him.

If I live at the eastern horizon or settle at the western limits,
even there Your hand will lead me; Your right hand will hold on to me.
PSALM 139:9–10

Living Beyond the Bubble

Aconcerned person pulled me aside after church and said, "Do you know what your daughter is doing?" I waited and held my breath. She continued, "Your daughter is hanging out with people who aren't Christians."

Oh, that. I sighed in relief. Yes, I knew about that. Because they hang out at our house too. They even spend the night. The woman was a little affronted.

Bubbles are created when we become hyper-vigilant about who stays in, or out of, our daily lives. But if Jesus is our example—and He is—then I'm not sure we should live in self-made bubbles.

Jesus loved people who were different and discarded by others. He listened to people and *saw* them, which led them straight into the arms of the Father. Jesus engaged in long conversations, and He walked straight into crowds where people adored Him, mocked Him, or were simply curious about Him. He showed compassion that was the lasting impression in every encounter.

Jesus remained true to Himself and His mission. He spoke truth and had very clear and honest words for those who lived in a bubble and demanded that they be popped. Jesus came to rescue humanity, and we are part of that plan.

You are the light of the world.
A city situated on a hill cannot be hidden.
MATTHEW 5:14

DECEMBER 11
Read and Repeat

My friend's son has stuttered his whole life. He went to specialists, but none have discovered the key to unlocking his speech so the words will flow.

He's an adult now, and everything he says and does is on constant repeat. So my friend prints out Scripture and hangs it all over her house, and she quotes it daily until the words take root. She asks him if he wants to learn Scripture with her.

So they memorize the verses together, read and repeat, read and repeat. He's already good at repetition, and the words take root in him too. These are the only words he speaks without a stutter. He quotes Scripture loud and clear, speaking the truth of God without pause.

Scripture is the key that unlocks the twisted tongue, just as it is the key that unlocks the twisted soul. My friend's son still stutters in conversation, but she holds close to hope. She's seen the transformative power of God's Word, and while the effect on his speech may be temporary, they are the words that set his spirit free.

And so they walk around the house . . . and they speak life together . . . Read and repeat. Read and repeat.

These words that I am giving you today are to be in your heart. Repeat them to your children. Talk about them when you sit in your house and when you walk along the road, when you lie down and when you get up. Bind them as a sign on your hand and let them be a symbol on your forehead. Write them on the doorposts of your house and on your gates.

DEUTERONOMY 6:6–9

From the Overflow of Our Hearts

Cozied up under my covers, the thoughts rolled silently off my tongue. I was swearing because of bitterness and jealousy. Those words are the overflow of my heart. I can't tame my tongue because I have a heart issue. My ugly is coming straight from inside my soul. So instead of praying, "Lord, help me tame my tongue." I'm praying, "Lord, give me a pure heart." Because if my heart is cleaned out, then the overflow will be good, uplifting words.

As I was pondering my heart, I thought about focusing on our children's hearts instead of trying to tame their tongues. Whenever I hear one of them speak with an edge, I ask, "What's going on? Can we talk about these words and what is behind them?" When I am able to see past the attitude, I can see the root cause. If I can help my children untangle the roots, then their words will change because their hearts will mend.

When left to myself, I follow my sin nature. When I'm not reading God's Word, I'm not thinking on good and lovely things. But when I pour God's Word into my heart, every single day, then His goodness is what pours back out.

A good man produces good out of the good storeroom
of his heart. An evil man produces evil out of the evil storeroom,
for his mouth speaks from the overflow of the heart.
LUKE 6:45

Duped by Darkness

Darkness can be alluring. It calls to us saying, "You won't get hurt. Come and see what I have for you. No one will ever know."

I, once, carefully hid a secret. Instead of eating in public, I didn't eat. And instead of eating in private, I also didn't eat. I starved myself. Little by little, I died internally, all the while trying to prove to the world that I had everything together. My mind felt much more comfortable in lies rather than in truth and a posture of repentance.

We often are aware of our mistakes but hide out of embarrassment. God doesn't desert us though—He loves us too much. He sees us hiding. He shines His light on the path to escape.

God's Word is that light. Through His Word, God leads and guides. Sometimes the light may seem dim, but it's still there, ready to lead us to hope, encouragement, and restoration. No matter what darkness you find yourself in, His light is there, waiting.

Jesus didn't abandon us on the cross and He won't abandon us today. And His glory and light extend far beyond the darkest shadows. He calls us to safe pastures. He calls us to truth. He calls us to light.

Your word is a lamp for my feet and a light on my path.
PSALM 119:105

DECEMBER 14
What It Means to Be Winsome

Before I began tutoring high school students, I observed another tutor's class for a day. The most memorable lesson came during a debate when the tutor challenged the class to think about what it meant to be winsome. I sneaked a peek at the dictionary app to find that *winsome* means "innocently charming."

The tutor stressed being winsome as more important than winning.

The desire to win serves us well if our only concern is a judge's score sheet, tally marks on a page, or getting the last word. But the desire to be winsome serves us well if we want to convert others and win them to our point of view. It's the mark of an evangelist or a peacemaker.

I heard a speaker recently who commanded the attention and respect of many simply by his presence. But when he opened his mouth, his words were tinged with disdain for those who disagreed with him. Even when his words rang true, his tone repelled. It was the opposite of winsome.

Although eternal salvation is accomplished through the shed blood and finished work of Jesus Christ on the cross and the quickening of the Holy Spirit, we can touch lives here and now when we live ours joyously, as winsome ambassadors for Christ.

By this all people will know that you are My disciples,
if you have love for one another.
JOHN 13:35

Shaped, Not Scorched

Did God really send us? It's a question I asked periodically after an intense season of serving. I was marked with anxiety and depression. I'll never be the same.

Others have asked if I misunderstood what seemed so clear at the time. I don't think so. When we moved our family to live on a ranch to foster many children, the decision was so beyond what I would have dreamed of on my own. Multiple opened doors along the way were unmistakable. Still, our experience left me utterly depleted.

Every day we faced a surreal number of challenges. Breakdowns occurred in material possessions, physical health, spiritual stamina, and emotional capacities. My new normal became the cry, "Lord, I need You." This sentiment changed everything in me. Never before had I needed to trust God so completely . . . so implicitly. Desperation led me to a brokenness only God could carry.

Looking back, it was easy to question our decision. Today, I see God's presence throughout. He walked us through far more than we ever thought we could handle and showed us His ability to do so tangibly.

Times of fiery trials are not times of God's neglect, no matter how we feel. They are times when we learn to trust His ways.

I will be with you when you pass through the waters, and when you pass through the rivers, they will not overwhelm you. You will not be scorched when you walk through the fire, and the flame will not burn you.

ISAIAH 43:2

With Broken Hearts and Wings

Every year a bird builds a nest in the rafters of our porch. One day my three-year-old daughter and I see the momma bird hovering with frantic cries. Our eyes transition to the tiny, broken bird, fallen from the nest too soon. I pull on gloves and tuck in the feathered baby as a tiny voice pipes up behind me, "Maybe God and da doctors can help the baby birdie, Mommy."

We pray God does help as she and I rock to sleep together that evening. Then I trace the edges of the scar that winds long around my baby's back, the one from the day she was pulled from my womb—the doctor cut into her heart and simultaneously sliced mine open too as I anxiously waited for news to come with assurances that hers never stopped beating.

And after so many hours spent sitting next to her tiny bedside, I know for certain that I'm grateful every single moment I have to look my little legacy of love in the face and teach her to fly.

Look at the birds of the sky: They don't sow or reap or gather into barns,
yet your heavenly Father feeds them. Aren't you worth more than they?
MATTHEW 6:26

The Friends We Invite

Hospitality, it seems, has been relegated to a lost art, a long forgotten practice, an old-fashioned notion. And it's been replaced by Pinterest perfection instead of people who gather around tables. But what about true, biblical hospitality? I long for a place in time when people were the point, not perfection.

The word for hospitality in the Greek—*philoxenia*—literally means "lover of strangers." In a nutshell, Scripture calls us to love strangers and to receive and embrace those who do not share our faith and our values.

When was the last time I hosted someone different from me? Different skin color? Different first language? When did I last host a smoker? (Do I even own an ashtray? Should I?) An unwed mother? A Buddhist? An adulterer? A Muslim? When is the last time I hosted someone who did not look, think, or act like me? When did I last embrace, listen to, take by the hand, receive, or accept someone who does not share my faith or my values?

When was the last time I invested in someone before they were all cleaned up? Jesus did this, many times. In fact, He invited me to have dinner with Him, long before I was all cleaned up. And, of course, I'm still in process.

But when He heard this, He said, "Those who are well don't need a doctor, but the sick do."
MATTHEW 9:12

DECEMBER 18
Redemption for the Nice Girl

Not long ago I left a comment on a blog post written by a friend, and she replied, saying, "Kristen, you're the nicest girl ever." And I roll my eyes—*Quit calling me nice!* Sinking back in my chair, I realize I've bought into the lie—that if you think I'm nice, maybe you don't think I'm smart or strong.

Sometimes nice doesn't feel like enough. Nice feels like a pushover, like the one you can't take too seriously. She doesn't own the dance floor, all wild and witty. Nice is vanilla-flavor boring.

But, then, for the person receiving the "niceness," such kindness tastes like double-chocolate heaven. Nice is powerful. Nice is the way hope turns its face to you, often unexpectedly. Nice is the cool drink of water that lingers on dry hearts.

If you're a nice one, don't eclipse your light by believing you aren't enough. An infinitely creative God makes room for infinitely creative personalities. They're all equally valuable and equally needed. We need those who know that nice isn't just something you do, but something you are.

This is the truth: nice, Jesus-loving folk are love-spreaders, grace-sharers, and gospel-livers. And living the gospel? Now, that's always a smart choice.

And we exhort you, brothers: warn those who are irresponsible, comfort the discouraged, help the weak, be patient with everyone.
I THESSALONIANS 5:14

A New Creation

When I first heard another woman share her testimony, I was captured by her stories of pain and rejoiced at God's redemption through it all. At the end of the talk, she invited those who didn't know Christ in a personal way to pray with her. My eyes squeezed shut and I fervently prayed. I expected something to happen, but I didn't feel anything. I thought I had done it wrong because my sin continued to entangle me.

Soon after, another woman shared how God had changed her life, and we were invited to pray. I once again begged God to come into my heart and change me too. *I must not be a new creation if my sin remained,* I reasoned.

But 2 Corinthians 5:17 revealed my failure. I thought that if I was truly saved I must also be "perfect." And I spent almost thirty years working hard at making myself perfectly presentable before God.

Only recently was I able to truly grasp the gift of salvation that has been mine all along. Such a burden was lifted when I finally stopped doing and started resting in the gift of Christ. I am fully flawed, yes, but because of Jesus, I am made new.

Therefore, if anyone is in Christ, he is a new creation;
old things have passed away, and look, new things have come.
II CORINTHIANS 5:17

DECEMBER 20
What Lies Ahead

Over the years, I've set goals and even planned toward their success, yet they've always seemed just beyond my reach. Lots of prayer and tears and more prayer followed as I've tried to figure out the underlying reason. I know intellectually what I need to do, but it's not been enough.

Sometimes, when I get tired of the discipline of work, I simply default to doing things that take me in the opposite direction of my goals: escapism.

When the pressure of being a wife, a mother, a businesswoman, a volunteer, and all the other hats I wear becomes too much, I attempt to escape the realities by looking in the refrigerator or skimming through e-mails.

In Philippians 3, Paul encourages us to press on—forgetting what lies behind us and focusing on what lies ahead. So I am making a day-by-day, moment-by-moment conscious decision not to allow myself to escape when I feel the pressures of my responsibilities.

I will keep pressing on, with my eyes on the joy waiting before me. I will disregard the discomfort I feel. I will think of my Savior, and I will look to Him when I grow weary. With His help and by His grace, I will not give up.

Brothers, I do not consider myself to have taken hold of it. But one thing I do: Forgetting what is behind and reaching forward to what is ahead, I pursue as my goal the prize promised by God's heavenly call in Christ Jesus.
PHILIPPIANS 3:13–14

God Wants Your Surrender, Not Your Strength

We all know to hold still when something hurts. It's our first instinct to pull into ourselves and try to brace that broken part. We protect our pain like a broken-winged bird, shielding our wings from flight. We know we are bound and yet we want to fight against the brokenness.

Stillness doesn't come by me naturally. I am frenzied, pained, or fatigued, but the stillness it takes to heal is elusive. I can quiet my limbs and my lips but not my mind. My mind fights when I'm backed into involuntary stillness.

In the chaos that surrounds being still, when the world moves on at a steady pace and we can't, it's hard not to push through.

But stillness often means waiting. No one wants to be passed. No one wants to feel as though they're going nowhere. But sometimes God tells us to be still because He's healing broken parts. He's building our strength. We need only to be still.

So many of us limp along and put on brave faces. But really, God isn't asking for our tenacity as much as our surrender. He's asking to carry us.

Youths may become faint and grow weary, and young men stumble and fall, but those who trust in the Lord will renew their strength; they will soar on wings like eagles; they will run and not grow weary; they will walk and not faint.
ISAIAH 40:30–31

DECEMBER 22
Enough Is Enough

I was eight years old the first time I heard I wasn't "enough." I wasn't enough to hang with the cool kids or play on the best team in gym class—thus began my journey of striving to feel like "enough."

This journey has been a precarious one—paved with lies and insecurities often laid by people haunted by the same struggle. And when comparison joins in as a constant companion, it is never, ever, ending.

"You aren't a good enough wife, mother, friend."

"You aren't smart enough or rich enough or spiritual enough."

"You aren't enough to be chosen by that company, that man, that friend, that group."

No success is enough to comparison's nagging voice. She will always point out someone smarter, brighter, and better qualified.

God wants you to know that He is enough for you both. All your days were ordained by Him. He will complete any good work in you because He is enough. He is enough, and He sustains you through whatever may come. Christ loved us enough that, even though He knew every single thing we would do to break His heart, He still died for us. And nothing can separate us from His love.

Who can separate us from the love of Christ? Can affliction or anguish or persecution or famine or nakedness or danger or sword? . . . No, in all these things we are more than victorious through Him who loved us.
ROMANS 8:35, 37

Trusting His Purpose

I'm in a season of life where a lot of things are up in the air. My family just moved to a new city, and while our home is cozy and our family is healthy, many things feel challenging. We're trying to make friends, find our place at a new church, and figure out rhythms and schedules. I know what needs to be done every day, but I still feel untethered. Confused. Lost. All of the externals in my life are in place, but inside, I feel purposeless.

Psalm 57:2 reminds me that the Lord knows the exact details of our current situations. When David wrote this psalm, he was in a challenging situation, but he knew that the Lord could fulfill the purpose he was created for. And as the psalm continues, David thanks God and praises Him. He declares God's love and faithfulness. Ultimately, David believed that God was the One who would complete the work that needed to be done in his life.

This, too, is how we can learn to live with purpose—cry out to the Lord, ask Him to fulfill His purpose in us, thank Him, praise Him, and declare who He is. God is secure in who He is and in who He has created us to be.

I call to God Most High,
to God who fulfills His purpose for me.
PSALM 57:2

On Giving My Heart a Good Scrub

We're getting ready to sell our house. We've replaced, repainted, and repaired places in our home we'd gotten so used to, we didn't see that they needed fixing.

As we clean up years of life lived within these walls, I'm finding that my heart needs a good scrub too. To toss lingering hurts and replace with forgiveness. To spackle up the cracks with gentle love notes from Scripture. To clean out the dark corners long neglected. To let light shine in.

What in my own heart have I grown so accustomed to that I don't even see anymore but may stand out to others? Only when I look at myself from the outside in am I able to name (more than) a few. I can see my first instinct is to defend myself instead of defending others. I can see the small chips on my shoulders have etched further into the bone. What I view as weariness, others may receive as complaint.

These quietly ugly characteristics have been given room to lurk, and it's time for them to leave. God isn't dwelling on the dusty, stale parts of my heart and I don't need to either. It's time to make my home sparkle . . . and I want that for my heart too.

Who is a God like You, removing iniquity and passing over rebellion for the remnant of His inheritance? He does not hold on to His anger forever, because He delights in faithful love.
MICAH 7:18

Mountain Whispers

I laced up my hiking boots, coated my skin with bug repellant, and loaded my backpack with the essentials: water, Bible, pen, and journal. I tucked the trail map in my pocket and closed the door to my mountain dorm. I was off on another adventure. Just me and God.

My ears were tuned to the tiny songbirds; my nose was tuned to the fragrance of woody sequoias mingled with sweet wildflowers and musky earth. And my heart was tuned to hearing God's voice.

Three months spent working and ministering in Kings Canyon National Park was a summer of learning. Learning how to do everything as unto the Lord during long shifts as a thankless busboy. Learning how to work with teammates so unlike me to put on Sunday worship services for park visitors. But more than anything, I started learning to awaken to God's wonder through creation.

The difficulties of that summer paled in comparison to the vividness with which I experienced God. At every turn I heard His whispers. Often I would come back from those nature treks sunburned, bug-bitten, hungry, and thirsty. But none of it mattered because I was awake to wonder.

For His invisible attributes, that is, His eternal power and divine nature, have been clearly seen since the creation of the world, being understood through what He has made. As a result, people are without excuse.
ROMANS 1:20

When You Worry You're Disqualified from Being Loved

My daughter comes to me with snot and tears streaked down her face and asks between wails, "Do you still love me, Mama? Even when I'm crabby?"

I slowly pet her back and say, "Zoe, I love you when you're crabby, and I love you when you're happy. I love you just as much when you're mean as I do when you're kind." And I hug her tighter. I want her to know this deep, reassuring promise of a love that isn't conditioned on good behavior. This love that doesn't keep a list of all she got wrong.

It's easy to keep our own score, though, isn't it? Yesterday I was late getting the kids up, I lost my temper, and we didn't properly hug goodbye, so today I'm a bad mom and don't deserve to be loved. Today everything ran smoothly and kids laughed and leaned through the minivan window and kissed me goodbye, so now I get to feel worthy.

But that kind of scorekeeping isn't love. God's love looks at everything we are and everything we've done and chooses to purposefully love us through it all. Because nothing can disqualify us from how Jesus loves us.

Love consists in this: not that we loved God, but that He loved us and sent His Son to be the propitiation for our sins.

I JOHN 4:10

One of the Most Important Things to Remember

The Scottish theologian Ian Maclaren shares one of my favorite life philosophies: "Be kind, for everyone you meet is fighting a hard battle." We've inherited a world marred by sin, which leads to brokenness. Believers and nonbelievers alike are walking wounded. I often find myself asking, "How can I be like Jesus?" whether in this circumstance or within the context of that relationship.

Sometimes it's easy, but other times it's downright hard. Loving others well is a daily offering and requires prayer and power from the holy work of the Spirit. That's because I, too, am walking wounded. Unless you're trusted and close, you can't see beyond my mask. I'll wear that smile and say I'm fine while feeling misunderstood, betrayed, or forgotten. I know I don't have the power to change others' behavior, but I can control my response.

My deepest desire is to honor the Lord, which demands I respond like Jesus. In the wake of atrocities committed against Him, the likes of which we'll never fully grasp, He always loved first, quickly forgave, and was for the very people who hurt Him. May we follow in His footsteps and learn to do likewise.

Then my enemies will retreat on the day when I call.
This I know: God is for me.
PSALM 56:9

DECEMBER 28
The Key to Successfully Handling Change

For decades my house was full of voices, laughter, music, and occasional sibling squabbles. We affectionately call ourselves "The Loud Family." Not one of us is an introvert. And then, just like that, everyone's on their own. And tonight there are no sounds. No one bounding down the stairs. No one hugging my neck. Only the silence.

What do I do now? is all I can think. With each changing season, we're faced with this question. It's scary and a little sad, but it's also brimming with new possibilities. My new normal doesn't have to be bad. It's just different. And change can be good in a different sort of way. In fact, with the right attitude and a plan of action, it can be great.

I've learned that the key to successfully handling change is to look forward with anticipation and look back with gratitude. I had to stop saying, "I wish it was . . ." and start saying, "I'm glad it is . . .".

So whether you're a new graduate, a new mom, a new employee, or a new empty nester, embrace the new season, thanking God for every moment of the old one.

Then I heard the voice of the Lord saying: Who should I send? Who will go for Us?
I said: Here I am. Send me.
ISAIAH 6:8

The Delight You Bring

The first time someone told me they delighted in me, I didn't understand what they meant. "What do you mean?" I had asked.

"I delight in you," the person replied. "I see you, and I know you make mistakes and are flawed, and I delight in you anyway."

That was a powerful moment for me because it reflected God so clearly. If a human could delight in me, wouldn't God's delight be even greater? God sees us exactly as we are. He sees our flaws and our strengths and takes delights in us.

How am I—a girl who is utterly imperfect, often screwing up and making innumerable mistakes—the source of the Almighty God's delight? It's an idea that doesn't compute in my brain.

But this is the truth: you and I bring God delight. Think of seeing your to-be husband at the end of the aisle, receiving your degree that you worked so hard to attain, or a hundred other moments. All those pale in comparison to the delight you bring God. He looks at you and sees a treasure, someone worthy and whole. Someone worth rescuing, something worth delighting in. *You* bring God delight. You are the source of His deepest joy.

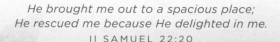

He brought me out to a spacious place;
He rescued me because He delighted in me.
II SAMUEL 22:20

The Purpose of Loneliness

Music off, television off, phone left on silent . . . I've been dabbling with the quiet because I need to hear from God, but the truth about the quiet is, it takes me to my rawest, loneliest places.

My mouth says I want to walk with God, but my actions crave a culturally acceptable numbness that keeps me away. I constantly struggle not to reach for the phone and scroll through Instagram. And I'm finding the lonelier I feel, the more I am left to deal with my own thoughts and what I really believe about God. I'm supposed to have the mind of Christ, but do I?

I've wondered, *How lonely was Jesus in His flesh?* I've imagined the communion Jesus kept with His Father—the kind of communion I want with Him too. So because of Jesus, I'm starting to embrace the lonely and asking Jesus to join me. Only then do I find myself truly not alone.

There is no people fix, no earthly father, no covering that will do other than the covering Jesus gives—the messianic fix.

What if we allowed the quiet, faced the lonely, and sat in it a bit?

Might that lonely place be exactly where the door is, the one on which we knock, the one Jesus promises to open?

For who has known the Lord's mind, that he may instruct Him?
But we have the mind of Christ.
I CORINTHIANS 2:16

Dwelling in the Rhythm of Grace

My family of three moved to ten acres with a farmhouse this year. We're overflowing with ideas about all this place can be, so I expected God would say, "Lots to do, girl. Let's get busy." Instead, God has whispered to my heart, "Dwell."

Dwell means to abide, nest, reside, and inhabit. God takes my hand like a patient Father and slows my pace to His as we walk in the garden. He's not in any hurry with His vision, and I feel grace pouring down, like a much-needed summer rain.

Dwelling is not an easy word for a woman with vision. It can sound like defeat in our day of hustle. But dwelling implies harmony, not isolation. God wants us to *be* with Him.

I'm learning that to dwell feels a lot like art. Absorbing colors, making memories, stepping into the picture God is painting, while choosing not to be so worried about framing it up for presentation.

I'm called to find a rhythm in daily life that's in sync with what He is about to do. So I'm working at being still to embrace the grateful heart God is trying to instill in me. I will dwell in the house of the Lord, forever. There's no rush.

I have asked one thing from the Lord; it is what I desire:
to dwell in the house of the Lord all the days of my life.
PSALM 27:4